ACTS OF INTERPRETATION

ACTS OF INTERPRETATION

Scripture, Theology, and Culture

Edited by

S. A. Cummins *&* Jens Zimmermann

WILLIAM. B. EERDMANS PUBLISHING COMPANY
GRAND RAPIDS, MICHIGAN

Wm. B. Eerdmans Publishing Co.
4035 Park East Court SE, Grand Rapids, Michigan 49546
www.eerdmans.com

27 26 25 24 23 22 21 20 19 18   1 2 3 4 5 6 7 8 9 10

ISBN 978-0-8028-7500-6

Library of Congress Cataloging-in-Publication Data

Names: Cummins, Stephen Anthony, 1958- editor.
Title: Acts of interpretation : scripture, theology, and culture / edited by
    S.A. Cummins & Jens Zimmermann.
Description: Grand Rapids : Eerdmans Publishing Co., 2018. | Includes
    bibliographical references and index.
Identifiers: LCCN 2018020965 | ISBN 9780802875006 (pbk. : alk. paper)
Subjects: LCSH: Bible—Criticism, interpretation, etc. | Bible—Hermeneutics.
Classification: LCC BS511.3 .A28 2018 | DDC 220.6—dc23
    LC record available at https://lccn.loc.gov/2018020965

Contents

Acknowledgments

Most of the essays in this volume were earlier presented in the form of public lectures in a series entitled "Scripture, Theology and Culture: Acts of Interpretation," organized collaboratively by the Canada Research Chair in Interpretation, Religion, and Culture (held by Jens Zimmermann) and the Religious Studies department (represented by Tony Cummins) at Trinity Western University, Langley, British Columbia. The lectures took place during the period from September 2013 to November 2014.

We gratefully acknowledge the Canada Research Council, whose funding for the Canada Research Chair program supported this lecture series and publication. The lectures by Dr. Peter Enns and Dr. Craig Bartholomew were also co-sponsored by the Canadian Scientific & Christian Affiliation and the Vancouver Area Science & Religion Forum.

The editors would like to thank Natalie Boldt for her administrative assistance with the public lecture series, and Kyle Parsons for his editorial work. We are also indebted to our colleague Dr. Craig Broyles for his linguistic and technical expertise. In addition, we are grateful for James Ernest's willingness to recommend this volume to the Eerdmans publishing committee, and we thank Mary Hietbrink, Justin Howell, and the editorial team at Eerdmans for their kind assistance in finalizing the manuscript.

Finally, we express our gratitude to each of the contributors for their warm collegiality, their patience throughout the publication process, and their fine essays. They are to be commended for their long-standing and collective commitment to the integration of Scripture and theology, and to its vital role in the church and the world.

Contributors

Craig G. Bartholomew
Director of the Kirby Laing Institute for Christian Ethics
Tyndale House, Cambridge

Hans Boersma
J. I. Packer Professor of Theology
Regent College

S. A. Cummins
Professor of Religious Studies
Trinity Western University

Peter Enns
Abram S. Clemens Professor of Biblical Studies
Eastern University

Stephen E. Fowl
Professor, Department of Theology
Loyola University Maryland

Joel B. Green
Provost, Dean of the School of Theology,
and Professor of New Testament Interpretation
Fuller Theological Seminary

Edith M. Humphrey
William F. Orr Professor of New Testament
Pittsburgh Theological Seminary

Charles Raith II
Vice President of Mission Integration
Mercy Health System

Christopher R. Seitz
Senior Research Professor
Wycliffe College, University of Toronto

Robert W. Wall
Paul T. Walls Professor of Scripture and Wesleyan Studies
Seattle Pacific University and Seminary

Jens Zimmermann
Canada Research Professor of Interpretation, Religion, and Culture,
Trinity Western University,
and Visiting Professor of Philosophy, Literature, and Theology,
Regent College

Abbreviations

AB	Anchor Bible
ACCS	Ancient Christian Commentary on Scripture
ACNT	Augsburg Commentaries on the New Testament
ACW	Ancient Christian Writers
ANF	*Ante-Nicene Fathers*, 10 vols. Edited by Alexander Roberts and James Donaldson. Buffalo, NY: Christian Literature, 1885–1887; reprint, Grand Rapids: Eerdmans, 1951–1956; reprint, Peabody, MA: Hendrickson, 1994.
BCOTWP	Baker Commentary on the Old Testament Wisdom and Psalms
BECNT	Baker Exegetical Commentary on the New Testament
CBQMS	Catholic Biblical Quarterly Monograph Series
CC	Continental Commentaries
CEB	Common English Bible
CO	*Corpus Reformatorum: Ioannis Calvini Opera quae supersunt omnia*, ed. W. Baum et al. Brunswick: C.A. Schwetschke & Filium, 1863–1900.
DBW	*Dietrich Bonhoeffer Werke*, 17 vols. Edited by Eberhard Bethge et al. Munich: Chr. Kaiser/Gütersloher Verlagshaus, 1986–99.
DBWE	*Dietrich Bonhoeffer Works*, English edition, 17 vols. Edited by Victoria J. Barnett, Wayne Whitson Floyd Jr., and Barbara Wojhoski. Minneapolis: Fortress, 1996–2015.
ESV	English Standard Version
IBC	Interpretation: A Bible Commentary for Teaching and Preaching

ICC	International Critical Commentary
JPS	Jewish Publication Society
JSNTSup	Journal for the Study of the New Testament Supplement Series
JSPSup	Journal for the Study of the Pseudepigrapha Supplement Series
LCC	Library of Christian Classics
LNTS	Library of New Testament Studies
NCB	New Century Bible Commentary
NICNT	New International Commentary on the New Testament
NICOT	New International Commentary on the Old Testament
NIV	New International Version
NPNF[1]	*A Select Library of Nicene and Post-Nicene Fathers of the Christian Church*, 1st series, 14 vols. Edited by Philip Schaff et al. Buffalo, NY: Christian Literature, 1887–1894; reprint, Grand Rapids: Eerdmans, 1952–1956; reprint, Peabody, MA: Hendrickson, 1994.
NRSV	New Revised Standard Version
OSHT	Oxford Studies in Historical Theology
OTL	Old Testament Library
PG	Patrologia graeca [= *Patrologiae Cursus Completus*: Series Graeca]. Edited by Jacques-Paul Migne. 162 vols. Paris, 1857–1886.
PTMS	Pittsburgh Theological Monograph Series
RSV	Revised Standard Version
SBL	Society of Biblical Literature
SBT	Studies in Biblical Theology
SFEG	Schriften der Finnischen Exegetischen Gesellschaft
Siphrut	Siphrut: Literature and Theology of the Hebrew Scriptures
SP	Sacra Pagina
SVTP	Studia in Veteris Testamenti Pseudepigraphica
WBC	Word Biblical Commentary
WUNT	Wissenschaftliche Untersuchungen zum Neuen Testament

Scripture, Theology, and Culture: Considerations and Contributions

S. A. Cummins

What is the Bible all about? How can Christians read it faithfully as inspired Scripture, in relation to the church's tradition and mission, while honoring its abiding Jewish heritage? And what is the significance of the Bible for the whole of humanity in today's complex and contested world? Not everyone is equally interested in tackling such questions. Many today do not know the Bible. Some misunderstand it. Others dismiss it as problematic and divisive. And even those who still pay attention to the Bible often privatize it (as *my* Bible), domesticate it (keep it "in house"), historicize it (see it strictly as an ancient text), marginalize it (abandon it to the particularly pious or to the experts), and in various other ways sell it short.[1]

Over the past generation or so, some who are committed both to the church and to the academy have addressed this situation. Biblical scholars, theologians, and others have tried to correlate three integral aspects of the Bible more effectively: it is an ancient and sacred text (Scripture); it discloses and testifies to the unfolding purposes of God, as experienced in the faith and practice of the people of God (theology); and it is concerned with all of humanity and the created order (culture). The work of these scholars

---

1. On the development of modern biblical studies in Western culture, compare, for example, Roy A. Harrisville and Walter Sundberg, *The Bible in Modern Culture: Theology and Historical-Critical Method from Spinoza to Käsemann*, 2nd ed. (Grand Rapids: Eerdmans, 2002); and the more focused studies by Jonathan Sheehan, *The Enlightenment Bible: Translation, Scholarship, Culture* (Princeton: Princeton University Press, 2007); Michael C. Legaspi, *The Death of Scripture and the Rise of Biblical Studies*, OHST (New York: Oxford University Press, 2011); and Alan J. Hauser and Duane F. Watson, eds., *A History of Biblical Interpretation*, vol. 3: *The Enlightenment through the Nineteenth Century* (Grand Rapids: Eerdmans, 2017).

has been expressed in ongoing deliberations about the nature and scope of historical criticism, developments in hermeneutics, and more recently in what is now often called "theological interpretation."[2]

What is theological interpretation of the Bible all about? It could be broadly taken to entail "diverse ways of engaging with the Bible theologically."[3] Yet the expression "theological interpretation" is now used in a range of particular ways to refer to a distinct interpretive perspective, disposition, or mode, and also to designate an approach, practice, program, and movement. Scholars have offered a number of working definitions;[4] and it is much discussed in an ever-increasing number of publications.[5] Yet even those empathetic to its cause express certain concerns. For example, they worry that theological interpretation may not reckon fully enough with important historical matters related to the Bible and its interpretation;[6] that it is not always clear on the main questions, issues, and prob-

---

2. Alternative or related designations include "theological exegesis," "theological hermeneutics," and "theological reading." Mark Alan Bowald, "The Character of Theological Interpretation," *International Journal of Systematic Theology* 12.2 (2010): 163–83, calls for greater rigor in the use of terms; he reserves "theological hermeneutics" for "the act of interpreting and/or reading in general" (i.e., "meta-hermeneutics") and "'theological interpretation'" for the specific act of reading Scripture" (162–64).

3. See Markus Bockmuehl, "Bible versus Theology: Is 'Theological Interpretation' the Answer?" *Nova et Vetera* 9.1 (2011): 41.

4. One of the most comprehensive is that of Michael Gorman: it is "biblical interpretation that takes the Bible not just as a historical and/or a literary document but as source of divine revelation, witness to God's creative and salvific activity, and/or (minimally) significant partner in the task of theological reflection—thinking about God and about the world and humanity in light of God." See his *Elements of Biblical Exegesis: A Basic Guide for Students and Ministers*, rev. and exp. ed. (Grand Rapids: Baker Academic, 2009), 144. Note also the definitional discussion by Kevin J. Vanhoozer, "What Is Theological Interpretation of the Bible?" in *Dictionary for Theological Interpretation of the Bible*, ed. Kevin J. Vanhoozer et al. (Grand Rapids: Baker Academic, 2005), 19–25; and R. W. L. Moberly, "What Is Theological Interpretation of Scripture?" *Journal of Theological Interpretation* 3.2 (2009): 162–63.

5. Among recent and helpful book-length studies, compare, for example, Craig G. Bartholomew and Heath A. Thomas, eds., *A Manifesto for Theological Interpretation* (Grand Rapids: Baker Academic, 2016); Stephen E. Fowl, *Theological Interpretation of Scripture* (Eugene, OR: Cascade, 2009); Joel B. Green, *Practicing Theological Interpretation: Engaging Biblical Texts for Faith and Formation* (Grand Rapids: Baker Academic, 2011); and Daniel J. Treier, *Introducing Theological Interpretation of Scripture: Recovering a Christian Practice* (Grand Rapids: Baker Academic, 2008).

6. Bockmuehl, "Bible versus Theology," rightly insists that intellectually responsible biblical and theological scholarship must include "historical, linguistic, and exegetical pursuits" (37). Others are particularly concerned that it lacks a commitment to biblical mean-

lems to be addressed;[7]and that it is often more theoretical than practiced.[8] Because of these factors, some find that it can be "a frustratingly disparate movement"[9] and offers only "a generally nebulous sense of what exactly we are talking about."[10]

These questions and concerns about the Bible and theological interpretation warrant careful continuing deliberation. However, they can only be addressed adequately within the wider context of Scripture, theology, and culture, as the setting within which readers claim, confess, and critique the Bible. To reflect further on this matter, I will begin by making several observations on the merits and limits of historical criticism. I will then move to broader considerations regarding the role of the Bible in relation to God's purposes, people, and world. Finally, I will conclude with an overview of the wide-ranging and concerted contributions found in this volume.

Historical Criticism and the Bible: Merits and Limits

Historical criticism remains the most prominent approach in contemporary biblical studies. Its practitioners realize that it "covers a range of methods" that are typically and collectively concerned that "texts should be interpreted in their historical contexts, in light of the literary and cultural conventions of their time."[11] John Barton, who is especially interested in the literary/philological dimensions of the biblical text (e.g., semantics, genre), prefers the designation "biblical criticism."[12] Yet, allowing for dif-

---

ing in "referential and intentionalist terms" and implies that historical criticism cannot be equally theological in its aims and interests; see John C. Poirier, "'Theological Interpretation' and Its Contradistinctions," *Tyndale Bulletin* 60 (2009): 105–18, quotation at 109 n. 11.

7. Cf. R. R. Reno, "Using the Fathers," *Journal of Theological Interpretation* 7.2 (2013): 168–69.

8. See Moberly, "What Is Theological Interpretation of Scripture?," 169–70.

9. D. A. Carson, "Theological Interpretation of Scripture: Yes, But . . . ," in *Theological Commentary: Evangelical Perspectives*, ed. R. Michael Allen (New York: T. & T. Clark, 2011), 204.

10. Bockmuehl, "Bible versus Theology," 39.

11. John J. Collins, *The Bible after Babel: Historical Criticism in a Postmodern Age* (Grand Rapids: Eerdmans, 2005), 4.

12. John Barton, *The Nature of Biblical Criticism* (Louisville: Westminster John Knox, 2007). See the review and critique of Barton's study by R. W. L. Moberly, "Biblical Criticism and Religious Belief," *Journal of Theological Interpretation* 2.1 (2008): 71–100.

ferent emphases and designations, what scholars have primarily in view is the disciplined use of widely recognized historical and literary interpretive methods. A key element involved is to discover the meaning of the text without being "constrained by prior convictions . . . drawn from an interpretative tradition," or trying to determine its truth in advance.[13] Practitioners readily recognize that the various methods used can on occasion conflict; that historical reconstruction, recovery of authorial intent, and other findings remain partial and provisional; that attaining objectivity in all of this is a complex matter; and that texts "may take on new meanings in changing circumstances."[14]

Nevertheless, historical criticism remains widely regarded as a central and important part of informed biblical exegesis. Many suggest that its focus on textual and historical rather than conceptual or theological analysis, especially as undertaken in academic and other public venues, helps create common ground for learning, conversation, and cooperation, rather than conflict and division along confessional lines.[15] Moreover, for Barton, biblical criticism doesn't have to be seen as "hostile to faith" because it "rests on the premise that truth is open to all comers, not the preserve of those 'in the know.'"[16] Indeed, its attentiveness to the text can foster "a religious approach to the world," discovered "not in the imposition of theological dogma, but in the recognition of what is actually there. Before theological interpretation comes the recognition of simple givenness, the appreciation of reality."[17]

Theologian Rowan Williams likewise appreciates the importance of historical criticism.[18] Yet he also draws on literary criticism to show that the rich nature of literary texts, and especially sacred texts, challenges any straightforward division between a text's representation of reality as simply given and a theological understanding of this reality. Texts are not "neutral archaeological site[s]" but "a *product*" of an author's interaction with the cultural context; and the biblical text "proclaims unambiguously its own

13. Barton, *The Nature of Biblical Criticism*, 124.

14. Cf. Collins, *The Bible after Babel*, 4.

15. On this, compare Collins, *The Bible after Babel*, 10; cf. R. R. Reno, "What Makes Exegesis Theological?" *Nova et Vetera* 9.1 (2011): 87–88.

16. Barton, *The Nature of Biblical Criticism*, 175.

17. Barton, *The Nature of Biblical Criticism*, 181–82.

18. See Rowan Williams, "Historical Criticism and Sacred Text," in *Reading Texts, Seeking Wisdom: Scripture and Theology*, ed. David F. Ford and Graham Stanton (Grand Rapids: Eerdmans, 2003), 217–28.

'produced' character."[19] Thus a key function of historical criticism is to show how texts are shaped and reshaped within a community's history, with all the material stages, internal dynamics, and ongoing interpretive challenges entailed: for example, intra-textual tensions, associations, the generation of evocative idioms and images, a sense of unfinished business, and the like.

According to Williams, keeping such tensions alive invites a "pathos of reading" that is integral and attentive to the continuing meaning and significance of biblical interpretation.[20] An informed and observant reading can, for example, help us see how a given biblical text such as Deuteronomy tackles difficult historical, theological, and cultural issues on its own immediate terms—requiring the reader to linger over rather than quickly leave behind such matters as simply "a stage in a longer story"—while also allowing for later developments that can add further challenging factors.[21] Indeed, at times what the biblical text conveys concerning God—for example, regarding grace, agency, relationships—may be intimated by means of inherent issues, questions, and unsettled matters. This can include fruitful interpretive tensions between dominant and dissonant voices whose interplay may become evident only within the Bible's wider composite witness.[22] Williams thus affirms a significant role for historical criticism, though in service of the theological aspects and ends of Scripture.

Williams's approach cautions students, preachers, and others who recognize how historical criticism can contribute positively to theological exegesis that it may also be used in ways that constrain and even compromise such a contribution. This is the case when historical criticism is deemed not only neccessary but sufficient, and is set up as "the gatekeeper of legitimate interpretation."[23] Those who adopt this approach may not only bracket out theological concerns in their initial reading, but also refuse to

---

19. Williams, "Historical Criticism and Sacred Text," 221, italics in original.

20. Williams, "Historical Criticism and Sacred Text," 221–22.

21. Williams, "Historical Criticism and Sacred Text," 222–23; quotation at 222. His remarks engage at points with Christopher R. Seitz, "Scripture Becomes Religion(s): The Theological Crisis of Serious Biblical Interpretation in the Twentieth Century," in *Renewing Biblical Interpretation*, ed. Craig C. Bartholomew, Colin J. D. Greene, and Karl Möller (Grand Rapids: Zondervan, 2000), 40–65, esp. 46–52.

22. Williams, "Historical Criticism and Sacred Text," 224–27.

23. See Brad East, "The Hermeneutics of Theological Interpretation: Holy Scripture, Biblical Scholarship, and Historical Criticism," *International Journal of Systematic Theology* 19.1 (2017): 47.

readmit them as legitimate products of rigorous exegesis. Francis Watson has noted that in public academic institutions, the label "historical criticism" can be used to demarcate the entire discipline of biblical studies, so that the discipline becomes understood largely in terms of texts within their contexts of origin and the exegete as essentially a historian.[24] This label can also be used as a polemical and anti-dogmatic device, criticizing and marginalizing theological concerns as not essential to biblical studies.[25]

Watson thus suggests that when "historical criticism" is construed in this way, it should be seen not as the normative and "neutral characterization of modern interpretative practice but as a rhetorical figure mobilized for transparent ideological ends." Moreover, it is being used in ways that limit and misrepresent "the variegated reality of interpretative practice itself."[26] Watson recognizes that biblical exegesis does include historical considerations, but he is also interested, for example, in the "immanent workings" of the biblical texts and in a dynamic "dialectic of distance and proximity" in which they can come alive and have an ongoing and extensive impact upon interpreters.[27] He suggests that an undertaking of this kind is better identified more broadly as "'biblical interpretation' and 'biblical scholarship.'"[28] And since such biblical scholarship has always been integral to the church's informed and faithful reading of the Bible, theological interpretation in this tradition can and should participate in and contribute to biblical and theological studies today.

Historical criticism has an important role to play. But when its practitioners take insufficient account of its limitations, and when they employ it in a proprietary fashion, then its claims and operation can become overextended and counterproductive. Furthermore, as Brad East has noted, greater account needs to be taken of various significant matters, such as the Bible's plenitude and powerful self-presentation; the church's longstanding and rich interpretive tradition; and the ongoing existence of a wide-ranging global church whose vital faith and practice are clearly not completely contingent upon a strictly historical-critical understanding of

---

24. Francis Watson, "Does Historical Criticism Exist? A Contribution to Debate on the Theological Interpretation of Scripture," in *Theological Theology: Essays in Honour of John Webster*, ed. R. David Nelson, Darren Sarisky, and Justin Stratis (London: T. & T. Clark Bloomsbury, 2015), 307–18, 312.

25. Cf. Watson, "Does Historical Criticism Exist?," 312.

26. Watson, "Does Historical Criticism Exist?," 308.

27. Watson, "Does Historical Criticism Exist?," 313–14.

28. Watson, "Does Historical Criticism Exist?," 318.

the Bible.[29] Indeed, we face a wider set of issues and concerns requiring a more comprehensive if contested consideration and engagement.

Life Together in the Real World:
Scripture and the Economy of God

Any understanding and correlation of Scripture, theology, and culture operates within some larger interpretive framework used to explain the way things are. From an explicitly Christian standpoint, this explanatory framework necessarily entails the will and work (economy) of the triune God—Father, Son, and Holy Spirit—in relation to humanity and the world, embracing the creation, redemption, and renewal of all things. This confessional and Trinitarian framework involves a particular, if still universal, outlook on life that not all share. Thus it requires a capacious rather than a restrictive explication in conversation with all concerned.[30] Nevertheless, a Trinitarian hermeneutic remains essential to a Christian understanding of the task at hand and needs a substantive account that expresses in careful and constructive ways what is involved.[31]

Divine and Human Agency:
Reality, History, and the Canon of Scripture

A Trinitarian hermeneutic includes wide-ranging if complex and contested claims regarding divine and human agency, and their relation to history, reality, and truth. And integral to all this are the Scripture-attested roles of Israel, church, and world.[32] Even when unacknowledged, all such matters

29. East, "The Hermeneutics of Theological Interpretation," 49–50.

30. See Bockmuehl, "Bible versus Theology," 43, who cautions that any stress on a "creedal and Trinitarian hermeneutical frame" leave room for constructive "conversations involving those of other faiths or of none."

31. Cf. Bowald, "The Character of Theological Interpretation," who calls for "thick confessional and dogmatic reflections on the character of the Trinity and the practices of reading [Scripture] which faithfully reflect that character" (162).

32. With particular reference to Paul and his Jewish context, cf. *Divine and Human Agency in Paul and His Cultural Environment*, ed. John M. G. Barclay and Simon J. Gathercole, LNTS 335 (London: T. & T. Clark, 2006). Note also the broad theological discussion on agency in Mark Alan Bowald, *Rendering the Word in Theological Hermeneutics: Mapping Divine and Human Agency* (Burlington, VT: Ashgate, 2007).

are always onstage, or at least waiting in the wings, whenever historical criticism is employed. While those undertaking contemporary biblical studies can, for example, often work with a modernist (i.e., a rather narrow and naïve) view of history and reality as "what really happened," or assume that the "facts" can somehow be entirely separated from anything that looks like "faith" (or other kinds of commitments), the biblical witness presupposes a thoroughgoing divine agency that includes humanity's participation in God's creation-wide purposes.[33] The same God who sustains creation is always involved in and through human history, not least in crucial episodes such as Israel's exodus; in the definitive divine self-disclosure in Jesus's incarnation and the epoch-turning events of his death and resurrection; and in the going forth of the gospel to all nations—all this with a view to an ultimate outworking encompassing a new heaven and earth. Indeed, Scripture's own outlook is that, in God's grace, history and humanity can truly participate in, be ordered toward, and finally be drawn up into a life and end "that transcends (without negating) history," into "eternal communion" with the triune God.[34]

If this is so, then biblical studies attentive to the Bible's own subject matter, including history, must also take account of the divine dimension in human life. And since "God is not part of the furniture of the world," interpreters seeking to discover the divine economy operative in history and humanity require a biblical scholarship that includes spiritual discernment, wisdom, and a readiness to wait, receive, and learn, in ways attentive and responsive to the purposes of God.[35] The Bible's own constitution requires this kind of reading, and thus one fundamental problem with historical criticism "is that it imposes limits on the reading of Scripture that are simply not suited to Scripture's own nature as an instrument of God's communicative presence in the world."[36] Scripture itself presents us with a

33. On history, cf. Joel B. Green, "Rethinking 'History' for Theological Interpretation," *Journal of Theological Interpretation* 5.2 (2011): 159–73.

34. Cf. Matthew Levering, "Linear and Participatory History: Augustine's City of God," *Journal of Theological Interpretation* 5.2 (2011): 175–96, 191. See further his *Participatory Exegesis: A Theology of Biblical Interpretation* (Notre Dame: University of Notre Dame Press, 2008).

35. On this, see Murray Rae, "Theological Interpretation and Historical Criticism," in *A Manifesto for Theological Interpretation*, ed. Bartholomew and Thomas, 94–109, esp. 103–9, quoted phrase at 107, which Rae notes "is variously attributed to Karl Rahner or to Donald M. MacKinnon" (107 n. 21).

36. Rae, "Theological Interpretation and Historical Criticism," 109. See also his "Read-

divine economy that includes God's generative and providential role in the human composition, transmission, and reading of the biblical texts.[37] Such divine involvement carries with it views of God's revelation, providence, Spirit, people, and world,[38] which together comprise important and inter-related elements within which Scripture exists and functions.

Integral to these elements is the Bible's formation and interpretation as a two-testament and canonical book. Its various parts share the same divine object, are centered in and bound together by Messiah Jesus, the divine Word and living Lord, and are shaped and sustained by the Spirit. It is this triune God—engaged in creation and humanity, Israel and the nations, the church and the world—who entails this inimitable biblical witness. Therefore, the Bible is not to be seen as simply a function of the religious history of Israel and Christian origins, but as an outworking of the providence of God.[39] Thus it is received, interpreted, and enacted as the canon—the rule, standard, measure—that normatively addresses and directs the faithful and holy people of God as they participate in God's rescue and renewal of the whole of humanity and the entire created order. So seen, the Bible is not like any other book but is in a unique canonical category of its own.

Understandably, privileging the Bible in this way raises various con-cerns among biblical scholars employing an encyclopedic approach to all of the available resources from the ancient Near Eastern, Second Temple Jewish, and Greco-Roman contexts. Certainly, interpreters must accu-

---

ing as Formation," in *Ears That Hear: Explorations in Theological Interpretation of the Bible*, ed. Joel B. Green and Tim Meadowcroft (Sheffield: Sheffield Phoenix, 2013), 258–62.

37. On the anterior role of divine action, see East, "The Hermeneutics of Theological Interpretation," e.g., at 33, acknowledging the influence of John Webster in n. 4.

38. Fowl, also engaging with John Webster's *Holy Scripture: A Dogmatic Sketch* (Cam-bridge: Cambridge University Press, 2003), notes, "The Spirit's work as the operation of God's providential ordering of things sanctifies the means and processes which lead to the production of scripture, turning them to God's holy purposes without diminishing their human, historical character"; see Stephen E. Fowl, "Scripture," in *The Oxford Handbook of Systematic Theology*, ed. John Webster, Kathryn Tanner, and Iain Torrance (Oxford: Oxford University Press, 2007), 345–61, at 351.

39. See, further, John Webster, "Canon," in *Dictionary for Theological Interpretation of the Bible*, ed. Kevin J. Vanhoozer et al. (Grand Rapids: Baker Academic, 2005), 97–100, on a theological account of the canon as transcendentally and providentially ordered; canoniza-tion as "a Spirit-directed process of discernment and judgment" (99), involving acceptance, reception, and compliance; and recognition that the canon shapes the life of the Christian community.

mulate, arrange, and assess in thoughtful fashion all the available biblical and extrabiblical data within their historical-cultural contexts. But scholars taking this approach can sometimes mistakenly assume that knowing all the data and their contexts of origins in itself adequately accounts for biblical meaning; and they may also fail to attend fully to what the biblical authors are doing, under the governance of God, in using the resources at hand to cast a common if complex theological vision. Moreover, those working with an encyclopedic approach inevitably come with their own assumptions, commitments, and interpretive frameworks, yet often provide little explanation for their continued "intensive focus on the canonical text."[40] Various thoughtful rationales may be offered—for example, that this is an ancient, classic, and immensely influential collection of texts. But the Bible's composition and content claim even more than this, offering a fundamentally theological basis for the texts' constitution as Scripture.[41] Understanding Scripture as canon also means taking the texts together as a whole, recognizing their canonical construction arising out of a real, shared history of a community: "the canon is a single (though complex) entity" with "mutually interpretative" elements, "because they testify to a single overarching work of God in the economy of creation and reconciliation: the canon is a whole because it refers to this unified divine work."[42] This entails interpreters taking account of its two-testament textual parameters and arrangements, and its intertextual, typological, and other associations, all of which have been taken up in the interpretive history of the church.[43] This and related considerations contribute to a canonical view of the Bible seen as "essential for building an accurate and consistent faith . . . [and] in forming the one, holy, catholic and apostolic church."[44]

---

40. Reno, "What Makes Exegesis Theological?," 89.

41. Cf. Moberly, "Biblical Criticism and Religious Belief," e.g., 86.

42. Webster, "Canon," 100.

43. See Christopher R. Seitz, "Canonical Approach," in *Dictionary for Theological Interpretation of the Bible*, ed. Vanhoozer et al., 100–102, together with his wider work on the biblical canon, including, for example, *The Character of Christian Scripture: The Significance of a Two-Testament Bible* (Grand Rapids: Baker Academic, 2011), esp. 17–91, 157–71.

44. See Robert W. Wall. "The Canonical View" and "The Canonical Response," in *Biblical Hermeneutics: Five Views*, ed. Stanley E. Porter and Beth M. Stovell (Downers Grove, IL: IVP Academic, 2012), 111–30 and 188–200, quotation at 111; see also Daniel Castelo and Robert W. Wall, "Scripture and the Church: A Précis for an Alternative Analogy," *Journal of Theological Interpretation* 5.2 (2011): 197–210.

Scripture, Church, and World

Inasmuch as the Bible arises in connection with God's covenant with Israel and the early church, fundamentally it is to be read in the context of the Spirit-shaped worship, life, and mission of the people of God. Reading the Bible as a privileged text in this way need not be seen as irrational or arbitrary. Rather, it is consistent with the divine economy, an integral aspect of which is the worshipping community who hears, discerns, and is faithful to the Bible's address, and so participates in its unfolding narrative and vision for humanity and the world. This participation entails a reading of the Old Testament that honors Israel's abiding heritage; that is centered in the Gospel narratives concerning Messiah Jesus, Savior and Lord; and that is faithful to the Spirit-empowered apostolic witness. Moreover, reading and being drawn into Scripture can be seen as "a sacramental act" because it both "points to something other than itself," which "is the grace of Jesus Christ," and "contains the grace it signifies," efficaciously conveyed to faithful readers.[45]

Such faithful reading has always functioned within Christian faith and practice, teaching and tradition, and creeds and confessions across the church historic and universal. Of course, how all of this has been delineated and correlated in detail has varied, with one's particular ecclesial location and tradition—Catholic, Orthodox, Protestant—among the significant factors involved. So, for example, Protestantism typically affords Scripture and its authority primacy over church tradition.[46] Included in Protestantism is the view that God has freely acted to provide the Word of God received by the church,[47] and that canonical Scripture shapes, addresses, and can critique the church and its tradition,[48] including creedal and doctrinal positions. Catholic tradition, as outlined by R. R. Reno in the course of advocating for theological exegesis, stresses "the principle

---

45. Darren Sarisky, "What Is Theological Interpretation? The Example of Robert W. Jenson," *International Journal of Systematic Theology* 12.2 (2010): 210.

46. On the varied nature of Protestantism and its approaches to tradition, see W. David Buschart, *Exploring Protestant Traditions: An Invitation to Theological Hospitality* (Downers Grove, IL: IVP Academic, 2006). Cf. Edith M. Humphrey, *Scripture and Tradition: What the Bible Really Says* (Grand Rapids: Baker Academic, 2013).

47. See, further, John Webster, *Holy Scripture*, 42–67; cf. Lewis Ayres, "'There's Fire in That Rain': On Reading the Letter and Reading Allegorically," *Modern Theology* 28.4 (2012): 616–34, esp. 624–27.

48. Webster, "Canon," 35.

of accordance" between the church and the Bible: "nearly all Christians presume that the supreme trustworthiness of Scripture as the Word of God dovetails with the doctrinal teaching, liturgical formation, and moral exhortation that emanate from the Church."[49] The Bible and the church are "on the same page," and Christians understand that biblical truth accords with that confessed and practiced in the church.[50]

Faithful reading in the church also entails engagement with and contributions from various conversation partners.[51] It is important to have a vibrant and mutually beneficial interaction between the Bible, doctrine, the church, and the wider world. Indeed, such is necessary for the health of the church and its integrity in the public sphere, including the academy.[52] And in this long-standing and continuing exchange there is much to be learned from a whole host of biblical interpreters and theologians, from the patristic period to the present day, who may function as exegetical exemplars, who provide theological parameters, who have wrestled deeply with life in their respective cultural contexts, and who can continue to be wise and challenging dialogue partners.[53]

On Interpreting Scripture

If indeed Scripture functions in service of God's economy, then its interpretation requires "a more theologically expansive and theoretically capacious hermeneutic" than normally found in contemporary biblical studies, one recognizing that divine agency informs and enriches Scripture's depth, scope, and outworking.[54] This hermeneutic certainly includes such basic and interrelated elements as its form and content, text and context, and

---

49. Reno, "What Makes Exegesis Theological?" Quotations from pages 78 and 77 respectively. Thus biblical interpretation ought to align well with what is deemed orthodox doctrine, 76.

50. Reno, "What Makes Exegesis Theological?," 90.

51. Cf. Angus Paddison, "The History and Reemergence of Theological Interpretation," in *A Manifesto for Theological Interpretation,* ed. Bartholomew and Thomas, 27–29.

52. Moberly, "Biblical Criticism and Religious Belief," 84, notes, however, that without the inclusion of its key religious dimension, the Bible "will deservedly lose its privileged place within the academy" (84).

53. See, for example, James A. Andrews, *Hermeneutics and the Church: In Dialogue with Augustine* (Notre Dame: University of Notre Dame Press, 2012), especially his concluding comments at 209–32.

54. East, "The Hermeneutics of Theological Interpretation," 38.

textual associations of various kinds. There is also, as Anthony Thiselton observes, "the inexhaustible, multilayered, multifunctional polyphony of biblical texts," this without allowing a "radical pluralism that brings anarchy."[55] Moreover, Thiselton's observation regarding polyphony prompts us to acknowledge and engage with spiritual interpretation. Indeed, this means recognizing that the Bible not only presents a divine narrative or drama, but is also a "book of signs" as providence unfolds and the Spirit speaks. Thus it invites new readings that participate in the unfolding purposes of God here and now.[56]

Spiritual (or figural and typological) interpretation is perhaps the least understood interpretive approach that remains crucial for a more capacious biblical hermeneutic. In its traditional fourfold form, it concerns the interrelated literal (including historical), allegorical, moral (or tropological), and anagogical (the ultimate) senses of Scripture. This approach aims to read Christ-centered Scripture richly within the divine economy in relation to Israel, the church, and the world: "For the medievals, the literal sense of the text opened out into a christological allegory, which, because Christ is the head of his body, opened out into tropological instruction and, because Christ is the King of a kingdom here yet also coming, into anagogical hope."[57] Spiritual interpretation allows that the Old Testament prefigures Messiah Jesus, and that the New Testament may read the Old Testament in the light of Jesus and the Spirit. In such interpretation, there need be no anachronism if it is accepted that the same Spirit attended the life and Scriptures of Israel, the life and ministry of Jesus, and the emerging early church and its covenant documentation; and, moreover, that "the church's creedal and dogmatic traditions are themselves exegesis of

---

55. So Anthony C. Thiselton, "Communicative Action and Promise in Interdisciplinary, Biblical, and Theological Hermeneutics," in *The Promise of Hermeneutics*, by Roger Lundin, Clarence Walhout, and Anthony C. Thiselton (Grand Rapids: Eerdmans, 1999), 138.

56. On these and other elements, see Richard B. Hays, "Reading the Bible with the Eyes of Faith: The Practice of Theological Exegesis," *Journal of Theological Interpretation* 1.1 (2007): 5–21, esp. 11–15.

57. So Peter J. Leithart, *Deep Exegesis: The Mystery of Reading Scripture* (Waco, TX: Baylor University Press, 2009): 207. This is cited by Matthew Levering, "Readings on the Rock: Typological Exegesis in Contemporary Scholarship," *Modern Theology* 28.4 (2012): 707–31, at 726. Levering, in reviewing certain studies by Richard Hays, Peter Enns, and Peter Leithart, notes that all variously indicate the significance of typological interpretation, both within Scripture itself and as it is interpreted today, with Leithart insisting that this can include speaking truly about the past (and, indeed, the present and the future) under God.

Scripture."[58] It thus follows that we may insist on a range of interpretive approaches—"figural, spiritual, moral, liturgical, devotional, doctrinal, creedal, canonical or other"—as necessary and normative in adequate and faithful reading of the Bible.[59]

Scripture, Public Theology, and Contemporary Culture

A rich reading of Scripture should aim to measure its breadth and depth, reckon seriously with life together, and enable a more faithful and complete participation in God's purposes for humanity and the world. Hence, an "in-house" approach to the Bible and the church that impedes or excludes meaningful ecumenical, interfaith, and public input and dialogue constrains Scripture's creation-wide vision and actualization under God.[60]

Of course, correlating Scripture and the Christian tradition with contemporary culture carries with it highly challenging and debated considerations. This includes agreeing upon a working definition of "culture." Kathryn Tanner suggests that culture entails "the whole social practice of meaningful action," including "the beliefs, values, and orientating symbols that suffuse a whole way of life."[61] And she notes that various approaches have been taken regarding the relationship between Christianity and culture.[62] Yet she contends that today it is not possible to view cultures as relatively "self-contained . . . unified wholes," with clear boundaries identifiable along group-specific (social, religious, etc.), nationalist, and/or geographic lines. Rather, in our postmodern and networked world, they are more internally diverse, perme-

58. On this sequence of statements regarding spiritual interpretation, see, further, East, "The Hermeneutics of Theological Interpretation," 40–43, quotation at 42.

59. East, "The Hermeneutics of Theological Interpretation," 52.

60. Cf. Bockmuehl, "Bible versus Theology," 42–47.

61. Kathryn Tanner, "Cultural Theory," in *The Oxford Handbook of Systematic Theology*, ed. Webster, Tanner, and Torrance, 527–42, quotation at 527. With particular reference to Christian theology expressed in cultural terms, it concerns "the meaning dimension of Christian practices, the theological aspect of all socially significant Christian action," which includes "going to church, protesting poverty, praying, and helping one's neighbour" (528).

62. Tanner, "Cultural Theory," 529: for example, preventing Christian distinctives from being assimilated into culture (post-liberals); correlating the Christian message with ever-changing cultural contexts (Tillich); concern "that Christianity has become irrelevant in a world going its own way" (Protestant liberals); alignment with movements of equality, liberation, etc. (liberation theologians). Still influential are the paradigms in H. Richard Niebuhr, *Christ and Culture* (San Francisco: Harper & Row, 1951).

able, interactive, and changeable.[63] Thus Tanner suggests that any attempts to talk in terms of a distinctive Christian culture is not best conceived socially—for example, by stressing "the church as a separate society" or, conversely, by connecting it too closely to another particular group. Rather, she thinks that it is best viewed in terms of what is and is not Christian, and notes that "Christian identity need not exclude overlapping activities and memberships," though it cannot simply be combined into such.[64]

Tanner helpfully outlines the complex and contested question of how we may consider Christian identity in relation to culture. Yet, in whatever precise way we understand this, it remains crucial that the church is committed to and actively involved in the common good. Angus Paddison, with a keen sense of the church as a cohesive body, calls for a Scripture-based and theologically astute public theology alert to the church's divine vocation and role in the world.[65] He takes Revelation 21:1–22:5 as a theocentric and cosmic vision of God's intention to make "all things new" (21:5), and as an invitation for the church "to stand in anticipatory solidarity with the world" that itself requires and is ready for transformation.[66] A Scripture-shaped public theology for the world includes a missionary concern for the fullness of life (John 10:10); a Christian faith that seeks the welfare of all, in which Christians are both faithful disciples and good citizens; and a fluid boundary between church and world, which encourages conversation, alliances, and attentiveness to both text and world. This public theology is "ecclesial without being ecclesiocentric"; and it seeks to persuade rather than coerce, based not on universal assent but on Scripture's capacity to speak to society's situation.[67]

---

63. Tanner, "Cultural Theory," 530–31.

64. Tanner, "Cultural Theory," 535–36; quotation at 535 and 536. Tanner may go further than some would in suggesting that, in a postmodern world, Christian culture does not cohere in common beliefs and values, but rather "is constructed piecemeal in the messy course of social relations" from disparate cultural materials and a "common concern to figure all this out" with a view to "the true character of Christian living" (539–40).

65. Angus Paddison, "Theological Interpretation and the Bible as Public Text," *Journal of Theological Interpretation* 8.2 (2014): 175–92.

66. Paddison, "Theological Interpretation and the Bible as Public Text," 179; in this reading of John's vision he draws upon the analysis of J. Alexander Sider, *To See History Doxologically: History and Holiness in John Howard Yoder's Ecclesiology*, Radical Traditions (Grand Rapids: Eerdmans, 2011), 45–55, which is interacting with the alternative readings of Oliver O'Donovan and John Howard Yoder.

67. Paddison, "Theological Interpretation and the Bible as Public Text," 178–85, provides a detailed delineation of public theology in terms of five key features; quotation at 184.

Such an approach offers a disposition and a way forward, inviting constructive interaction with our contemporary culture in its various expressions. To revisit a notable case in point, ideally conversations across the church and academy on the nature and role of the Bible today will contribute to the world at large. The academy can provide broad resources and expertise; address issues of intelligibility, offer insight, and propose correction; and do so mindful of its own varied interpretive frames, interests, and ends. And the same can be true of contributions from many other spheres of public life. The church, in living out its vocation and seeking to serve society at large, must be attentive to such scholarly and other contributions. Yet it must also remain true to its common and continuing faith and practice, including its rich theological and spiritual tradition. Inasmuch as Scripture claims to truly render reality under God, then it is to be read historically and theologically in relation to God's purposes for his people and the entire world.[68]

On the Essays That Follow

Most of the essays in this volume were previously presented on separate occasions as public lectures held during the period from September 2013 to November 2014 at Trinity Western University, a Canadian Christian university. The audience largely comprised undergraduate, graduate, and seminary students, and a cross-section of interested people from the wider community, most with connections to various local and largely Protestant and broadly evangelical churches. Those who attended are mindful that reading the Bible is shaped by ecclesial, educational, and other contexts and traditions, and that it involves its various historical, literary, and theological dimensions. Yet they also recognize that it is an ongoing challenge to discern and appropriate all the resources and practices required to embody and enact a Scripture-shaped vision for a faithful life today.

The contributors are specialists in Old Testament, New Testament, and Christian theology, with a common commitment to the constructive correlation of Scripture, theology, and culture, in service of both the church and the academy—without claiming their complete concurrence with everything said above on this wide-ranging subject. Each author was afforded a fairly free hand in selecting a specific topic. There was no in-

---

68. Cf. Rae, "Theological Interpretation and Historical Criticism," 109.

teraction with one another's presentations or ensuing essays. It will be evident, explicitly and implicitly, that the essays share certain common perspectives, interests, and approaches. Yet they are tackling specific issues in particular ways. And they may not align in all respects; such is the complex nature and scope of all that is in play. The contributors have all participated in this undertaking long enough to appreciate the importance and demands of what is entailed; to have made a significant contribution; and to envisage and chart proactive, practiced, and constructive ways forward.

Given what has been said here about Scripture within the economy of God, these essays, which combine broader reflections on key interpretive issues and case studies on important and contested biblical texts, together offer "acts of interpretation" resonating in various ways. Thus, for example, Scripture is understood to be "living and active" (Heb. 4:12) and a communicative and formative act of God. It bears witness to the acts of God in history and to all entailed in the composition of Scripture itself; and it does so in ways that attest that God's antecedent agency graciously operates in and through human participation.[69] These essays also recognize that Scripture's faithful interpretation entails informed, rigorous, and ongoing exegetical engagement with the biblical text—involving the actualization of God's Word in the lives of its readers, the church, and the world.

Part 1 focuses on Scripture and its interpretive frameworks in terms of various important and interrelated considerations and correlations. Stephen Fowl, pursuing an issue he has variously considered elsewhere, offers "A Proposal for Advancing the Theological Interpretation of Scripture" (Chapter 1). Among his initial observations is the limited capacity of various historical-critical practices, and of newer critical approaches, to work together to deliver cohesive and compelling readings of Scripture, and so to address the ever-pressing, complex question of Scripture's meaning and significance. The resulting and remaining tensions and challenges offer an opportunity for theological interpretation to establish its worth by making an informed and constructive contribution. Toward this end, Fowl takes up three important considerations. First, he advises that we work with a broad definition of theological interpretation that, inasmuch as Scripture serves the divine drama of salvation and the Christian life, should be centered on those interpretive habits and practices that keep these theological concerns primary. Second, he suggests that it is now time for a "less fevered" evaluation of the relationships between theological interpretation

---

69. Cf. East, "The Hermeneutics of Theological Interpretation," 33.

and historical criticism. Instead of making overheated claims on both sides, interpreters may profitably use various practices, while keeping the theological aims and ends of Scripture in view throughout. Third, if theological interpretation is to flourish into the future, how will theological interpreters be formed? Fowl makes a case for the cultivation of interpretive virtues: in particular, charity, not least in maximizing interpretive agreement and clarifying disagreement; and prudence (practical reason), in developing professional proficiency in service of the Christian life. He concludes by referencing his own educational context in reflecting on some of the ways in which academic institutions might invest in the formation of theological interpreters.

Jesus often engaged Israel's Scriptures in ways that startled his contemporaries and still puzzle today. And indeed, historically, the many rich dimensions of the Bible have been illuminated and faithfully understood from within various interpreting contexts and communities. Yet as Joel Green observes in "A Discursive Frame for Reading Scripture" (Chapter 2), the modern discipline of biblical interpretation can often work in ways that contract and constrain the ability to appreciate the Bible as God's Word. By way of addressing this situation, Green considers in turn certain frames for reading Scripture that are operative within different communities, each promising a more robust and transformative encounter with the Bible. There is, for example, a "Default Frame" that claims that the Bible need not be interpreted, only read—"what the Bible says, we think, we believe, and we do"—and yet may actually employ any number of particular and problematic dispositions, such as autonomy, individualism, and pragmatism. A "Scientific Frame," seeking neutrality and critical distance, has focused on the Bible as an ancient rather than a sacred text, its truths to be unpacked by the academy's historians rather than the church's theologians. The "Contextual Frame" tries to hold together the previous two frames by moving from what the text meant then to what it means now, but this approach carries its own challenges and concerns. Finally, Green proposes a "Discursive Frame," locating biblical interpretation within a Spirit-guided church and its participation in God's mission to the world. In this frame, it is canon and creed that constitute the primary criteria for biblical interpretation.

Both the historical study of the Old Testament (e.g., of Genesis) and scientific models of origins have exerted considerable pressure on traditional Christian beliefs, calling into question not only the reliability of Scripture but, for some, even the truth of the gospel. Peter Enns, in his thought-provoking "The Bible, Evolution, and the Journey of Faith" (Chapter 3), observes that a common Christian response is to address this problem through various *ad hoc* solutions that try to hold together certain biblical (and evangelical) and scientific (and evolutionary) accounts of creation. However, Enns suggests that such attempts often produce their own sources of stress and can impede attempts to correlate biblical scholarship and scientific inquiry with intellectual and spiritual integrity. He contends that a preferred way forward is to feel the force of the various challenges raised by historical—including extrabiblical—and scientific investigation and to embark on a spiritual journey of rethinking one's perhaps too-familiar conceptions of Scripture and even of God. Enns advocates an incarnational model of Scripture, reading it in relation to its ancient contexts and canonical formation and within the Christian tradition. And he urges that, rather than resist taking such a spiritual journey—by ignoring the challenges, avoiding conversations and critique, and becoming disengaged—one should undertake it as an essential function of Christian faith seeking understanding.

The chapters in Part 2 engage in acts of interpretation that are variously attentive to doctrine, canon, and literary form, tackling a range of notable biblical texts and documents. Among the most formative and challenging texts in the Bible is Genesis 1:2, which Craig Bartholomew takes up in his "Genesis 1:2 and the Doctrine of Creation" (Chapter 4). Much is at stake here. For example, does the text indicate, as some scholars have suggested, that God creates with preexisting matter ("a formless void and darkness") rather than *ex nihilo* ("out of nothing")? And could it also be inferred that the world was created only after a primordial conflict with Chaos, thus intimating that evil existed eternally rather than emerged within God's good creation? Bartholomew addresses such contentious questions in dialogue with two leading twentieth-century theologians, Karl Barth and Dietrich Bonhoeffer, together with current work on the still influential so-called *Chaoskampf* motif (a conflict between God and Chaos). While rejecting a primeval reality alongside God, Barth nonetheless reads Genesis 1:2 as standing in contrast to 1:1, as "the shadow side of creation" yet to be addressed by the Word of God. But Bonhoeffer, with notable precedent in Christian tradition, instead regards Genesis 1:2 as following directly from 1:1 as "the progressive movement of the act of creation." Negotiating his way through the interrelated exegetical and doctrinal issues in play, Bartholomew finally regards Bonhoeffer as closer to all that is entailed. And he substantiates his own position with a rich exegetical and theological reading of Genesis 1:2, set within Genesis 1:2–2:3, and attentive to what this programmatic text has to say concerning God, creation, and redemption.

Reading biblical writings in relation to their various canonical associations can bring into view important aspects of their nature and significance that interpreters may otherwise miss on a strictly historical assessment. Christopher Seitz demonstrates this point in "A Canonical Reading of Ecclesiastes" (Chapter 5), which approaches this challenging Old Testament text canonically from a series of interrelated standpoints. He first notes the unusual character of the protagonist's designation as "Qoheleth" (Eccles. 1:1, 12, etc.) and argues that it is best seen in relation to Solomon's depiction in 1 Kings 8 as one who gathers, prays, and blesses Israel, encompassing all that transpires under the all-seeing eye of God in heaven. Seitz then considers the meaning and thematic significance of the key recurring term *hebel,* and Qoheleth as one who has experienced the world's *habel habalim*—that which is "not to be grasped . . . not within our control"—yet in the midst of this can still see God's good purposes at work. Seitz follows this with an assessment of the contested correlation between Proverbs and Ecclesiastes' use of proverbs (e.g., at Eccles. 12:9–11), which he regards as complementary: taken together, they attest that wisdom, though difficult to attain, must be pursued if "God is to be feared and life found in him." In sum, as these connections between Ecclesiastes, 1 Kings 8, and Proverbs indicate, and as the Jewish and Christian interpretive tradition well knew, interest in the discrete witness of a biblical text is best served when seen within the broad and rich field of canonical associations.

The New Testament canon comprises a collection of collections—for example, the Gospels, the Pauline Letters, and the Catholic Epistles—and all are irreducibly integral to its apostolic witness to God's Word and to the church's continuing faith and practice. However, as Robert Wall notes in his "What's 'Catholic' about the 'Catholic' Epistles Collection?" (Chapter 6), many modern scholars have viewed the Catholic Epistles—James, 1–2 Peter, 1-2-3 John, and Jude—as a diverse and arbitrary anthology of largely independent documents. Countering such a view and developing further his important and continuing work in this area, Wall begins by examining the formation and form of the Catholic Epistles. He contends that their inclusion contributes to the New Testament's "aesthetic excellence"—that is, to its completeness and coherence as Scripture—and so safeguards its full apostolic witness, orthodox use, and universal application. Indeed, the sevenfold sequence and shape of the Catholic Epistles is not arbitrary or incidental, but engenders intertexts and offers an inner logic that enables readers to recognize and realize more fully their combined contribution. He also considers their unifying Christology, which attests to a direct and intimate apostolic access to the historical Jesus and risen Messiah, an epistemic claim that secures the authoritative collection and underwrites its Christology against false claims. In short, Wall's essay explicates the literary aesthetic and theological integrity of the Catholic Epistles and shows the collection's crucial contribution to and completion of the apostolic witness and the biblical canon.

Revelation or the Apocalypse of John continues to capture the imagination of lay readers and academics alike. Its language and imagery, sources and traditions, social setting and purpose, all fascinate and confound. Edith Humphrey, in "Mixing Wine with Water: Enjoyment and Expectation through the Style of the Apocalypse" (Chapter 7), observes the text's literary, cultural, and theological dimensions and provides an incisive analysis of two of its most extraordinary and central scenarios. The first focuses on the two witnesses in chapter 11; the second involves a woman, a child, and a dragon in chapter 12; and, taken together, they cast considerable light on the complexity and profundity of the Apocalypse overall. Humphrey adeptly deploys Northrop Frye's anatomy of literary levels or "modes" to show how the text boldly blends folk story with myth or divine story in ironic and thought-provoking ways. Notably, in depicting the key actors and action, the text creatively reconfigures and combines various figures and literary forms from the Hebrew Bible and other ancient Jewish and Greco-Roman sources. This gives considerable depth and even a level of discomfort to the narrative and theological drama in view. And, remarkably, at the heart of all this is the Messiah, who, though "a mere child, a humble figure," is nonetheless exalted to the throne of God. Revelation's rhetorical artistry requires that its readers appreciate how its stylistically mixed modes incorporate "legend into serious theology," offer "wine mixed with water," and invite their participation in the unfolding divine drama.

The chapters in Part 3 recognize that Scripture has always been read in the context of the continuing faithful Christian community and that contemporary readers can benefit by keeping company with its rich interpretive tradition. Not everyone is persuaded that we can learn much from how early Christians read the Bible. Indeed, in relation to the allegorical readings of the church fathers, two pressing questions arise in both the academy and much of the church today: what is the justification for "speaking other" than the words themselves say, and isn't allegorizing "an arbitrary imposition of our own preconceived notions onto the biblical text"? Responding to such questions, Hans Boersma, in "Reading the Exodus Story with Melito and Origen" (Chapter 8), shows that the fathers read Scripture in light of the new realities of Christ and the life and worship of the church, an interpretive approach they saw as rooted in the Bible itself. And Boersma illustrates this by reference to Melito of Sardis (died ca. 180) and Origen of Alexandria (ca. 185–ca. 254). They understood all things as unfolding under the providence of God; and so, for example, they viewed the Passover/exodus narrative in Exodus 12 as inextricably linked to Christ and the church. Indeed, it may even be said that Christ is already sacramentally present within the Old Testament text and that, as God's people, not least in baptism and the Eucharist, later readers are also taking the exodus journey. As such, allegorical reading aims to offer not an unrelated "other" reading, but rather to reveal the deeper and more expansive meaning that is already inherent in Scripture itself. In this way, allegorical reading attests to the significant and sacramental role Scripture plays within God's purposes for the church and the world.

Undertaking rich readings of Scripture within the continuing Christian tradition, including those attentive to Catholic and Protestant dialogue, will require what Charles Raith II calls "ecumenical *ressourcement*": "asking old questions of old sources in new ways." As an instance of such *ressourcement*, in "Reading Paul's Letter to the Romans with Aquinas and Calvin" (Chapter 9), Raith revisits the readings of Romans in the commentaries of Aquinas and Calvin—two towering theologians who have significantly shaped the Catholic and Protestant traditions and engages especially their understanding of salvation. He shows that a comparison sensitive to their respective historical contexts and underlying theological concerns reveals agreement on the key issue in Romans: that we are justified through the mercy of God alone, by virtue of Christ's sacrifice and redemption on our behalf. Yet Raith also recognizes differences between Aquinas and Calvin on justification. But rather than settling for these differences or defending his own Reformed tradition, he asks the question, "How can the Reformed reading of Romans be enriched by that of Aquinas?" Reading Scripture together should not reduce and relativize, nor merely repeat and reassert. Rather, under God's guidance, the theological resources available can be drawn together, heard anew, deepen perspectives, and expand one's heritage. And this approach will advance the faithful interpretation of Scripture, promote Christian unity, and above all attest to the saving and life-giving truth of the gospel.

Finally, Jens Zimmermann, in "Reading the Old Testament with Dietrich Bonhoeffer" (Chapter 10), explains Bonhoeffer's christological reading of the Old Testament as demonstrated in his exegesis of Genesis 1–3 and the Psalms. While Bonhoeffer consciously reads the Old Testament rather than a "Hebrew Bible," he nonetheless observes a tension between the two Testaments. Zimmermann shows how the eschatological ultimate-penultimate schema that grounds Bonhoeffer's theology also undergirds his Old Testament exegesis and governs the relation of the two Testaments. Bonhoeffer did not deny, of course, that Jesus himself consciously takes up and transforms Israel's story by presenting himself as the fulfillment of God's messianic promises to his people. But he did deny that a reader can take this transformation for granted, can accept it secondhand as a settled truth. Rather, each reader has to work through, reexperience, and appropriate for himself or herself this history to understand the full weight of Jesus's own affirmation that "salvation is from the Jews" (John 4:22). According to Bonhoeffer, "whoever wishes to be and perceive things too quickly and too directly in New Testament ways is to my mind no Christian. One cannot and must not speak the ultimate word before the penultimate." It is not by leaving the Old Testament behind but by staying within this story of which Christ is the culmination that we will understand who Jesus is, and who God is. "Only when one knows that the name of God may not be uttered may one sometimes speak of grace [. . .]. Only when one accepts the law as binding may one perhaps sometimes speak of grace."[70] In Bonhoeffer's theological exegesis, past and present horizons are fused in a way that the whole of the past horizon constantly stands before us in its difference to elucidate our present understanding of God. Therefore, it is only by staying with Jesus within the Jewish narrative that we can ever grasp who Jesus really is.

---

70. "Letter to Eberhard Bethge" (Dec. 1943), *Letters and Papers from Prison*, *DBWE* 8, 213.

PART 1

Interpretive Frameworks

CHAPTER 1

A Proposal for Advancing the Theological Interpretation of Scripture

Stephen E. Fowl

Establishing an Academic Practice

Before moving to more substantive matters, I would like to begin by briefly noting the reemergence of patterns of theological interpretation within the academy. Thus, I will begin with a truism, albeit a truism that took me a long time to appreciate. Although I could not have recognized this when I finished my PhD, the rich tradition of Christian theology from the patristic period down to the present is soaked in Scripture, even if it is sometimes hard to recognize. In fact, for the great majority of the church's history, you could not really be counted as a theologian if you were not a master of the sacred page, if you did not have a deep knowledge and sharp facility with Scripture and its interpretation. Indeed, I would go so far as to say that at its best, throughout its history, theology has always been a mode of scriptural exegesis.

You don't have to be an expert to see that biblical interpretation during the patristic, medieval, or early modern period looks very different from the biblical interpretation I was trained to do in graduate school. One way of accounting for this difference, the way I was at least implicitly taught by virtually all my professors, was that premodern biblical interpretation was

---

This is a slightly condensed/revised version of my "Historical Criticism, Theological Interpretation, and the Ends of the Christian Life," in *Conception, Reception, and the Spirit: Essays in Honor of Andrew T. Lincoln*, ed. J. Gordon McConville and Lloyd K. Pietersen (Eugene, OR: Cascade, 2015), 173–86; and Stephen Fowl, "Theological Interpretation and Its Future," *Anglican Theological Review* 99.4 (2017): 671–90; used by permission.

simply a form of error. Just as physics has moved on from debates about phlogiston in the seventeenth century,[1] we biblical scholars have left those failed interpretive remains behind.

I understand how this argument works in physics. Theories about phlogiston were replaced by theories about oxygen. Those superior theories both accounted for the data that had been observed and allowed scientists reliably to anticipate future data. Theories about oxygen did the same job, answered the same questions, that theories about phlogiston did and did so better and with fewer residual difficulties and anomalies. It is harder to make this case with scriptural interpretation over time. That is, it is harder to claim that modern biblical criticism is a clear advance over premodern biblical criticism.[2]

One way of making this claim is to say that modern biblical criticism leads readers to the meaning of biblical texts better than premodern biblical criticism did. Biblical critics reach the meaning of a text by mastering a number of ancient languages and some modern languages, and also by studying the histories, cultures, and societies within which the biblical texts are set and within which the biblical texts were written. In addition, and most importantly, by developing a facility with a number of critical skills that are often lumped together under the name "historical criticism," one will be able to uncover the meaning of biblical texts in ways that premodern biblical interpreters did not and could not do. Although I cannot recall anyone ever saying it quite as directly as this, this view was certainly widely assumed when I was beginning my graduate training in the early 1980s.

In the intervening time, a number of things have rendered this account implausible to many scholars, including me. For example, many of the practices of historical criticism were shown to be badly flawed in their assumptions and methods. The best example is gospel form criticism.[3]

---

1. In the seventeenth century, scientists proposed that combustible materials contained an element called phlogiston that was released during combustion.

2. This point is made most forcefully by David C. Steinmetz, "The Superiority of Pre-Critical Exegesis," *Theology Today* 37.1 (1980): 27–38. Reprinted in Stephen E. Fowl, ed., *Theological Interpretation of Scripture: Classic and Contemporary Readings* (Oxford: Blackwell, 1997), 26–38.

3. See Erhardt Güttgemanns, *Offene Fragen zur Formgeschichte des Evangeliums; eine methodologische Skizze der Grundlagenproblematik der Form- und Redaktionsgeschichte* (München: C. Kaiser Verlag, 1970). This volume was translated as *Candid Questions Concerning Gospel Form Criticism: A Methodological Sketch of the Fundamental Problematics*

Scholars have demonstrated that the assumptions that made gospel form criticism work were misguided, particularly the assumptions about the transition of discrete stories about Jesus from oral to written exposition and about the ways language functions in different contexts. This change in itself is not surprising. Gospel form criticism was the methodical working out of a set of theories. In the course of investigating those theories, they proved to be inadequate. This is how knowledge is tested and developed in any field. The failure of gospel form criticism is not in and of itself a problem if it is replaced by new theories and methods that can do the same things better, just as theories about oxygen replaced theories about phlogiston. It is not clear to me, however, that such a theory has emerged or can emerge.[4]

There could be a number of reasons for this. It may simply be that, with more time and new data, we will come up with a better account of how various passages functioned in their original oral contexts and how the evangelists ultimately took up and shaped them with their own communities' interests in mind to produce something like the canonical Gospels. I am not confident this will happen. Rather, there is a growing recognition that we do not really have a clear and reliable picture of how the Gospels were produced. Although each of the canonical Gospels became associated with specific churches,[5] there seems little chance of discerning whether and how these specific communities played any role in the production of those Gospels. Moreover, it is less clear that the

---

of Form and Redaction Criticism, trans. William G. Doty, PTMS 26 (Pittsburgh: Pickwick, 1979). Both the German and the English translation make for difficult reading. This may in large measure account for the limited influence of Güttgemanns's criticisms. When coupled with insights from speech-act theory and anthropological work on the transition between oral and written cultures, however, very few if any of the fundamental assumptions of gospel form criticism survive.

4. See Klaus Berger, "Rhetorical Criticism, New Form Criticism, and New Testament Hermeneutics," in *Rhetoric and the New Testament: Essays from the 1992 Heidelberg Conference*, ed. Stanley E. Porter and Thomas H. Ulbricht, JSNTSup 90 (Sheffield: Sheffield Academic, 1993), 390-96.

5. In response to Richard Bauckham's argument that scholars should abandon redaction-critical approaches that focus on the "communities" of the evangelists, in favor of a recognition that the Gospels were written for all Christians (see note 6), Margaret M. Mitchell has noted that, in the early church, certain readers tended to associate specific Gospels with specific churches. This in no way supports the redaction critical project, but it does raise a helpful corrective to some of Bauckham's claims. See "Patristic Counter-Evidence to the Claim that 'the Gospels Were Written for All Christians,'" *New Testament Studies* 51.1 (2005): 36-79.

evangelists wrote with the interests of particular communities in mind.[6] Further, although Markan priority still seems secure, the Q hypothesis has come under increasingly sharp and sophisticated criticism.[7] Our newly won ignorance in these areas opens up the prospect for rethinking this aspect of study in ways that would completely obviate form criticism. We obviously will need to wait for further developments here. For my purposes, it is enough to note this is an example of a practice of historical criticism that is being eclipsed. As a result of these and other tensions internal to the practice of historical criticism, its claims to deliver the meaning of a biblical text are less plausible now than they ever have been.

In addition, it became clear that the other various practices that went under the name "historical criticism" did not actually work together to produce a single result called "meaning." The more proficient we became at these various practices, the clearer it became that their results were rarely compatible with each other. That is not to say that the results of each of these practices were false. Rather, it meant that these results could rarely, if ever, be combined into some summative result called the meaning of a biblical text. When you add to that the advent of new critical practices that were entering biblical studies from fields such as classics, history, literature, and sociology, the beginning graduate student's hope of finding the meaning of the biblical text became even more remote.

Finally, and most importantly, those working in fields such as philosophical hermeneutics began to show us that the notion of the meaning of a text was a lot more complex than we once thought.[8] Initially, there was great resistance to addressing these philosophical claims. If the practices of historical criticism had been as internally cohesive and coherent as was

6. This is the point variously argued in Richard Bauckham, ed., *The Gospels for All Christians: Rethinking the Gospel Audiences* (Grand Rapids: Eerdmans, 1998). See also the collection of essays edited by Edward Klink III, *The Audience of the Gospels: The Origin and Function of the Gospels in Early Christianity*, LNTS 353 (Edinburgh: T. & T. Clark, 2010).

7. See Mark Goodacre, *The Case Against Q: Studies in Markan Priority and the Synoptic Problem* (Harrisburg, PA: Trinity Press International, 2002).

8. No single scholar puts these philosophical issues on the agenda of biblical scholars more profoundly than Anthony C. Thiselton. See, in particular, *The Two Horizons: New Testament Hermeneutics and Philosophical Description with Special Reference to Heidegger, Bultmann, Gadamer, and Wittgenstein* (Grand Rapids: Eerdmans, 1980) and *New Horizons in Hermeneutics: New Testament Hermeneutics and Philosophical Description* (Grand Rapids: Zondervan, 1992).

once thought, these more philosophical arguments about meaning might have been kept at arm's length. In the absence of such cohesion and in the presence of newer critical practices, the questions about the nature of textual meaning were too pervasive, too compelling, and too important simply to ignore. Arguments among biblical scholars about the meaning of a text became very intense. That intensity remains and often grows whenever someone has a stake in claiming that there is only one meaning of a biblical text and all other interpretations are either erroneous or something subsidiary or derivative.

The large institutions that support biblical scholarship have, for the most part, not directly confronted these intense arguments. Instead, they simply allow a variety of interpretive interests and approaches to have their own space. This policy does not resolve any serious theoretical issues, but it allows us all to continue to operate in the absence of any coherent way of resolving the various challenges to historical criticism noted above. This is not to say that the intensity of arguments over historical criticism and its alternatives have completely dissipated. Rather, it simply means that these arguments are now generally carried on by discrete groups arguing among themselves.

I take it that, despite its own inner tensions, arguments over historical criticism and the subsequent fragmentation of biblical scholarship into numerous discrete interests are at their root very specific examples of the larger fate of arguments about textual meaning that one finds in other disciplines. One can still pursue a grand unified theory of textual meaning and methods for attaining or displaying it, but I am not optimistic of success here. Although some might consider this a crisis, for those who are interested, as I am, in reinvigorating forms of biblical interpretation that are genuinely theological, this fragmented state of affairs is more like an opportunity.

Although Christians have always read Scripture theologically, within the guild of professional biblical scholars, these practices had largely fallen out of favor with the rise of historical criticism, beginning in the late eighteenth century.[9] By the time of the methodological ascendance of historical criticism, its practices were often seen as the only viable scholarly option, and they largely worked to keep theological considerations at arm's length. Whereas in premodern times theologians were required to display

---

9. See Michael C. Legaspi, *The Death of Scripture and the Rise of Biblical Studies*, OSHT (New York: Oxford University Press, 2010).

facility with Scripture, by the time of historical criticism's ascendancy, one could be either a theologian *or* a biblical scholar, but not both.[10] That disjunction persists down to today and is rigidly enforced in the structure of most graduate-school curricula.

As I already mentioned, however, the fragmentation of biblical scholarship has provided an opportunity to reinvigorate practices of theological interpretation. Here is what I mean: since no one set of interpretive considerations can guarantee access to textual meaning, it becomes difficult to deny a place to most thoughtful ways of interpreting Scripture. Theological considerations can no longer be ruled out of court simply for being theological. The past twenty years have witnessed a significant growth in scholarship directed toward what might be called the theological interpretation of Scripture.[11] Within the profession of biblical studies, there has been some opposition to these developments. This opposition, however, seems primarily directed at and driven by poorly done examples of theological interpretation or inept arguments about the place of theological interpretation as a scholarly practice. To the extent that this is true, theological interpreters should be as opposed to poor practice and inept argument as anyone else. These are not, however, principled objections.[12] There cannot be substantial methodological objections to theological interpretation done well apart from prior agreements about method in biblical studies that would rule out theological considerations. Such agreement is lacking and is not likely anytime soon.

It would be foolish to say that theological interpretation of Scripture is now the dominant mode of biblical interpretation in the academy. It is not. I do think it is safe to say that theological interpretation has sufficient support among scholars and the institutions that support

10. The conceptual roots of this can be traced at least to William Wrede, "The Tasks and Methods of 'New Testament Theology,'" in *The Nature of New Testament Theology: The Contribution of William Wrede and Adolf Schlatter*, ed. Robert Morgan, SBT 2.25 (London: SCM, 1973), 68–116. See also the discussion in Stephen E. Fowl, *Engaging Scripture: A Model for Theological Interpretaion* (Oxford: Blackwell, 1998), 13–21.

11. The *Journal of Theological Interpretation* has published continuously since 2007. There are several major commentary series devoted to theological interpretation that have already published numerous volumes. There are at least two SBL groups that work primarily in this field, and their sessions are usually very well attended.

12. See the initial essay by Ron S. Hendel, "Farewell to SBL: Faith and Reason in Biblical Studies," *Biblical Archaeology Review* 36.4 (2010): 70–74, and the subsequent discussions in such places as http://www.brookelester.net/blog/2012/4/12/farewell-to-sbl-revisited -biblical-studies-religious-faith-a.html.

them and that it seems set to continue as a distinct scholarly activity for some time to come. Given this reality, I would like to address some of the issues currently facing theological interpreters of Scripture as they move into the future. The first of these issues concerns debates around the nature and practice of theological interpretation. These debates are largely matters of self-definition. There may be less to say here than one might first think.

The second concerns the relationships between theological interpretation and the other practices of biblical scholarship, particularly those that still go under the name "historical criticism." When theological interpretation of Scripture was trying to get a foothold in the academy, there was a good deal of overheated rhetoric from both theological interpreters and historical critics about either the necessity of or the bankrupt nature of historical criticism. I think the time is right to reflect on these relationships in less fevered tones.[13]

Finally, in the light of these other two discussions, I would like to propose some considerations and concerns for those interested in the growth and formation of theological interpreters of Scripture. In this regard, I believe there are some reasons for concern and some opportunities for further thought.

Defining Theological Interpretation: Less May Be More

Many new academic ventures are marked by extraordinary methodological self-consciousness and great fussiness over self-definition and boundary marking. Theological interpretation of Scripture was no different in this respect. Although theological interpretation of Scripture was new to the modern university, it was not a new practice. To the extent that I have participated in these arguments, I have tried to point out that rather than starting something new, scholars should speak in terms of reviving something older, a practice or sets of practices that used to be considered normal but had largely been eclipsed. Clearly, one should not fantasize about the past and then seek to repeat slavishly something that never was.

---

13. Joel B. Green's essay, "Re-thinking 'History' for Theological Interpretation," *Journal of Theological Interpretation* 5.2 (2011): 159–74, reflects a similar concern. I am less certain that the various sets of interests he ascribes to his three types of historical criticism can be retained as clearly as he seems to indicate.

Although such attention need not define theological interpretation, it seems wise to me that the aims of contemporary scholars interested in theological interpretation should be directed to discerning and reflecting on the habits and practices of those premodern interpreters who saw scriptural interpretation as one of the central tasks of theology, not as a separate discipline distinct from theology. Those habits and practices would need to be made serviceable for our modern contexts and related to other interpretive habits and contexts, but this did not and does not require an overly narrow definition of theological interpretation or a distinct interpretive method for it.

In this regard, it is striking to note that, unlike our own time, premodern interpreters produced very few works on interpretive method. Origen's *On First Principles* and Augustine's *On Christian Doctrine* come immediately to mind. In addition, in the medieval period, Nicholas of Lyra and Thomas Aquinas write what might be called methodological reflections, though Aquinas's reflections are part of a much larger theological endeavor. One can also learn much from the debates between Erasmus and Luther. There are, no doubt, others besides these that come to mind. Nevertheless, in comparison with the modern period, there are very few works dedicated to what might be called interpretive method. Moreover, despite the various differences between Origen, Augustine, Aquinas, and Luther, they all share an approach that does not treat scriptural interpretation as an end in itself. Instead, what they all seem to share is the view that Scripture is to be interpreted in the light of the larger ends of the Christian life. They use different idioms to describe this end. Some invoke the vocabulary of salvation; others speak of ever deeper love of God and neighbor, or ever deeper union with the triune God or deeper friendship with God. These differing vocabularies can lead one to think that there are many different views about the end of the Christian life, but that would be a mistake. There is enormous agreement on this matter; no one of these idioms rules out the others. Moreover, given the fact that there is an in-built element of mystery about the precise nature of humanity's ultimate end in God, it is not surprising to find a variety of ways of describing this.

Nevertheless, by focusing on the end or purpose of the Christian life, one can see that scriptural interpretation is never an end in itself for believers. Scripture becomes one, perhaps the primary, gift of God for drawing believers toward their ultimate end. Scripture has a role to play in the divine drama of salvation. To use Augustine's image, it becomes the vehicle on which one rides toward one's true home along the road laid down by

Christic.[14] Reading Scripture theologically, then, involves those habits and practices that will enable believers to interpret Scripture in ways that will enhance rather than frustrate their progress toward their ultimate end in God.

I recognize that this is a very open-ended account of theological interpretation. That it is so is not simply a factor of the space constraints on this essay. There is little to gain and much to be lost by trying to offer too narrow a definition of theological interpretation.[15] In fact, I would be very happy for all to adopt the view that theological interpretation is that interpretation that keeps theological concerns primary. Keeping theological concerns primary means that Scripture or scriptural interpretation does not become a source, tool, or means to attain some other goal or project that is not theological—that is, not serving the ends of ever more faithful faith and practice so that Christians might be drawn into ever deeper love of God and neighbor.

Although a definition such as this one is capable of bringing rigorous scholarly forms of interpretation, as well as homilies and congregational Bible studies, all under the umbrella of theological interpretation, I am primarily interested here in scholarly forms of interpretation. In this respect, I would also at least propose for further discussion the view that one need not personally share the doctrinal and theological convictions of Christians in order to reflect on and even display the ways those convictions may influence and be influenced by scriptural interpretation. Jews, Muslims, and those with no religious faith at all, could, in principle, interpret Scripture theologically. Indeed, one can only think that believing Christians would benefit from such intellectual generosity extended by those who do not share their theological convictions yet are still willing to engage in the practice of helping display how such convictions shape and are shaped by scriptural interpretation.

When it comes to the life and practice of specific Christian communities, there may well be aspects of this scholarly work, whether done by

14. See Augustine, *On Christian Doctrine*, trans. and intro. D. W. Robertson (New York: Macmillan, 1987), 1:39.

15. Stanley Porter is simply one of the most recent scholars to press this issue. See "What Exactly Is Theological Interpretation of Scripture and Is It Hermeneutically Robust Enough for the Task to Which It Has Been Appointed?" in *Horizons in Hermeneutics: A Festschrift in Honor of Anthony C. Thiselton*, ed. Stanley E. Porter and Matthew R. Malcolm (Grand Rapids: Eerdmans, 2013), 234–67. For a list of others who press this question, see Green, "History," 163 n. 4.

believers or nonbelievers, that they will not be able or want to engage. Further, there may be additional forms of interpretive expression that are crucial to the lives of these communities that are not part of the standard scholarly discourse. In addition, within such communities, there may be different standards and procedures for authorizing interpreters and specific interpretations from those of the academy. These realities should not obscure the prospect of non-Christians or nonbelievers engaging in the scholarly practice of theological interpretation of Scripture. At the same time, I realize that there are not likely to be many such scholars. Nevertheless, engaging in debate over a suggestion such as this one could be extremely useful for clarifying the nature and scope of the practice of theological interpretation of Scripture, at least at a scholarly level. Moreover, I think that whether it is this issue or others, engagement in discussion and debate over focused and specific questions regarding the practice of theological interpretation will be the most fruitful way to clarify the definition or definitions of theological interpretation.

Theological Interpretation and Historical Criticism: No Need for War

My second area of concern is to chart some of the relationships between theological interpretation of Scripture and some of the other types of biblical interpretation common in the academy. In my narration of the rise of contemporary interest in theological interpretation, I hinted that when theological interests were trying to assert themselves into the scholarly mainstream, advocates for theological interpretation often made overheated claims about the bankruptcy of historical criticism. At the same time, there has also been an outpouring of articles by scholars arguing that allowing theological concerns a hearing within such institutions as the Society of Biblical Literature will have a deleterious effect on biblical scholarship.[16] These, too, tend to rely on overheated claims about such things as scholarly objectivity, historical integrity, and so forth. Often each side points to poorly executed or poorly defended examples of whatever it is they are arguing against. This seems to be not so much an argument in favor of one sort of interpretation over another as an argument in favor of doing whatever work one does better. As long as each side continues

16. See note 12 above.

to make overheated claims about the logical necessity of their approach relative to all others, we can expect a lot of rhetorical heat, but little hermeneutical light.

For those of us who are both interested in theological interpretation and recognize the legitimacy of other interpretive interests and practices, the question remains, how should theological interpreters engage other forms of biblical criticism? The short answer is: theological interpreters can and should make use of historical, literary, social-scientific, and all other types of biblical interpretation as long as they understand that such work needs to be subsidiary to the task of keeping theological concerns primary. Scholars can and will interpret biblical texts from a variety of interpretive interests, employing diverse interpretive practices. They can and will offer these interpretations as ends in themselves or contributions toward larger historical, literary, or social-scientific projects. This is all to the good. Theological interpreters should read, engage, and learn from such works. This is because theological interpreters can and should make use of them when and as they can help in the tasks of theological interpretation. The practice of engaging and making use of the best work of those who don't share one's theological convictions has a long history in the church. Origen, for example, argued for a deep and thoughtful engagement with pagan philosophy to the extent that it helped Christians think about Christianity better. He used the trope of the Israelites plundering the Egyptians in Exodus to justify this practice.[17] Many have followed in his footsteps.

If theological interpretation of Scripture is marked by a sustained interpretive commitment to keep theological concerns primary in one's interpretation, it seems plausible that one can and should make *ad hoc* use of other interpretive habits, practices, and results. This raises questions about how to make such *ad hoc* use of other interpretive habits, practices, and results without sacrificing the primacy of theological concerns. Answering this concern will push me toward my next point, which is concerned with the formation of future theological interpreters. There is no method or procedure that will guarantee success here. Just because there is not a method, however, does not mean that we cannot think methodically about these questions and come up with some insights. Rather than pursuing a method to keep all of the various interpretive interests of biblical scholars in some

---

17. See Origen's letter to the as yet unbaptized Gregory Thaumaturgos. "Letter to Gregory," paras. 1 and 2 in PG 11:88–89. See also the discussion in Fowl, *Engaging Scripture*, 181–83.

sort of proper order, theological interpreters would be better served by working to cultivate a set of interpretive virtues that will help them make wise judgments about how to keep theological concerns primary in their interpretive work. I would also like to suggest that the formation of any virtue, interpretive or otherwise, requires institutional contexts that will nurture such virtue in scholars. Recognition of this latter point will lead to my final consideration.

The Formation of Interpretive Virtues:
Charity and Practical Wisdom

First, although I am certain that theological interpreters of Scripture should cultivate numerous virtues both moral and intellectual, two in particular come to the forefront. These are charity and prudence, or practical reason. At their best, these two virtues work together to help theological interpreters engage the wide variety of biblical interpretation while working to maintain the primacy of theological concerns. Further, although I will discuss each of these virtues as if they were discrete things, they ultimately must be manifested along with other virtues in a more or less unified human life.

Charity in interpretation is always directed toward maximizing agreement between interpreters. The point of this is not to reduce disagreement because disagreements are bad and upsetting. Rather, charity assumes that if interpreters read each other's works in ways that maximize their agreements, then both the nature and the scope of their disagreements will be clearer and more capable of resolution. Such charity is particularly important when dealing with interpreters and interpretations that come from times, places, and cultures far different from our own. When we seek to maximize the agreements between ourselves and such interpreters, we diminish the temptation simply to reduce those interpreters to inferior versions of ourselves who can be easily dismissed. In this respect, when historical critics emphasize the temporal and cultural "strangeness" of the Bible, they are emphasizing a necessary, but not sufficient, aspect of interpretive charity. They see the importance of understanding interpreters and interpretations on their own terms.

This is a necessary, but not sufficient, aspect of interpretive charity because the charitable interpreter will not simply desire to display the strangeness of alternative interpretations. In addition, the charitable interpreter will want to present alternative interpreters and interpretations in the most positive light possible. This might require going above and beyond the work done by those who hold these alternative views; this may involve doing more for one's argumentative opponents than they did for themselves. Nevertheless, if one is to produce a better interpretive alternative, then one must build upon and extend the strengths of alternative views without replicating their weaknesses. Doing this requires one to address the strongest possible version of any alternative. It should be clear from this discussion that charity is not about artificial forms of humility. It does not require one to support weak or erroneous interpretations in favor of keeping interpretive peace. There is no reason for charitable interpreters to shy away from disagreement or argument. Indeed, this side of the eschaton, Christians can expect that disagreement and debate will mark all their engagements with Scripture. In such a situation, charity is that virtue that will give us the best chance of resolving our disputes well.

The second virtue to examine is practical reason or prudence. If you pick up a journal in the field of biblical studies or attend a professional conference of biblical scholars, two things would strike you. First, the material under discussion is both exceedingly diverse and complex. Second, those who are fully participating in the discussions and debates are able to address the diversity and complexity relatively well. They are able to figure out where the critical issues lie; they can make judgments about the weight and relevance of particular claims; they can come to a conclusion that they can defend, revise, or abandon in the light of new evidence or superior arguments. What this shows, in part, is that these scholars have been more or less well formed to be particular types of readers.

It is simply the case that one cannot successfully and proficiently enter into these professional discussions and debates without prior formation. This is because there is a great deal of technical information to master. This is not the whole story, however. This technical information is not self-interpreting. It does not organize itself; it cannot identify its own problems, tensions, and underlying patterns. Professional proficiency presumes technical mastery. Such proficiency is distinguished from technical mastery, however, by the professionals' abilities to engage in interpretive debates and discussions. In the course of such engagements, they are able: to reformulate the issues as needed; to marshal evidence both arguing for its relevance to a particular issue and showing how that evidence should lead to specific conclusions; to defend, refine, and reformulate views in the light of counter-claims; and, in all of this, to advance a particular interpretive debate or discussion.

The virtue that enables one to move beyond technical mastery to professional proficiency is what Aristotle would call *phronesis*, or practical reasoning or prudence. Although it is rarely specified this way, the graduate formation of biblical scholars is primarily an exercise in cultivating the virtue of practical reasoning. The aim of this is so that scholars can deploy their technical knowledge and skills in ways that are appropriate to specific problems, contexts, and audiences. The prudent or practically wise scholar perceives the relevant similarities between complex problems and already agreed standards and then moves by analogy to use already proven standards to elucidate the unknown or the contested.

Given that theological interpretation of Scripture is marked by debates, discussions, and arguments about how to interpret and embody Scripture so as to enhance Christians' prospects of worshipping and living faithfully before God, cultivating the virtue of practical reasoning or prudence will be as important as cultivating interpretive charity. This is so that the technical skills and knowledge of the scholar can fruitfully be displayed, deployed, and directed toward the larger ends of the Christian life. Without practical reasoning, it is too easy to displace theological concerns from their primacy in theological interpretation.

Forming Theological Interpreters

How are such virtues formed and cultivated in people? For professional biblical scholars, this formation takes place in graduate school and in the course of becoming a full-fledged member of the academy. Theological interpreters of Scripture can and should benefit from such formation. Although the formative work that graduate schools and the academy more generally provides is quite strong, it tends not to do as good a job in developing both the technical skills and knowledge attendant to theological interpretation and the precise ways in which one needs to be formed to be a charitable and prudent theological interpreter. In large part, this is because the skills and knowledge distinctively related to theological interpretation will cross the disciplinary and departmental boundaries that currently shape most institutions. There is much work to be done here with regard to the curricula and aims of graduate education that will develop theological interpreters of Scripture. Historical and systematic theologians will need to work with biblical scholars and others in ways that graduate training does not equip them to do well.

One might well ask, if the academy does such a poor job of forming theological interpreters, how would I account for the presence of current theological interpreters? Apart from any detailed surveys, I would suggest that contemporary theological interpreters have benefitted from sets of contingent circumstances and contexts that have formed them. Without denigrating such circumstances and contexts, this is not a systematic and intentional pattern of formation. I believe it is now time to focus on just such a systematic and intentional set of processes.

In this light, we must not forget that the aims of theological interpretation will always have an eye on the church, on that primary context where Christians argue, debate, and discuss Scripture with the aim of deepening their love of God and neighbor. Having said that, I think I can assert without much argument that, in regard to both of these virtues that are crucial to theological interpretation, the academy does a much better job than the church in cultivating charitable and prudent interpreters.

Although the practices of theological interpretation of Scripture have always operated in some form within ecclesial contexts, it now appears that the practices of theological interpretation have established some space within the modern academy, and much of the institutional support for such interpreters comes from academic institutions. The various institutions of the modern academy do a relatively good job of forming many of the requisite skills, habits, and dispositions biblical scholars need. For the most part, these institutions are neither interested in nor well placed to form the specific skills, habits, and dispositions required to form theological interpreters of Scripture. Further, although churches benefit from the presence and work of contemporary theological interpreters of Scripture, and although one might argue that such scholars are essential to the long-term health of the church, churches have not generally invested in the formation and sustenance of such scholars. Moreover, given the current questions surrounding the state and future of higher education and related concerns and questions about seminary education, there is, perhaps now more than ever, a need to enrich and fortify institutions within which theological interpreters of Scripture can be formed, in ways that impart, within an ecclesial context, both the requisite technical mastery of languages, history, philosophy, and doctrine and such interpretive virtues as charity and prudence. The primary question is, who will invest in such formation? Further, in the absence of such investment, will there be sufficient younger scholars who will be formed and supported to carry this practice on into the future?

If the formation of theological interpreters of Scripture is to be more systematic or intentional, one obvious option is to found new academic institutions or new departments or programs within existing institutions. A central aim of such institutions, departments, or programs would be to form theological interpreters of Scripture in ways that impart both the requisite technical mastery of languages, history, philosophy, and doctrine and such interpretive virtues as charity and patience so that this practice may continue to grow and flourish into the future.[18] The structural and economic realities of higher education in colleges, universities, and seminaries make it seem unlikely that new ventures will be sustainable for the foreseeable future.

One might argue that current seminaries are precisely the places where such formation might flourish. I am sure that such formation happens in seminaries. I would, however, also note a couple of structural factors that may work against this. First, seminary faculties are, for the most part, drawn from the PhD programs of major research universities. Such graduate training encourages disciplinary specialization within which it is difficult to develop the wide-ranging exposure to church history and Christian doctrine needed to interpret theologically. Given this, it will be difficult, but not impossible, for seminary faculty to help seminarians overcome the disciplinary boundaries that were so important in their own training.

A second set of challenges are those structural ones facing the residential seminary model—especially free-standing seminaries. Here is simply one form of this challenge: among mainline denominations, there are fewer and fewer congregations that can support full-time clergy. In that light, it becomes difficult for a student to justify things typically involved in going to a residential seminary, such as giving up a job, moving a family, and taking on debt to finance training that is not likely to lead to a full-time job. There are a number of ways of responding to these challenges. As far as I can tell, none of the proposed responses will enhance the prospects for a seminary's survival, and none of these will enhance the prospects of forming theological interpreters of Scripture.

---

18. Although the formation of theological interpreters is not its only aim, the ThD program at Duke Divinity School is an example of the type of formation across the theological disciplines that I advocate here.

Although they, too, face many challenges, there may be opportunities within church-related colleges and universities that bring together reflective Christian faith and serious academic study. Such masterful, charitable, and prudent contexts could profoundly participate in the formation of theological interpreters of Scripture—at least at the undergraduate level. Here, however, such institutions face the same challenge that seminaries do, in that their faculties are also drawn from graduate programs that foster disciplinary specialization.

Given that the structure of graduate education is not likely to change substantially in the near future, there may be scope for forming theological interpreters within already existing departments and faculties. With that in mind, here are some ideas that institutions might take in order to enhance the prospects for forming theological interpreters of Scripture. For example, there could be a foundational course that all students take and all faculty teach. I think there are numerous benefits for students when such a course exists. For the purposes of this essay, I want to concentrate on the ways in which such a course can help in the formation of faculty who are theological interpreters of Scripture.

In my own context, this course is Introduction to Theology. All students at Loyola, regardless of their majors, must take Introduction to Theology. All faculty members in our department must teach this course. It is a point of pride for us that we all have a stake in this course. At the same time, we all were trained in fairly narrow theological specialties. No one really comes to this course fully prepared to teach it. We do not use a common textbook. We do not employ a common syllabus. Instead, we have a variety of rules of thumb that we observe with each other. Remember, these are rules of thumb to be used prudentially. Teach to your strengths. If you are in patristics, do not try to teach this course as if you were a philosophical theologian. There is a strong preference for primary texts over secondary texts and for whole texts over portions of texts. In terms of content, we agree that we will cover a wide variety of Scripture, a text from the Christian tradition, and something contemporary. In addition to the natural overlap in our syllabi, each year we pick a common text for all of our sections. We are on a three-year rotation between biblical texts, texts from the tradition, and contemporary texts. Some texts from past years include Isaiah, Philippians, Gregory of Nyssa's *The Life of Moses*, Bonaventure's *The Life of St. Francis*, Catherine of Siena's *Letters*, Dietrich Bonhoeffer's *Letters and Papers from Prison*, and Martin Luther King Jr.'s "Letter from a Birmingham Jail."

As a biblical scholar, one of the first benefits I have derived from teaching this course is that I have been formed to see my work with Scripture as part of a larger theological enterprise. Even if we do not have a single departmental theology, and even though we might articulate the end of that theological enterprise differently from each other, our common teaching helps us see ourselves as participants in a common theological enterprise. It is important to note that, in this enterprise, there is no clear division of labor. The biblical scholars are not simply providers of raw material for the theologians. Instead, we each bring our special types of expertise to this common theological enterprise. If anything, Scripture plays a normative, if not always explicit, role in all our conversations. This is not to say that the findings of professional biblical scholars always have the last word. Rather, Scripture is often, but not always, the generative source for the conversations. The interpretation of Scripture tends to regulate both discussion and any provisional conclusions. Scripture can also direct the conversation in new ways, particularly through its history of interpretation or through powerful contemporary interpretations. Importantly, scriptural interpretation is not simply the purview of the Bible expert, either. All are expected to be able to talk about the Bible even if they are not biblical scholars. Likewise, I am treated as a competent or potentially competent interpreter of Augustine, Aquinas, or Martin Luther King Jr.

I understand that, for some institutional contexts, such an integrated theological approach is not possible or even desirable. Nevertheless, in those contexts where it may be both desirable and possible, the common teaching of a single course in theology can be especially formative for those who want to interpret Scripture theologically.

It is important to recognize that each member of our department has had to go well outside his or her graduate training in order to teach Introduction to Theology. On the one hand, we hire people for their specialized graduate training in specific fields. We need them to mediate the best and most current scholarly discussions in their subfields to the rest of us. On the other hand, they need to have the capacities to overcome the hyperspecialization of current graduate training. This, of course, requires a healthy sense of and respect for what one does not know, combined with the confidence not to be paralyzed by this. In this respect, the support of one's colleagues is essential. Grace and good humor can go a long way toward encouraging folks to venture beyond the boundaries of their graduate education.

Moreover, theology at its best is a thoroughly communal endeavor. This, of course, is not a new idea. The realities of our curriculum, however, have indelibly impressed this truism on me over the years. Every day, for as long as I have been at Loyola, we gather for lunch together. In our current building, all our offices surround a lounge area with sofas, soft chairs, and two tables with chairs around them. Each day, at least some of us will gather at the tables with our food. This is completely voluntary; nobody is there every day; people come when they can and leave when they have to. We don't always talk about theology. But day in and day out, as often as not, folks will come to lunch just having taught a text that was new to them or just about to teach a text that is new to them. As they eat lunch, they can partake of both the wisdom of those who have expertise in those texts and the experience of those who have taught the text to Loyola students over a number of years. Quite simply, our curriculum doesn't work without our daily lunches. More personally, I would not be the theologian I am today apart from those lunches.

These reflections all come from the dual observations that theological interpretation requires a particular type of formation that is different from the formation that most graduate programs in biblical studies provide and that there are few programs or resources dedicated to such formation. They are offered not as the final word on these matters. Rather, my aim is to point out that this is a significant and neglected discussion to which current theological interpreters might now direct their attentions.

CHAPTER 2

A Discursive Frame for Reading Scripture

Joel B. Green

Readers of the Gospels can easily find themselves alternating between awe, surprise, and downright bewilderment at Jesus's words. This is especially true in scenes where the evangelists cast Jesus in conversation, whether with friend or foe. Among the responses that baffle are those occasions where Jesus asks, "Haven't you read . . . ?"—followed generally by his reference to some well-known scriptural text or another (e.g., Mark 12:10, 26, CEB). Actually, these exchanges are perplexing in two ways. First, it may not be clear why Jesus asks such a question, since it is obvious that his conversation partners have in fact read those scriptural texts. After all, Jesus typically poses this question to those whose lives revolve around the reading and interpretation of those Scriptures. It would be like asking a theology professor, "Haven't you read Barth?" It would be like asking a New Testament theologian, "Haven't you read Bultmann?" The answer must be, "Yes, of course!" Second, the point at which we might really be perplexed is how Jesus arrives at the conclusions he reaches from these well-known passages from Israel's Scriptures. We know these texts, we might say, but we did not know that this is their significance. Clearly, Jesus has *framed* those texts in ways that are strange to our ears, surprising in light of Israel's interpretive traditions.

I am reminded of the many times I have accompanied my wife, Pam, to get a picture framed. We might have secured an antique portrait of the Durham Cathedral or landed a nice reproduction of Pieter Bruegel's *Tower*

This essay was originally presented as a lecture for the series "Scripture, Theology, and Culture: Acts of Interpretation," Trinity Western University, September 2013. I am grateful to Kellie Adamian for her invaluable assistance in preparing this essay for publication.

of Babel, and we needed a frame. Invariably, at the framing store, I would be drawn to such-and-such a frame, Pam to another. In fact, a number of frames "worked" well enough with the picture in question, but each caused us to see the same print in a different way. After all, a picture is many things—colors, textures, potentially multiple focal points—and different frames can diminish or draw out different features. The question is, what features of this picture do we want to showcase?

Moving a little more toward the abstract, those of us who are interested in "how institutions think" can frame those institutions, like a university or a coffee shop or a dot.com, so as to draw attention to their organizational structures, or to the talents of their people, or to the distribution and use of power, or to the values they want to instill.[1] Organizations are all of these things and more, but, often serving different needs, different people visualize them through different frames and therefore see different things. In the same way, the Bible is many things—a collection of books, a literary artifact, a conglomerate of sources, a stage in the tradition history of a developing faith, a theological treatise, a grand narrative, and more. Different frames highlight different characteristics of these texts, while cloaking others.

With regard to reading the Bible, the problem on which I want to reflect is this: Although different communities might choose to frame the Bible in different ways, the modern discipline of biblical interpretation has tended to narrow our options in ways that are not only problematic but actually hazardous to those of us who turn to the Bible as Christian Scripture. The forms of study generally taught in Western colleges and universities, as well as in Christian seminaries, have done little to cultivate transformative encounters with Scripture. This should not be surprising, since the protocols accredited by and within the academy are not particularly concerned with nurturing theological formation and scriptural wisdom. Biblical studies in the modern era has tended to frame the biblical materials in ways that are at best unfriendly and at worst downright hostile toward our reading the Bible as God's word. Accordingly, I want to examine some common ways we have learned to frame the biblical materials, before proposing a frame with the potential to take more seriously the Christian Scriptures' home within the church.

---

1. Cf. Lee G. Bolman and Terrence E. Deal, *Reframing Organizations: Artistry, Choice, and Leadership*, 5th ed. (San Francisco: Jossey-Bass, 2013).

JOEL B. GREEN

A Word about "Framing"

By way of orientation, I need first to say another word or two about "framing." In the field of cognitive linguistics, "frame" refers to the larger patterns within which we locate, experience, and make sense of terms, concepts, and experiences. Consider these words: "Number 41." When we hear these words, what we make of them depends on our framing—for example, whether we are standing in line for a bagel; watching our favorite, left-handed defenseman for the Vancouver Canucks; or trying to distinguish between US presidents named "Bush." In these examples, the same words, "number 41," have been framed differently and so are understood to signify different things.

As Vyvyan Evans and Melanie Green put it in their textbook on *Cognitive Linguistics*, "frame" refers to "a schematisation of experience (a knowledge structure) . . . represented at the conceptual level and held in long-term memory. The frame relates the elements and entities associated with a particular culturally embedded scene from human experience."[2] We associate terms for things, feelings, and experiences with whole patterns of thought and belief. As a result, like dropping a stone into a peaceful lake, thinking of a single object has a ripple effect, setting in motion an entire experience structure. What set of experiences comes to mind when we hear the word "driver," for example? This depends on the frame signaled by our context. Are we talking about why my computer refuses to communicate with my printer, powerful market forces that will undermine my investments, or who will be drinking club soda at Saturday night's party? Similarly, setting a Bible on a podium will excite different expectations as a prelude to a lecture on ancient Israelite religion at the University of British Columbia than it will have at Coastal Church, Vancouver.

The Default Frame

Let us consider, then, three common frames within which the Bible is read.[3] The first I will call the "Default Frame." This is the frame I encoun-

---

2. Vyvyan Evans and Melanie Green, *Cognitive Linguistics: An Introduction* (Edinburgh: Edinburgh University Press, 2006), 222.
3. This general framework was inspired long ago by my reading of C. René Padilla, "The Interpreted Word: Reflections on Contextual Hermeneutics," *Themelios* 7.1 (1981): 18–23.

48

FIGURE 2.1 THE DEFAULT FRAME

The arrow indicates the uninterpreted transfer of the biblical message to the contemporary setting.

tered explicitly soon after I went to seminary. Walking down the halls of the church where I was an associate pastor, I was talking with a couple of people about what I was learning. One of them took me aside and corrected me, saying, "Joel, we don't really *interpret* the Bible. The Bible *doesn't need to be interpreted. It just needs to be read.*" This, then, is the default position: what the Bible says, we think, we believe, and we do.

Even if this is for many Christians the default position, even if this has been the *de facto* practice on display in many Bible studies I have witnessed, it actually does not work very well. Consider, for example, the scene in John 13, where Jesus washes his disciples' feet and then says, "I have given you an example: Just as I have done, you also must do" (John 13:15, CEB). These words at least seem pretty straightforward. Indeed, with these words, Jesus has provided us with as strong or direct a command as we read elsewhere: "'This is my body, which is for you; do this to remember me.' . . . 'This cup is the new covenant in my blood. Every time you drink it, do this to remember me'" (1 Cor 11:24–25, CEB). Yet how many of us participate in the Lord's Supper or the Eucharist? And how many of us engage regularly in the washing of each other's feet? Typically, when I ask these questions in classrooms and churches, everyone responds in the affirmative to the first question, but only a smattering of hands is raised in response to the second. Why is this? Apparently, many who are committed generally to the Default Frame work at other times with an alternative hermeneutic, and this allows them to respond immediately (and obediently) to the one text but not to the other.

Another example is Romans 16:16: "Greet each other with a holy kiss" (my translation). Here is another directive, plainly spoken. Its meaning seems unambiguous. Yet we rarely find it practiced, at least in the Western church. This suggests to me again that even those who are happy enough most of the time with the Default Frame easily shift to other hermeneutical approaches, allowing them to set aside what seems to be the plain sense of the text. (And in this case, we are dealing not only with Romans 16:16 but with a cadre of New Testament texts that speak of holy kissing or the kiss of love.[4])

The Default Frame has important emphases that we should not overlook. For example, this approach emphasizes an accessible Bible; anyone can read it. It emphasizes the perspicuity or clarity of Scripture: the Bible speaks plainly; its message is not obscure. And it supports a strong emphasis on "application."

But there are also some shortcomings, the most important of which I can formulate as a question: As we use the Default Frame in our engagement with the Bible, is it actually the Bible that we hear? Does the Bible get to speak with its own voice; or do I take seriously enough that, when I read Scripture, I read Scripture within the commitments I have learned as a child of the Western world and through the lens bequeathed to me by my socialization in this world and through my education? What might it mean to read the Bible as people deeply formed in the Western world? Painting with the broadest of brushes, we might expect the following dispositions to shape the readings of those reared in the West:

- Subjectivity: I evaluate this text in relationship to my experience.
- Autonomy: I decide how, or even whether, this text applies to me.
- Individualism: I turn to Scripture with concerns about my salvation and my walk with Jesus.
- Pragmatism: I want the Bible to tell me what to do, to give me three things to do; I generally don't read the Bible to learn what kind of person to be.
- Libertarianism: I have direct access to this text, quite apart from that hermeneutical community called the church—present, past, or global.

If such dispositions as these are widely shared among readers of the Bible, then can it be said that, when we read the Bible, we simply hear what it says unfiltered by our own proclivities, needs, and allegiances? Other problems could be enumerated, too. Thus, the Default Frame neglects the historical rootedness of the biblical materials. And, as I have already mentioned in my references to John 13 and Romans 16, this approach is selectively ap-

---

4. For the significance of holy kissing, see Joel B. Green, "Embodying the Gospel: Two Exemplary Practices," *Journal of Spiritual Formation and Soul Care* 7.1 (2014): 11–21.

FIGURE 2.2 THE SCIENTIFIC FRAME
The addition of the shaded circle around the biblical message symbolizes the embedding of this message in a historical context, and the removal of the arrow indicates the loss of any concern with contemporary significance.

plied. Undoubtedly, at least for many, these shortcomings of the Default Frame have made the Scientific Frame all the more attractive.

The Scientific Frame

In his book, *The Death of Scripture and the Rise of Biblical Studies*, Michael Legaspi tells the eighteenth-century story of the Bible in search of a home.[5] What he develops is an early portrait of the Scientific Frame. Note the innovations in our diagram when we compare it to the Default Frame. (1) Here we see that the biblical message must be understood in its context, with "context" understood above all in historical terms. (2) Moreover, we find no arrow moving from the "biblical message" to the "contemporary message," since, after all, historical inquiry as such is not particularly concerned with (and may actually deny) the ongoing significance of the biblical materials. Reading according to the Scientific Frame prioritizes "what it meant," not "what it means."

For Legaspi, in the early modern era, the Bible was orphaned by cultural forces that removed the Bible from its home in the church. The weakening of notions regarding, and commitments to, scriptural authority resulted in the Bible's dislocation from its privileged status and therefore its ecclesial home. Where would study of the Bible find new lodgings? As

5. Michael C. Legaspi, *The Death of Scripture and the Rise of Biblical Studies*, OSHT (New York: Oxford University Press, 2010).

Legaspi tells the story, serious study of the Bible bounced from one foster family to another until it was finally adopted into the home of nineteenth-century historicism. This led to certain perspectives on reading the Bible. For example, first, the Bible should be read "like any other book."[6] Second, approaches to reading the Bible would emphasize interpreter neutrality. Third, theologians identified the chief critical problem of reading the Bible in historical terms, as "historical distance." What separates us from the words of the Bible is the vast chasm between past and present, and, by implication, between fact and narrative, and between history (what really happened) and theology. Accordingly, "truth"—long the property of theology and philosophy—now fell into the custody of historians. Moving forward, "what is true" would be identified more and more with what history tells us "really happened." If people previously regarded the Bible as bearing witness to the truth because the Bible was inspired testimony to God's perspective on the world, now the biblical materials would witness to the truth only insofar as they represented events as they actually occurred.

The eighteenth and nineteenth centuries saw a move away from framing our engagement with the Bible primarily in theological terms toward framing our engagement with the Bible primarily in historical terms. These centuries witnessed a concomitant move away from framing the Bible as a unified collection giving us access to God's voice toward framing the biblical materials as individual testaments, then as disparate books, and then as discrete sources. Those taking this path would find themselves studying less the Bible than the New Testament, less the New Testament than the Gospel of Matthew, less the Gospel of Matthew than the (hypothetical) source document Q, and less the (hypothetical) source document Q than the (hypothetical) layers comprising the (hypothetical) source document Q, and the (hypothetical) Q community (or communities) alleged to have produced and to have shaped its life in relation to these (hypothetical) documents. This Scientific Frame would come to rule biblical studies in the modern world—up to and including the turn of the twenty-first century.

Let me illustrate further. When I was in seminary, I took a course in a spring semester concerned with "New Testament Christologies." On the Wednesday afternoon of Holy Week, our seminar met for the purpose of discussing the New Testament formulae regarding the death and resurrection of Jesus. As that class session was coming to an end, a student

6. Cf. R. W. L. Moberly, "'Interpret the Bible Like Any Other Book'? Requiem for an Axiom," *Journal of Theological Interpretation* 4.1 (2010): 91–110.

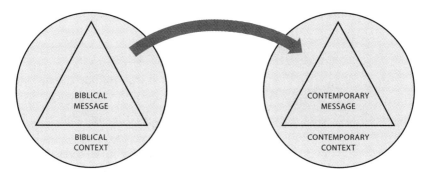

FIGURE 2.3 THE CONTEXTUAL FRAME
Here shaded circles show that not only the ancient message but also the contemporary reader are embedded in their own contexts, while the restoration of the arrow indicates an interest in nevertheless drawing contemporary significance from the ancient message.

addressed these words to our professor: "Thank you, Dr. So-and-So. Thank you for putting this material on the schedule for this week. This discussion has been so helpful as I prepare my sermon for Good Friday." Our professor responded by shaking his head and saying, "I can't believe I've done this. I try so hard not to be relevant." We students laughed, but he did not, and for good reason. After all, as he would say to me in another context, the moment a New Testament scholar declares his or her interests, at that moment he or she gives up any claim to "neutral scientific exegesis." This explains why, according to the Scientific Frame, we see no concern for moving from what the Bible meant to what the Bible might mean today.

The Contextual Frame

Our third frame, the Contextual Frame, is a critical and imaginative attempt to hold together the Default Frame, with its emphasis on contemporary significance, and the Scientific Frame, with its emphasis on listening carefully to the past. From this vantage point, we must understand the biblical message in its context; in order to speak that message today, we must also take seriously our own contexts. We might hear in the background those words often attributed to Karl Barth, that we should read the Bible and the newspaper together.[7]

7. Whether Barth actually said these words is unclear. See http://barth.ptsem.edu /about-cbs/faq.

We see here an important emphasis on specificity, both "then" and "now." And some will appreciate the biblical-theological impulses on display in this emphasis on moving from "what it meant" to "what it means."

What might, at first blush, appear to be helpful, though, is actually quite troublesome. This is because the Contextual Frame problematically imagines that "what it meant" can be determined through neutral, objective study, as though our contemporary interests or allegiances have no role in shaping what we see as we read the Bible. Moreover, this kind of framing leads to the long-held and widely shared understanding that biblical interpretation is properly an exercise in baton-passing: from the biblical scholar, who is concerned (only) with grammatico-historical exegesis, to the theologian and ethicist and preacher. Is it really true that God can speak today only after history has first determined what God has said?

Let me introduce an interlude at this point. From my vantage point, we have been dealing thus far with an implicit and deeply problematic modeling of how communication takes place. Even with its fairly obvious deficiencies, this model has continued to infiltrate much of our reading of the Bible. Here is how it works. A sender forms an idea, encodes it in some form for transmission through a channel; the receiver receives it, decodes it, and re-forms the idea. And, presto, the idea re-formed in the receiver's mind is the same idea that was first formed in the sender's. Our own experiences with family or friends provide us with endless illustrations of the failure of this model. At an intuitive level, we know that this is not actually how communication works. Moreover, if we have engaged at all in intergenerational or other forms of intercultural exchange, the liabilities of this model will have become even more transparent. We know instinctively that more is going on than a simple process of one-way traffic, from one mind to another, and our interactions with even our closest friends and family serve repeatedly to disconfirm the usefulness of this model. This model treats communication as though we all have exactly the same experiences and share the same background, as though the recipient is passive, as though hearing from "the other" would not have the potential to change us, and as though communication were always one-way. Even if this model has been discredited in communication studies, even if at an instinctual level we know it does not work, it nonetheless remains the case that many of us have framed our engagement with Scripture in just these terms.

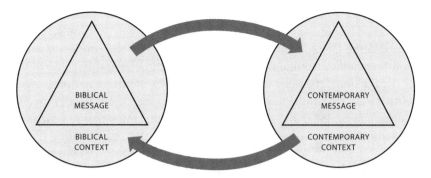

FIGURE 2.4 THE DISCURSIVE FRAME (PART 1)
The addition of a second arrow, from the contemporary setting back to the ancient setting, recognizes the ways in which contemporary readers carry their questions and assumptions back to the biblical text, producing a circular dialogue beween readers and text.

The Discursive Frame

A step forward, then, would be my introduction of a fourth frame for reading Scripture. I refer to the Discursive Frame. I am borrowing the word "discursive" from discourse theory, with its central interest in "language in use." Accordingly, I am concerned with what happens when actual readers read the Bible as an instance of "language in use." Understanding our engagement with the Bible in this way, we see immediately our need to acknowledge that we are not passive recipients of the Bible's meaning; hence, we acknowledge the interests we bring to the text, our readerly interests. We do not come naked to the text, but bring with us not only our prior expectations of the text, but also any number of assumptions about the way the world works, what God can or cannot do, our understandings of time and authority and science, and so on.

Why is it important that we take seriously our interests, our allegiances, and our taken-for-granted view of things? Let me give an example or two. Over the past three or four decades, as I have listened to teachers, I have heard again and again this appeal to "common sense": "Now, a common-sense reading of this text would be. . . ." Every time I hear those words I wonder: Common to whom? Or, more sharply put, whose sense gets to be "common"? Invariably, the answer is: "the speaker," of course (and people like him or her). The same problem arises often enough when someone working with a debated text refers to what the text "clearly" or "obviously" says.

Mark Allan Powell writes of an informal research project he conducted, in which he asks similar questions of a single text in three different contexts.[8] He first read the parable of the Prodigal Son (Luke 15:11–32), then asked his audience why the younger brother was in trouble. An audience in the United States responded typically that the younger brother found himself in trouble because of his wicked behavior, because of his sin. In Tanzania, the representative answer drew attention to the younger brother's lack of support. No one helped him at his time of need! Powell's audience in St. Petersburg, Russia, spoke of the famine that had gripped the land. Which of these is correct? Which is the right reading of the younger son's situation in Luke 15? Careful readers of Luke's Gospel will know that they are all "correct," that is, that each of these emphases is supported by the details of the parable Jesus relates. "What do they hear?" Powell asks. This is a good question precisely because the answer cannot be taken for granted. In the present case, diverse cultural assumptions and socio-economic experiences led to different responses. The text is the same, the textual background is the same, but the readers have changed, and these different readers hear the text differently.

Again, for centuries people have been mapping the world. Today, we have photographs of our planet from outer space. Surely, we know what the world looks like. Yet our frames for portraying the world make a difference in what we see—whether we draw the map based on population density, HIV prevalence, global internet usage, military spending, or even happiness. Analogously, we tend to find in the Bible what we went looking for, whether we sought solace or theological support or moral direction.

We have heard it said, "A text without a context is a pretext." But now we learn that no text is ever read apart from a context. Every reading is contextually situated. The question is, within or in relation to what context will a text be read? Reflecting on the Discursive Frame, we begin to see that there are multiple possibilities for grasping the relationship between the contemporary and biblical worlds, and thus between the contemporary message and the biblical message. In short, readers matter.

Let me press further by reflecting more deeply on this issue of "context." From the vantage point of the Scientific Frame, "context" must be understood especially in historical terms. Adopting a Contextual Frame, "context" is expanded to account for all sorts of possibilities, whether geographic or socio-economic or religious, or some other. With respect to my interest in this essay with "reframing Scripture," I want to urge that

8. Mark Allan Powell, *What Do They Hear? Bridging the Gap between Pulpit and Pew* (Nashville: Abingdon, 2007).

those of us who want to read the Bible as Christian Scripture must locate our reading within the church. This includes the liturgy, prayer, and public reading of Scripture, but it also includes how we engage in biblical studies—a reality that raises a pivotal question: What difference ought it to make that we read the Bible within the church, as church people? This question deserves far more work than it typically receives. This is because of the truism that the approaches to studying the Bible taught in most colleges and universities and seminaries in the United States and Canada have nothing to do particularly with reading the Bible *as the church's book*.

Let me illustrate with reference to the Nicene Creed, which tells us that the church is one, holy, catholic, and apostolic. If we take seriously this confession that there is only one church, historically and globally, that the church is set apart, that the church is universal, and that the church is moored to the apostolic kerygma witnessed in the Scriptures and confessed in the Rule of Faith, then what might this entail for our reading of Scripture? Among the possible responses we might give to this question is this one: If the church is genuinely "one," then the church addressed in Paul's First Letter to the Corinthians, the church in Langley, British Columbia, and the church of the eschaton—these are all the same church. And if this is true, then the primary distance to be overcome in our reading of the Bible is not *historical* (as with the Scientific Frame) but *theological*. We may profitably ask, therefore, whether we have been formed theologically such that we are ready to allow Scripture to tell us who God is and who we are.

Raising questions about theological formation inevitably leads to the much larger question of the role of the Holy Spirit in our formation for reading Scripture. I tend to think about the relationship between the Holy Spirit and our engagement with Scripture along four lines.[9] First, we come to Scripture dependent on the Spirit. As we invite the Holy Spirit into the interpretive process, we deny our autonomy as readers of Scripture and affirm our dependence on the Spirit and on the community of God's people generated by the Spirit (against any notions of self-autonomy and self-legislation). Second, we acknowledge the role of Scripture in our sanctification—in our becoming more Christ-like, more fully human, more holy. As the Holy Spirit is the divine agent of sanctification, so the Spirit is at work in shaping us for reading the Bible as Scripture—that is, in forming in us dispositions and postures such as those of invitation, openness, and

---

9. Cf. Joel B. Green, *Seized by Truth: Reading the Bible as Scripture* (Nashville: Abingdon, 2007), 94–100.

repentance. An integrated life of devotion to God, conversational intimacy with God, our capacity to enter into prayer as submission, our willingness to participate in a repentance-oriented reading of Scripture—these orientations and concomitant practices are the fruit of the work of the Spirit in our lives. Third, we recognize that the Spirit has been and continues to be engaged in the formation of God's people. As the Spirit of Christ was active in the generation of Scripture, so, in our actualization of the Scriptures, the Spirit points us to Christ and forms the church in Christlikeness. Fourth, we take seriously the role of the Holy Spirit in the long history of God's people as they have sought to interpret and embody the Scriptures. The ongoing work of the Spirit includes the Spirit's forming us as, and within, an interpretive community of faithfulness—God's people continuous through history and across the globe.

Not incidentally, this emphasis on the formation of readers of Scripture has as a corollary our mitigating the contemporary fascination with and hyper-concern for "right method" in studying the Bible. Stated plainly, reliance on method, any method, is inadequate for faithful reading of Scripture. Let me illustrate. As an early riser, I often find myself dressing in the dark. Sometimes, I find that I have failed even though I have done everything correctly as I put on my shirt. I take a button, insert it through the hole, give it just the right twist so that the button is fixed in place. I do this repeatedly, with each button, one at time. Having finished the job, however, I discover that my shirt is wrongly buttoned—a wonderful column of buttons, but each in the wrong buttonhole. Methodologically, my approach was infallible. I did all the right things. I used the right techniques. I did what I have practiced doing for decades. But I started in the wrong place. Formation for reading the Bible as Scripture, I am urging, entails a decidedly theological starting place.

If we take seriously the formation of the reader and the reader's location within the church, then we cannot assume that the answer to our ills is the discovery of or commitment to a new interpretive technique. Importantly, nor can I ever be satisfied with an interpretive path that leads first to reading the Bible and only then inquires into the significance of this biblical text for the church. Instead, we begin with the Christian formation of readers. And we begin with the location of our interpretive work within the church. We ask, "How does the life of the church in the world make a difference in our reading of Scripture? What difference does it make that we read from within the community of faith instead of from outside of it?"

Revised in this way, the Discursive Frame situates our interpretive work within the context of the church under the guidance of the Spirit, with

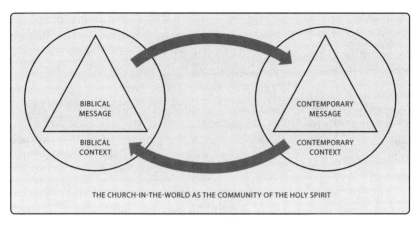

FIGURE 2.5 THE DISCURSIVE FRAME (PART 2)

The addition of a shaded region around the whole of the preceding diagram represents the theological understanding that the whole hermeneutical process takes place within the guidance of the Holy Spirit.

the church itself located with reference to its presence and mission in the world. The Discursive Frame thus presses for any number of hermeneutical emphases that have not found an easy home among biblical interpreters whose work is framed scientifically or even contextually. Chief among these today might be interests in theological interpretation of Scripture, a missional hermeneutics of Scripture, or spiritual interpretation of Scripture.

Validity in Interpretation

I recognize, of course, that the interpretive interests I have introduced will have surfaced significant problems for some. Let me address what I take to be the most worrisome of these concerns. I refer to the question of how we might adjudicate among different readings of the Bible. How do we know when a reading of a text is valid (or good)? What criteria do we use? If we have learned the protocols of biblical studies in the modern era, then we have learned that the meaning of a biblical text is constrained historically. But if we have learned this lesson, then one of the challenging consequences of my attempt to reframe Scripture is that it might seem to deconstrain meaning and thus to open the door to unrestrained subjectivity. Without the bedrock provided by historical inquiry as the foundation for verifying what a text means, is each of us left to our own meaning? The only viable prophylactic against anything-goes-ism in reading the Bible is the Scientific Frame, is it not? How will we know whether we have produced or encountered a good reading of Scripture rather than a bad one? An acceptable one, rather than an unacceptable one?

Apart from the allegedly firm anchor offered by modern reading strategies that prioritize "what the author intended" or "what the text originally meant," how can we decide what a text *really* means? Without such landmarks, are we not at the mercy of anyone who tells us that the Bible says this or that?

Simply put, when we take up the Bible as the church's Scriptures, we recognize that we do not depend on even our most talented historians to portray for us what is true. Within the church, we recognize that those interpretive winds that would toss us to and fro are already tamed by canon and creed. In fact, reading from within a Discursive Frame as I have sketched it, it seems to me that we can affirm a range of criteria for sorting between good and bad readings. To encourage discussion on this very point, I urge that an interpretation of the Bible *as Christian Scripture* can be regarded as more or less faithful according to the degree that it:

1. Accounts for the text in its final form, without depending on a cut-and-paste job that refabricates the text in order that it might fit a prior theory
2. Accounts for the text as a whole and is consistent with the whole of the text, without deliberately masking unfortunate aspects of the text that continue to haunt the interpreter
3. Is consistent with the general rules of language, including considerations of a philological, syntactical, and grammatical sort
4. Accounts for the cultural embeddedness of language, allowing the text to have its meaning fashioned in light of its sociocultural assumptions
5. Is "ruled" by its canonical embeddedness
6. Is set within the boundaries of the "rule of faith" and the "rule of love"; as Augustine wrote, "So any who think they have understood the divine Scriptures or any part of them, but cannot by their understanding build up this double love of God and neighbor, have not yet succeeded in understanding them."[10]

---

10. Saint Augustine, *On Christian Teaching*, trans. and ed. R. P. H. Green, Oxford World's Classics (Oxford: Oxford University Press, 1997), 1.86 (p. 27, translation altered).

Regarding this last point, I might add that in my own, Wesleyan-Methodist tradition, we would follow John Wesley in affirming that a faithful reading of Scripture is one coherent with the church's faith as set out in the church's creeds—the Apostles' Creed, the Nicene Creed, and the Athanasian Creed—but acknowledge that orthodoxy is not enough. We would follow Wesley in affirming that a faithful reading of Scripture is one that is put on display in one's right actions—but acknowledge that orthopraxy is not enough. A faithful reading of Scripture is one that turns the hearts of God's people to God and neighbor in love—that is, in orthokardia, right-heartedness. These three—orthodoxy, orthopraxy, and orthokardia—these are the marks of a faithful reading of Scripture.

Conclusion

People turn to the Bible for assorted reasons and with a variety of aims. My remarks should not be taken as a protest against this diversity. My concern, rather, has been to carve out fresh space for an approach to biblical studies that is neither naïve nor scientific, and to do so by prioritizing the hermeneutical concept of "framing" over modern interests in right method. Indeed, I have urged that method is and must be secondary, a derivative consideration, dependent both on how we frame the work of biblical interpretation and, relatedly, on the criteria by which we determine good (or faithful or valid) readings of scriptural texts.

It is nonetheless true that the Discursive Frame I have sketched grows out of my disquiet with the Scientific and Contextual Frames. I trust it will be just as clear that I regard the path forward as marked less by turning the clock back to a premodern era and more by learning from the strengths and liabilities of these other ways of framing engagement with the Bible. The Discursive Frame thus highlights the importance of what readers bring with them to the task of reading the Bible. And because of my interest in reading the Bible as Christian Scripture, I have developed those readerly interests especially in terms of location and formation. Working within these interpretive horizons, the whole enterprise of studying Scripture is set within a particular interpretive community, the church (which is itself situated missionally and redemptively vis-à-vis the world), and carried along by the Holy Spirit. This does not open the gates to interpretive libertarianism; the removal of authorial intent or original meaning from the interpretive throne does not mean that people are left to read what is right in their own eyes. Rather, the Discursive Frame as I have sketched it, in relation to reading the Bible in and for the church, occasions critical judgment of our interpretive efforts on the basis of a number of interrelated literary, sociocultural, and theological-ethical benchmarks.

CHAPTER 3

The Bible, Evolution, and the Journey of Faith

Peter Enns

The challenges presented by evolution to a biblically anchored Christian faith constitute a vital and timely topic of discussion. With the New Atheist phenomenon of recent years and the much-publicized human genome project—ironically headed by an evangelical Christian, Francis Collins—the compatibility of evolution and a biblically centered faith has been much on the minds of Christians.[1] My own interest in this topic has not been to find a definitive solution to this challenging issue. My interest is in encouraging a conversation by accepting the challenge of evolution and to think differently about the kind of information the Bible is prepared to provide. Though potentially destabilizing, the challenge of evolution cannot be marginalized or dismissed but requires genuine engagement and contemplation. A process like that typically results in a change of thinking.[2]

1. Among New Atheist authors, Richard Dawkins has likely been the most influential on the popular level; see his *The God Delusion* (New York: Bantam, 2006; Boston: Mariner, 2008); and *The Greatest Show on Earth: The Evidence for Evolution* (New York: Free Press, 2009). Francis S. Collins's argument for the compatibility of evolution and Christian faith is *The Language of God: A Scientist Presents Evidence for Belief* (New York: Free Press, 2006).

2. Nicholas Wolterstorff's words are apropos: "The scholar never fully knows in advance where his line of thought will lead him. For the Christian to undertake scholarship is to undertake a course of action that may lead him into the painful process of revising his actual Christian commitment, sorting through his beliefs, and discarding some from a position where they can any longer function as control. It may, indeed, even lead him to a point where his authentic commitment has undergone change. We are profoundly historical creatures" (*Reason within the Bounds of Religion*, 2nd ed. [Grand Rapids: Eerdmans, 1984; repr., 1999], 96–97).

Some Foundational Factors

My approach rests on accepting two factors. The first is an evolutionary model of cosmic, geological, and human origins. For a vast majority of scientists across the ideological spectrum, an evolutionary model has had tremendous success for the last several generations in explaining how the universe (not simply life on earth) came to be.[3] The second factor is our ever-growing understanding of the historical and cultural contexts of the Bible. Data from the ancient worlds of the biblical authors have been subject to no small measure of analysis and interpretation, and those discussions have been framing and continue to frame our understanding of the meaning and nature of the biblical texts of origins. In addition to Genesis 1–2, other texts that speak of creation (such as in Job and Psalms) are also relevant, and a full Christian accounting demands engagement with Paul's comments on Adam (in Rom. 5:12–21 and 1 Cor. 15:22). I see these two factors—evolutionary theory and the study of Scripture in historical context—as nonnegotiable conversation partners for modern-day Christians who are navigating the intersection of biblical literature and evolution. Whatever other factors might also be brought into the discussion (and I don't deny there are others), these two are my point of departure.

I realize that these are also the very factors that have generated the disquiet among Christians. Both have been caricatured since the nineteenth century as "attacks" upon the Christian faith, the memory of which is deeply ingrained in conservative and evangelical collective consciousness.[4] These tensions are still very much at play and no doubt help explain the strong feelings that this topic continues to generate. I do not wish to add to hostilities, but neither do I feel we can, or should, avoid difficult conversations about whether evangelicalism might have painted itself into a theological corner by advocating a posture of resistance rather than synthesis, and how best to move forward.

In my view, neither the established theory of evolution nor the modern study of Scripture can be marginalized, let alone dismissed. They reflect a

3. A 2009 Pew study concludes, "Nearly all scientists (97%) say humans and other living things have evolved over time—87% say evolution is due to natural processes, such as natural selection. The dominant position among scientists—that living things have evolved due to natural processes—is shared by only about [a] third (32%) of the public." http://www.people-press.org/2009/07/09/section-5-evolution-climate-change-and-other-issues/.

4. Peter Enns, *The Evolution of Adam: What the Bible Does and Doesn't Say about Human Origins* (Grand Rapids: Brazos, 2012), 3–76.

general learned consensus of thought among those trained in these fields. Since I have no training in the sciences, I confess without hesitation that I cannot offer anything remotely resembling an informed judgment on these matters, and so I have decided to accept the overwhelming consensus that humans did not begin with a single pair specially created *de novo* by God several thousand years ago.[5] And little is gained, in my opinion, from trying to minimize the distance between a scientific model of human origins and the ancient biblical stories of creation.[6]

With respect to biblical studies, although I do not claim a full grasp of all the issues, I do feel more informed to speak. In my opinion, the study of Scripture in context alone presents sufficient challenges to traditional readings of the biblical stories of origins without bringing evolution into the discussion. Simply put, every ancient culture we know of tells *stories* of origins that reflect *their own ancient view* of the world. It strains credulity to the breaking point to think that Israel and Israel alone escaped this story-telling mentality and instead gave us something closer to a historical report, let alone a report that can (or should) be aligned somehow with scientific models. To respond, as some do, by saying that divine inspiration by definition guarantees the "factuality" of the biblical accounts over against these other ancient stories is not convincing to me. That view assumes that it is the mark of a divinely inspired text to stand aloof from the surrounding culture. I strongly reject this view and will return to it below.

---

5. Thoughtful yet nontechnical works that I have found particularly helpful are: Darrell R. Falk, *Coming to Peace with Science: Bridging the Worlds Between Faith and Biology* (Downers Grove, IL: InterVarsity, 2004); Keith B. Miller, ed., *Perspectives on an Evolving Creation* (Grand Rapids: Eerdmans, 2003); Karl W. Giberson and Francis S. Collins, *The Language of Science and Faith: Straight Answers to Genuine Questions* (Downers Grove, IL: InterVarsity, 2011); Denis O. Lamoureux, *Evolutionary Creation: A Christian Approach to Evolution* (Eugene, OR: Wipf and Stock, 2008); and Richard Dawkins, *The Greatest Show on Earth*.

6. I am, however, quite happy to concede that there is a hermeneutical factor at play in both the analysis of evidence and the conclusions drawn from that analysis; the work of scientists is not free of perspective and potential distortion. Yet given the consensus among scientists concerning evolution, held by those who span the ideological spectrum, I do not feel it is profitable to try to neutralize that consensus by claiming some higher hermeneutical awareness, especially when offered by those not trained in the relevant scientific fields. The final word on evolution has certainly not been written, but the theory is so well established that its general characteristics can and should be accepted as true and therefore highly relevant for engaging the historical value of the biblical accounts.

I am where I am on the Christianity-evolution discussion because I do not feel at liberty to neutralize the significance of these two factors, regardless of how much theological discomfort they might generate. And to anticipate my comments below, these two destabilizing factors are not to be seen as challenges to the Bible or to Christian faith, but to traditional understandings of how the relevant biblical texts should be understood. These traditional understandings typically include the assertion that the Garden of Eden narrative is an account of historical events, if even minimally, and are perpetuated and defended in evangelical and fundamentalist iterations of the Christian faith, rooted in presumably universal Reformation and post-Reformation dogmatic categories.

Recreating Adam

It is worth stressing that evolution does indeed present very difficult challenges to any iteration of the Christian faith. The dilemma cannot be solved simply by "pinning the evolutionary tail onto the evangelical donkey," as it were.[7] And I wince when I hear casual claims that, when the dust settles, we will see that any conflict between evolution and evangelical Christian faith was all along more apparent than real. I don't think such optimism is a realistic assessment of the gravity of the problem and therefore will not provide a long-lasting and intellectually compelling way forward.[8] Some will disagree, of course, but I feel I need to search elsewhere for suitable answers.

As I have followed this discussion over the last several years, it seems to me that the attempt to graft together evolution and evangelical Christi-

7. Or as Denis Lamoureux put it, "Tacking Adam on the tail end of evolution" (private communication). Lamoureux's two books on Christianity and evolution are, in my view, among the best at bringing a balanced summation of the central scientific *and* hermeneutical factors: *Evolutionary Creation*; and *I Love Jesus & I Accept Evolution* (Eugene, OR: Wipf and Stock, 2009).

8. For example, see the following comment by N. T. Wright appearing in https://biologos.org/about-us/endorsements/: "Christians and secularists alike are in danger of treating 'Darwin vs. the Bible' as just another battlefront in the polarized 'culture wars'. This grossly misrepresents both science and faith. BioLogos not only shows that there is an alternative, but actually models it. God's world and God's word go together in a rich, living harmony." I certainly agree that the discussion must transcend the culture war mentality, and I applaud BioLogos in these efforts, but the claim that Scripture and evolution "go together in a rich, living harmony" requires greater nuance than this blurb suggests—some of which I hope to outline below.

anity is driven by a nonnegotiable theological need among evangelicals to retain a historical Adam in some genuine sense of the word "historical." I would further suggest that the pressure to do so comes not so much from the need to read Genesis literally,[9] but from the fear that anything other than a historical Adam will render null and void Paul's argument in Romans 5:12–21, where the obedience of Christ offsets the disobedience of Adam—if Adam is not a single historical man, Paul's analogy dissipates into mist. I understand the theological motivation for this, but retaining a historical Adam solely to preserve a perceived theological necessity will eventually fail to persuade. Adam as first man created by God *de novo*, whose disobedience in time and space alone plunged the human drama into sin and misery, cannot easily work alongside evolution, which says there is no *de novo* first man, and violence and death were part of the earthly drama long before anatomically modern humans came on the scene (about two hundred thousand years ago). The historical Adam of evangelical theology and an evolutionary model of origins cannot simply coexist. One or the other must be adjusted somehow.[10]

There are no doubt subtleties and differences of opinion about what sorts of adjustments evangelicals feel they need to make and how deep those adjustments should go, but for Christians who accept biological evolution, the adjustment routinely involves redefining "Adam" in a way that is more compatible with evolution. I see the following two means of doing so as most prominent. First, Adam and Eve, rather than the biological first pair of fully developed humans, are understood as Neolithic farmers whom God had chosen among all others at some point in time, perhaps tens of thousands of years ago.[11] These Neolithic farmers are "first" but only in a theological sense: they are chosen by God to be the representative heads of humanity rather than the biological heads. As the representative first

9. This point is warmly and routinely conceded by evangelical scholars. See, for example, Richard F. Carlson and Tremper Longman III, *Science, Creation and the Bible: Reconciling Rival Theories of Origins* (Downers Grove, IL: InterVarsity, 2010), and John H. Walton, *The Lost World of Adam and Eve: Genesis 2–3 and the Human Origins Debate* (Downers Grove, IL: InterVarsity, 2015).

10. For a recent defense of the necessity of a historical Adam to preserve the truth of the gospel, see Hans Madueme and Michael Reeves, eds., *Adam, the Fall, and Original Sin: Theological, Biblical, and Scientific Perspectives* (Grand Rapids: Baker Academic, 2014).

11. Denis Alexander calls this the "Homo divinus model"; see "How Does a BioLogos Model Need to Address the Theological Issues Associated with an Adam Who Was Not the Sole Genetic Progenitor of Humankind?" (http://biologos.org/uploads/projects/alexander _white_paper.pdf).

pair, their rebellion cast the stain of sin onto all other humans laterally, not simply linearly (their descendants, as in the traditional view of Adam), and throughout time. This view might be analogous to holding all Americans responsible for an administration's foreign policy. Second, others take the human genome project as their point of departure, according to which the current human population could only have come from a gene pool no smaller than a population of about ten thousand. "Adam and Eve" then becomes a collective term for a historical first gene pool rather than individuals.

For both of these options, evolution is accepted and the historical nature of a "first" pair (of some sort) is maintained, and I appreciate the respect shown for both, but these adjustments produce for me an uneasy détente and raise three red flags. First, as mentioned above, the question of a historical Adam is not simply a conversation between science and Genesis, but with a third partner, biblical scholarship, which on its own has effectively reoriented many traditional expectations of what Genesis and the Adam story are prepared to deliver. Even without evolution, biblical scholarship is enough of a factor to challenge historical expectations of Genesis.

Second, it is ironic that the attempt to preserve the general historical validity of the biblical Adam story, and therefore the ever-looming concern for biblical authority, yields an "Adam" that the biblical writers and their audience certainly would not have recognized. A modern framework (Neolithic farmers and gene pools) has been imposed onto an ancient text, rather than reading the text with ancient eyes. It is not clear to me how evangelical doctrine is preserved by posing such an unbiblical Adam.

Third, and more importantly, these "adjusted Adams" are often accepted as valid merely because they are deemed *possible*. As the argument goes, since science cannot *disprove* God choosing two Neolithic farmers to be Adam and Eve, then there is no real reason not to accept this as *possible* and *therefore* a *valid* means of reconciling Adam and evolution. This line of reasoning troubles me a bit because it is entirely *ad hoc*—a hypothetical is created to ease the pressure generated by a perceived dogmatic need. It is never logically sound to fill holes in an argument by introducing hypothetical scenarios created simply for that purpose, and evangelicals would not allow atheists, Muslims, or theological liberals to defend the coherence of their system by positing an *ad hoc* and unfalsifiable "possibility."

Is Science "over" the Bible?

That being said, I can understand a possible rejoinder: "Aren't we just putting science and biblical scholarship *over* the Bible to determine what the Bible can mean? Are we not putting the word of God *under* the authority of what fallible humans perceive in the uncertain fields of their time-bound and fallen intellectual pursuits?" This is an important point to address, but I think it should be framed differently. None of us comes to the Bible with a blank slate. Even the apparently straightforward claim to be simply following "what the Bible says" is already working from a particular set of associations about *how* "what the Bible says" should be understood. We all interpret the Bible within a network of categories shaped by our own time and place, some of which we are conscious of and many more that lie beneath our waking thoughts. I feel this is part of the inescapability of human limitations, which is why I prefer to speak of theological pursuits as journeys we take rather than permanent structures we build.

Also, the warning not to put science or historical studies over the Bible already makes a false assumption: namely, that the Bible is prepared to comment on scientific issues and when it does, it is to be followed as an act of faithful obedience to God. But this is the very stance that needs to be demonstrated rather than assumed. Furthermore, when such a stance is adopted, confirmation bias is not far behind—privileging data that confirms the default position. Information that calls into question that default position is either resisted, or, as we glimpsed a moment ago, answered by asserting the *possibility* of an *ad hoc* alternate scenario. Anywhere else, this would be called overt confirmation bias.

Without suggesting that I am somehow unaffected by my own moment in time and place, I would contend that extrabiblical information actually helps in several important ways when it comes to the topic of the Bible and evolution. First and foremost, our thinking about what we have the right to expect from the biblical texts of origins is adjusted. Extrabiblical information can "calibrate" the expectations we bring to the biblical texts in question. So, things like genomic studies, the fossil record, and other ancient stories of origins help us see that scientific or historical information are not the proper default expectations of the Adam story. When the conversation turns in this direction, we have come to the question of the authority of the Bible. In many quadrants of Christianity where evolution is particularly threatening, the operative articulation of biblical authority is biblical inerrancy. In my opinion, preserving inerrancy has been a major—if not *the* major—factor in why this topic is of such concern among evangelicals. Despite how the word is nuanced, however, "inerrancy" is not a word that does justice to Scripture's character and so is, for me, a theological dead-end.[12]

When I open the Bible and read it, I see a diverse collection of texts from different times and places that present various and sundry hermeneutical and historical challenges that can't be captured within an inerrantist model of Scripture. Maintaining inerrancy requires constant and stressful vigilance in order to remain viable, which suggests that it may not be a model that matches the data. I continue to think that an incarnational model of Scripture, such as I outlined in *Inspiration and Incarnation*, offers a more compelling and less dissonant paradigm for explaining why the Bible looks so very "untended."[13] An incarnational model of Scripture suggests that the God-man Jesus can be a model for understanding the nature of the Bible. It is an uncontroversial point among evangelicals that Jesus as God incarnate fully bears the marks of humanity, specifically that of ancient, first-century Palestine. Similarly, the Bible, though inspired by God, fully bears the marks of the historical settings of the various ancient authors—our willingness to affirm the full humanity of Jesus (the Word) without apology could help us see Scripture (the word) in an analogous light. An incarnational model describes the tenor, the character of Scripture by means of the central element of the Christian faith, what C. S. Lewis called the "irreverent doctrine" of the incarnation.[14] Along with Lewis, I believe that Scripture as God's word necessarily and unashamedly comes to us from the vantage point of the localized and limited understanding of its ancient authors. Thinking of Scripture this way, I believe, reflects a fundamental confession of Christian faith: God became flesh.

To be absolutely clear, I am not suggesting that an incarnational model of Scripture is the only, or even best, way to think about the Bible at all times. It is, rather, a heuristic device designed to help readers come to terms with the fact that the various and diverse writings of the Bible

12. A discussion and debate about various views of inerrancy can be found in J. Merrick and Stephen M. Garrett, eds., *Five Views on Biblical Inerrancy* (Grand Rapids: Zondervan, 2013). I contributed an essay and responses, along with R. Albert Mohler Jr., Michael F. Bird, Kevin J. Vanhoozer, and John R. Franke.

13. Peter Enns, *Inspiration and Incarnation: Evangelicals and the Problem of the Old Testament*, 2nd ed. (Grand Rapids: Brazos, 2012).

14. C. S. Lewis, "Introduction" to *Letters to Young Churches: A Translation of the New Testament Epistles*, by J. B. Phillips (New York: Macmillan, 1953), vii–viii.

look and act like ancient literature and should unashamedly be treated as such. The same or similar notion can be expressed by other models.[15] I also readily acknowledge the importance of other reading strategies of Scripture, where an incarnational model might be less beneficial—such as devotional or spiritual readings. But when the topic turns to the connection of Scripture and history, which is the heart of the evolution-Bible debate, I see much value in an incarnational model. It is a heuristic device designed to help readers come to terms with Scripture's historical contextualization. It provides theological language to help us corral misguided expectations of what Scripture needs to deliver and thus gives theological permission for readers to allow ancient expectations to shape their own expectations. This view of the nature of Scripture invites us—better, incites us—to embark on a liberating hermeneutical-theological journey, which is at the same time spiritual, where we can explore without fear how the ancient context and ours interact. To put it another way, an incarnational model is not prescriptive, delimiting what Scripture *can* mean (as an inerrantist model functions), but opens the door for descriptive possibilities.

A Journey with Three Companions

Thinking of Scripture this way frees one up to explore, without guilt or fear, possible solutions to our vexing problem. Regardless of the theological substructure one chooses, however, allowing the full "humanity" of Scripture to shine forth without embarrassment or complaint is a crucial first step on the journey of exploring how to engage the relationship between Scripture and evolution. One way of articulating the journey metaphor is to envision three traveling companions engaging in a vibrant conversation along the way, each participant of which needs to be heard as we seek to interpret Scripture well with respect to evolution. The three travelers are (1) the historical context of Scripture, (2) the canonical context of Scripture, and (3) Christian tradition. We can only sketch these issues here, but the voice of each of these traveling companions is vital, and none in isolation is determinative.

15. For example, I find compelling an ecclesiastical model of Scripture, where the diverse and even contradictory nature of the various biblical writings is analogous to the diverse voices in the church that nevertheless remain in fellowship as one body.

The first voice is the **historical context** of Scripture, which includes the various ancient Near Eastern contexts of the Old Testament and the Second Temple Jewish and Greco-Roman Hellenistic contexts of the New Testament. Of perennial importance here is the significant amount of literature discovered over the last one hundred fifty years or so that has formed a valuable, even paradigm-shifting, backdrop against which to view the biblical texts. This is not the place to rehearse the specifics, but well known for their impact on our understanding of the opening chapters of Genesis are Enuma Elish, the Epic of Gilgamesh, the Atrahasis, and the Myth of Adapa.[16] The value of the first three is not what they have to say directly about the creation of the first humans, but the general similarities Genesis 1–11 bears to these older stories. Atrahasis in particular reflects the narrative of Genesis: creation—population growth—offense against the divine realm—cataclysmic flood. Also, similar to the Adam story, Gilgamesh's quest for immortality includes a scene where access to a life-giving plant is thwarted by a serpent. More explicit in this regard is the Babylonian Myth of Adapa, a "fall of man" story involving the themes of wisdom and immortality. It goes without saying that these stories evince crucial differences when laid side by side. But the larger point should not be lost, namely that these stories, including the biblical one, breathe the same ancient air in terms of their depiction of origins, which can and should rightly be called "myth," which I define as *an ancient, premodern, prescientific way of addressing questions of ultimate origins and meaning in the form of stories involving the divine realm.*[17] To be sure, the Adam story has its own unique theology, as all these stories do. Nevertheless, holding the biblical story at arm's length from these older ancient Near Eastern stories is unreasonable. Rather, these texts help us calibrate the genre of the biblical "primeval history."

The same principle holds for Paul. He, too, was a man of his time, and how he understood Adam should not be isolated from the hermeneutical environment in which he was educated and within which he thought. Paul's creative handling of his Scripture is easily documented and hard to

16. These texts are routinely rehearsed in most any introductory volume on Genesis. I find the following two articles by Daniel C. Harlow to be among the most helpful for introducing the issue clearly and succinctly: "After Adam: Reading Genesis in an Age of Evolutionary Science," *Perspectives on Science and Christian Faith* 62.3 (2010): 179–95; "Creation According to Genesis: Literary Genre, Cultural Context, Theological Truth," *Christian Scholars Review* 37.2 (2008): 163–98.

17. For a fuller discussion, see Enns, *Inspiration and Incarnation*, 28–30.

marginalize as an occasional quirk. It is, rather, reflective of his Judaism, which by Paul's time had already enjoyed a long history of creative, midrashic exegesis.[18] Paul's interpretation of the Adam story is not an objective exposition of what the biblical story is about, but an exercise in actualizing the story for a new purpose. Acknowledging as much is simply to acknowledge that Paul thought and wrote as a first-century Jew—albeit one who was a servant of Christ—but nevertheless a first-century Jew and not a twenty-first-century Christian. And if we recall our incarnational model, Paul's cultural setting is not window dressing or some unfortunate baggage for us to remove, but the vehicle through which we hear God.

The second voice, not entirely distinct from the first, is **canon**, which involves three interpenetrating concentric circles of canonical meaning: *the surrounding literary context, Old Testament theology*, and *New Testament theology*.

(1) *The surrounding literary context.* The immediate context of the story of Adam raises perennial challenges to seeing Adam as the first human and that his disobedience led to inherited sinfulness for all. For example, if Adam and Eve are the first two humans, what are we to make of the creation of multiple males and females in Genesis 1:27? Similarly, if Adam and Eve are the first humans, who are these others that Cain fears will take his life, how could Cain find a wife, and what need would he have to build a city? And what are we to make of the nagging fact that inherited sinfulness, a core element of traditional readings, is not mentioned as a punishment in Genesis 3? And why is the promised punishment of "death" to Adam "on the day" he eats of the tree of knowledge seemingly carried out in his exile ("driven out") from the garden (Gen. 3:24)? An allegedly "plain" reading of the Adam story raises interpretive questions that are difficult to pin down and that sometimes run afoul of conventional understandings of this story. Adam and Eve are not alone, and whatever the disobedience, it did not plunge humanity into a state of sinfulness. Any interpretation of the Adam story that does not adequately address these (and other) factors will not be compelling.

18. On Paul's use of the Old Testament, see Donald Juel, *Messianic Exegesis: Christological Interpretation of the Old Testament in Early Christianity* (Philadelphia: Fortress, 1987), and Steve Moyise, *Paul and Scripture* (London: SPCK, 2010). On the interpretive environment of Second Temple Judaism, see James L. Kugel, *Traditions of the Bible: A Guide to the Bible as It Was at the Start of the Common Era* (Cambridge: Harvard University Press, 1998), and James L. Kugel and Rowan A. Greer, *Early Biblical Interpretation* (Philadelphia: Westminster, 1986).

Likewise, Paul's handling of Adam in Romans 5:12–21 presents numerous well-known interpretive conundrums that complicate any plain reading, not the least of which is verse 12: "death spread to all because all have sinned." Though sin entered the world through one man (Adam), resulting in death, the responsibility is on each one of us and not simply to be placed at the feet of Adam.[19] But later in the passage, Paul draws the not entirely clear analogy between Adam and Jesus. Through Adam, *all* are *condemned* and *many* are *made sinners*, whereas through Jesus, *all* receive *justification and life* and *many will be made righteous* (Rom. 5:18–19). How Romans 5:12 and 5:18 square with each other is difficult to discern. A further complication is Paul's curious use of "all" and "many," not to mention his departure from Genesis in assigning "condemnation" as a consequence of Adam's disobedience—unless by that he means the fact of death (see 5:16–17) rather than eternal separation from God.

Another factor is simply discerning how Paul's rhetoric in Romans 5 fits into that larger picture of his purpose for writing Romans. If the New Perspective on Paul has aided in our understanding of this letter (and I think it has), then Paul's main agenda in Romans as a whole is to place Jewish and Gentile Christians on the same footing before God, as it were, rather than giving a timeless systematic theological exposition.[20] Paul's use of the Adam story is a creative and elsewhere unattested reading to illustrate that sin is not a Jewish problem that can be addressed through faithfulness to Torah, but a universal problem culminating in death, which can be addressed only through the resurrection of the Messiah. To sum up, Paul's use of the Adam story is hardly straightforward, and assuming that it is cripples the discussion over evolution.

(2) *Old Testament Theology.* Working outward in the concentric circles of canonical meaning, we have Old Testament theology, allowing for the Old Testament's own internal history of development and theological

---

19. Augustine, relying on the mistaken Latin translation of his time, famously misread Rom. 5:12 as saying "*in him* all have sinned" rather than "*because* . . . ." The correct reading of 5:12 is consistent with what we find in Second Temple sources, e.g., 2 Baruch 45:15 and 2 Esdras 3:7. See Jesse Couenhoven, "St. Augustine's Doctrine of Original Sin," *Augustinian Studies* 36.2 (2005): 359–96.

20. See for example, E. P. Sanders, *Paul and Palestinian Judaism: A Comparison of Patterns of Religion* (Minneapolis: Fortress, 1977); James D. G. Dunn, *Romans*, 2 vols., WBC 38A and B (Dallas: Word, 1988); J. R. Daniel Kirk, *Unlocking Romans: Resurrection and the Justification of God* (Grand Rapids: Eerdmans, 2008); N. T. Wright, *What Saint Paul Really Said: Was Paul of Tarsus the Real Founder of Christianity?* (Grand Rapids: Eerdmans, 1997).

diversity. I see several factors that challenge the conventional evangelical reading of the Adam story.

First, the absence of Adam's explicit mention in the Old Testament outside of Genesis 2–5, with the exception of 1 Chronicles 1:1, suggests that he is not a central character in Old Testament theology. Specifically, the Adam of the conventional reading of Romans 5—Adam as the source of universal death, sin, and condemnation—is not how Adam is presented in Genesis 2–5 or in the Old Testament as a whole. Adam does have a larger role in Second Temple Judaism than in the Old Testament,[21] but the conventional reading of Romans 5 seems to be unduly influenced by Augustine's misreading of Romans 5:12.[22]

Second, Adam seems to anticipate, even embody, Israel's long story of struggling with God, a notion that, according to Genesis 32:28, is embedded in the very name "Israel" ("strive with God" or "God strives").[23] Both Adam and Israel are miraculously created by God (Adam from dust and Israel out of slavery) and brought to live in a lush land (Adam in the Garden of Eden and Israel in the lush land of Canaan). Staying in the land is contingent upon obedience to divine command (for Adam the command not to eat of the Tree of Knowledge and for Israel obedience to the Mosaic Law). And disobedience results in exile from the land not only for Israel but for Adam (Gen. 3:24). And since Israel's exile is a kind of "death" (see Ezek. 37:1–14 and Deut. 30:15–20), the promised punishment of death to Adam in Genesis 2:17 is executed in 3:24. This parallel suggests that Adam is a preview of Israel, which raises the serious option that the biblical writer presented Adam as a metaphorical figure, a miniature Israel, not the first literal historical human. Such a reading would essentially neutralize the tension between evolution and Genesis.

Third, we see in the Garden story echoes of wisdom, namely the book of Proverbs. The serpent's *craftiness* and the woman's naïveté in Genesis 3 echo the opening verses of Proverbs, which promise *craftiness* (*'ormah*,

---

21. For example, according to 2 Baruch 23:4 and 48:42–43, Adam is the cause of humanity's "corruption" (death), a topic not enjoined in the Old Testament outside of the Adam story in Genesis. See also 2 Esdras 3:4–27.

22. Again, see Jesse Couenhoven, "St. Augustine's Doctrine of Original Sin."

23. This reading goes back explicitly to medieval Judaism: Gen. Rab. 19.9, "Just as I led Adam into the garden of Eden and commanded him and he transgressed my commandment, whereupon I punished him by dismissal and exile . . . so also did I bring his descendants into the land of Israel and command them, and they transgressed my commands and I punished them by dismissal and exile." On Adam and Israel, see, further, Enns, *The Evolution of Adam*, 65–70.

Prov. 1:4, same root as in Genesis, 'arum; NRSV "shrewdness") to the naïve. Likewise, wisdom is a Tree of Life in Proverbs 3:18 (see also 11:30). These echoes suggest that the story of Adam and Eve is, once again, illustrative of Israel—here not in terms of the Mosaic Law but Israel's wisdom journey from childlike naïveté toward godly wisdom. Read this way, the story of Adam and Eve is not about the descent of two ontologically sinless first humans.

Fourth, allusions to creation in Job and the Psalms echo mythic themes known in other ancient stories of origins: the ancient Near Eastern cosmic battle motif (the defeat of chaos/water), which leads to the formation of habitable space;[24] the slaying of the mythic monsters Rahab and Leviathan (Job 26:12–13; Pss. 89:9–10; 74:13–14); and the rebuking and fleeing of the waters (the "deep" of Gen. 1) at the sight of the warrior Yahweh (Ps. 104:7). Although these psalms do not mention Adam and are more comparable to Genesis 1, they contribute to our understanding of how ancient Israelites (at least in the texts we possess) understood primordial history, which was in mythic terms.

(3) *New Testament Theology.* For Christians, the outer circle of canonical meaning is *New Testament theology.* It may help to think of the New Testament not as "Bible: Part 2" but as an engagement of Israel's long story by early Jewish followers of Jesus who saw him as the climactic covenantal act of God for his people. The New Testament explicates the Christian narrative by transforming and transposing Israel's story in the light of Christ, especially his resurrection, which we have already glimpsed with respect to Paul's exposition in Romans 5. Paul's fresh reading of the Adam story is required by the unexpected advent of a crucified and resurrected messiah.

Finally, along with the first voice (the surrounding literary context) and the second (the canonical context), we also have the third voice, the **Christian Tradition**. To clarify, I mean "Tradition" in two senses. The first is "Tradition" (capital T), which many call the "grand tradition," captured in the ecumenical ancient church creeds. The second is "tradition" (lowercase t), which is the particular, localized (geographically and chronologically) iteration of Christianity we call home, either broadly defined as Orthodox, Roman Catholic, or Protestant, or further subdivided or sub-subdivided somehow. Put another way, *Tradition* speaks to the gen-

24. Richard J. Clifford, *Creation Accounts in the Ancient Near East and in the Bible,* CBQMS 26 (Washington D.C.: The Catholic Biblical Association of America, 1994).

eral uniformity of the Church whereas *tradition* speaks to the inevitable diversity of Christian thought throughout history and across the world at this very moment.

None of us, as Christian thinkers, fly above our cultural context. All Christians are part of localized traditions, and each of these traditions is *a* voice in the conversation, not the judge. A localized tradition becomes the judge of the other voices only when we mistake our tradition for the Tradition. The various Christian traditions are genuinely good-faith iterations of the gospel, but the gospel *as we see it*, invariably informed and influenced by various factors and accidents of history, known and unknown. We are not always the best judges of where our own theological iterations obscure truth or help reveal it. Speaking for myself, my own spiritual and intellectual journey has led me to be more and more comfortable walking by faith, not by sight, and to accept that I see things provisionally, not as they necessarily are, even as I hold to Christ, or better, Christ holds to me. Hence, the theological challenges of a nonhistorical Adam are, for me, not a conversation stopper but a starter.

Confusing *tradition* with *Tradition*

In my experience, the contextual factor that most often proves challenging to evangelical iterations of the nature of Scripture is the voice of *historical context* (the first voice). This may seem unfair, given that historical context plays an important role in evangelical biblical interpretation. In fact, it is fundamental to grammatical-historical exegesis, and simply glancing at evangelical study Bibles and commentaries will make that point quickly enough. But judging by the last two centuries, the study of history often challenges one's Christian tradition (lower case t). This is precisely what has happened with respect to Adam over the last several generations. I have observed the tendency to suspend historical inquiry in favor of doctrinal preservation when the historical challenges become too acute.

An illustration of this all-too-common phenomenon concerns a review of *The Evolution of Adam* by evangelical theologian Hans Madueme.[25]

---

25. The review was originally posted online on "The Gospel Coalition" website (http://themelios.thegospelcoalition.org/article/some-reflections-on-enns-and-the-evolution-of-adam-a-review-essay) and later was published as Hans Madueme, "Some Reflections on

Theological concerns, the author argues, should necessarily override any sort of historical investigation when the two conflict, if one wishes to be faithful to the gospel, a point conveniently summarized at the very end of the review:

> I recognize the force of the mainstream evolutionary consensus, and I know that it raises tough questions for the viability of a historical Adam and the doctrine of the fall. But I am constrained by Scripture, tradition, and weighty theological considerations.[26]

The reviewer freely acknowledges the problematic nature of the scientific evidence for his theology, yet he feels "constrained" by his theological precommitments to abort further dialogue. This solution simply will not do if one wishes to engage the problems of theology rather than run from them, and one will forgive this reader for thinking the review could have been greatly shortened had the author simply opened with this statement rather than closed with it.

The Bible is many things and can be read in many ways, as I mentioned above, and I do not chide theologically driven readings. But I also think that engaging the Bible in its historical contexts, though challenging, cannot be dismissed or discounted because of the theological tensions it may generate. It must be integrated. To put it this way is not to deny that the Bible is God's word—as some might say—but to affirm by faith that God's word is, as a plain matter of fact, spoken through the idioms, attitudes, assumptions, and general worldview of the ancient authors. As I see it, this means that understanding the abiding theological validity of the Adam story in Genesis and Paul's interpretation of that story in Romans is hard work—at least it should not be assumed to be self-evident, transparent, and easily aligned with our theologies. Our theological discomfort should certainly be articulated and brought to the table, but theological discomfort should not be used as an excuse to abort the journey altogether.

Enns and *The Evolution of Adam*: A Review Essay," *Themelios* 35.2 (2012): 275–86. My response can be found at http://www.peteenns.com/spinning-our-wheels-a-response-to-a -review-of-the-evolution-of-adam-with-apologies-to-those-with-a-500-word-1–6-minute -internet-attention-span/.

26. Madueme, "Some Reflections on Enns and *The Evolution of Adam*," 286.

A Glimpse at the Larger Picture

In conclusion, I would like to highlight three big-picture, theological is-sues that in my experience are too often left unarticulated but need to be brought more overtly into the conversation about evolution and the Bible. The first issue is the perennial question of *the role of extrabiblical information in biblical interpretation*. Extrabiblical information is too often engaged either reluctantly, defensively, or in piecemeal manner, where a dominant factor in whether one integrates the information is the theolog-ical fallout it would cause. To use the language of systematic theology, I am speaking here of the perennial question of the relationship of general and special revelation for exegesis and theology. If God is present and active in both categories, how do the two inform each other? The Bible-evolution question raises this issue to a new level of urgency, at least for evangelicalism.

The second issue, overlapping with the first, concerns the Bible's au-thoritative role in the church; that is, the well-known problem of the *Bible in the modern world*, which has framed many conflicts over Scripture for more than two centuries. How do we bring into meaningful conversation (1) attitudes toward the Bible that were largely shaped and promulgated in the context of Reformation and post-Reformation dogmatics, with (2) genuine advances in our knowledge of antiquity that inform and frame modern study and that push to a breaking point some of these traditional boundaries? At the end of the day, the real challenge in managing these sorts of conversations is sociological and not simply theological. Attitudes toward Scripture have performed central gatekeeping functions that define group boundaries. When group identity is at stake, at least in my experi-ence, much heat is generated and less light. A necessary dimension of this discussion is to be explicit about often unstated deep fears of loss of iden-tity. There is little hope for movement if the emotional dimension is not addressed and people feel that before them is only further disintegration rather than an opportunity to grow in faith.

The third issue, particularly pertinent to evangelicalism, concerns the extent to which its view of the Bible should be *open to critique from within or from the outside*. To put it directly, is evangelicalism's doctrine of Scripture the final word and most faithful expression of historic Christian faith? Or is it a paradigm, a way of understanding God's truth that can and should be open to constructive self-criticism when the occasion arises? Should evangelicalism engage and seek wisdom from other iterations of the Christian faith where neither the Bible nor Adam create the same degree of disquiet?

In processing this issue along with several others over the last decade or so,[27] I have come to the view that seeking finality and certainty in our theological articulations, which I think provides fuel for the fire in the evolution debate, is misguided and unhealthy. Instead, judging by the diverse nature of Christian theology past and present, theological articulations are the fruit of deep thinking while also inevitably in process and never beyond change. Such is to be human, and few issues have brought this process to light in recent years more than the challenge of evolution for Christian faith.

---

27. I discuss this at length in *The Sin of Certainty: Why God Desires Our Trust More Than Our "Correct" Beliefs* (San Francisco: HarperOne, 2016).

PART 2

Interpreting in Accord with Doctrine, Canon, and Literary Form

CHAPTER 4

Genesis 1:2 and the Doctrine of Creation

Craig G. Bartholomew

The renaissance of theological interpretation of the Bible is an exciting and potentially very significant development in our time, as this volume demonstrates.[1] Because this renaissance is emerging amidst the continued dominance of historical criticism as the default mode for biblical interpretation, and more immediately in the wake of literary and postmodern approaches, an immense amount of work remains to be done if theological interpretation is to mature and reach its full potential.

I have proposed that we think of modern biblical interpretation in terms of four major turns:[2] the historical, evident in modern historical criticism; the literary, from the 1970s onward; the postmodern, from the 1980s onward; and most recently, the theological turn. No turn erases those that are earlier; indeed, in one way or another, all form part of the ecological mix of contemporary interpretation. Yet each raises important questions about the others, many of which still have to be satisfactorily explored amidst the smorgasbord of postmodern pluralism. If, as I think is right, theological interpretation is not just another method of interpretation but claims to embody the appropriate contours within which to read Scripture, then the major task of evaluating and sifting the earlier turns, weeding out ideological baggage, and appropriating genuine insights, becomes its responsibility. I do not think we can retreat behind historical criticism; its insights have been many, and progress has been made in myriad areas, so

---

1. See also Craig G. Bartholomew and Heath A. Thomas, eds., *A Manifesto for Theological Interpretation* (Grand Rapids: Baker Academic, 2016).

2. Craig G. Bartholomew, *Introducing Biblical Hermeneutics: A Comprehensive Framework for Hearing God in Scripture* (Grand Rapids: Baker Academic, 2015), 237–50.

that text after text will need to be reexamined in order to show the (often) richer insights theological interpretation yields. It is in the latter spirit that this chapter focuses on Genesis 1:2.

The Theological Importance of Genesis 1:2

Why Genesis 1:2? There is much at stake theologically in how we read this verse.[3] Many continue to translate Genesis 1:1-2 in a way that leaves open the possibility of *Elohim* (God) using *preexisting matter* with which to create. So, for example, the NRSV translates 1:1-2:

> In the beginning when God created the heavens and the earth, the earth was a formless void and darkness covered the face of the deep, while a wind from God swept over the face of the waters.[4]

This translation leaves wide open the possibility that the formless void and darkness of 1:2 is preexistent matter, and if 1:1-2 teaches that God used preexisting matter, then clearly this denies *creatio ex nihilo* and means that something exists alongside God prior to creation. As James Orr reminds us, theologically this is an important issue.[5] If anything in the "creation" exists apart from God, then our trust in God's execution of his plans, in his providence, in the triumph of his kingdom, in his working all things together for the good, is undermined. To confess the contingency of all things is simply another way of confessing that God created everything. Things would not depend on God were he not their creator.

However, there is more to this than just preexisting matter. As we will see in our engagement with Karl Barth, many see in Genesis 1:2 evidence of a threat to creation, with evil already present as a possibility. It is here that the *Chaoskampf* motif of Hermann Gunkel (1862-1932) has been so

---

3. On Hermogenes's use of Genesis 1:2 to support his view that God created from preexistent matter and on Tertullian's reply, see Andrew Gregory, *Ancient Greek Cosmogony* (London: Bristol Classical, 2011), 233. On the different views held by Justin Martyr, Clement of Alexandria, Tatian, and Theophilus, see Helen Rhee, *Early Christian Literature: Christ and Culture in the Second and Third Centuries* (London: Routledge, 2005), 52-53.

4. Unless otherwise stated, the NRSV is used throughout this chapter.

5. James Orr, *The Christian View of God and the World as Centring in the Incarnation: Being the Kerr Lectures for 1890-1891*, 2nd ed. (Edinburgh: Elliot, 1893), 145.

influential. As he notes in his *The Legends of Genesis: The Biblical Saga and History*, "Thus the account of creation in Genesis i. is scarcely to be called a story; and yet, from v. 2 and 26, . . . we can conjecture a form of the account . . . in which the world is created after a conflict of God with Chaos."[6] Gunkel himself, as far as I can see, does not clearly assert that chaos was necessarily preexisting matter according to Genesis 1, but the logic of such a view is compelling, and many others have made this connection.[7] Once again, this has major implications for Christian belief that insists that evil emerges in God's good creation as a possibility but is not coeternal with God. To articulate the problem succinctly: historical critics have raised important issues about Genesis 1:2, and these call for attention by any renewal of theological interpretation.

Karl Barth and Dietrich Bonhoeffer: Dialogue Partners

Fortunately, we do not have to reinvent the wheel when it comes to a theological reading of this verse. Karl Barth's *Church Dogmatics* is unique in its combination of rigorous theology with extensive biblical exegesis, a combination that we need to recover today. It is almost unimaginable to think of a contemporary theologian including some one hundred thirty pages of exegesis on Genesis 1–2, and yet this is precisely what one finds in the *Church Dogmatics*.[8] As Barth's Christocentric theological framework takes hold, he does more, much more, and not less, exegesis. And this includes close attention to Genesis 1:2.

Barth's theological style of interpretation was dismissed by scholars when he published his *Epistle to the Romans* (1918), as was Dietrich Bonhoeffer's *Creation and Fall: A Theological Exposition of Genesis 1–3* when it was published in 1937.[9] Neither biblical scholars nor theologians knew

---

6. Hermann Gunkel, *The Legends of Genesis: The Biblical Saga and History*, trans. W. H. Carruth (Chicago: Open Court, 1901), 74.

7. See, for example, Walter Brueggemann's comments in his *Genesis*, IBC (Louisville: Westminster John Knox, 1982), 29. Cf. also Steven DiMattei, *Genesis 1 and the Creationism Debate: Being Honest to the Text, Its Author, and His Beliefs* (Eugene, OR: Wipf and Stock, 2016), 13.

8. Karl Barth, *Church Dogmatics*, ed. G. W. Bromiley and T. F. Torrance, trans. G. W. Bromiley et al. (Edinburgh: T. & T. Clark, 2004). Abbreviated hereafter as *CD*.

9. Karl Barth, *The Epistle to the Romans*, trans. Edwyn C. Hoskyns (Oxford: Oxford University Press, 1933); Dietrich Bonhoeffer, *Creation and Fall: A Theological Exposition of*

what to do with this style of theological interpretation of Scripture. We are now amidst a partial renaissance of so-called theological interpretation of the Bible, and, I would suggest, it is to Barth and Bonhoeffer that we need to look for some of the best and most creative examples of what theological interpretation might look like. This is not, of course, to say that we need to follow them slavishly, but it is to assert that they are on to something in their work that we need to be aware of, receive, and translate into our contexts today. Like Barth, Bonhoeffer attends to Genesis 1:2, but, intriguingly, he reads it in a very different way. Thus, in this chapter, I use Barth and Bonhoeffer as dialogue partners to explore this notoriously difficult text.

Genesis 1:2 in Context

Genesis 1:1–2:3 is the opening salvo of the entire Bible, as well as of Genesis and of the Pentateuch. In my reading, it stands outside of the first of ten *toledot* ("generations of") headings that indicate the literary structure of Genesis.[10] I take Genesis 2:4a as the *toledot* heading for what follows and not for what precedes.[11] There has been much discussion about the genre of Genesis 1:1–2:3. I agree with Westermann that it is *narrative* first and must be read as such.[12]

I translate Genesis 1:1 as "In the beginning God created the heavens and the earth."[13] Genesis 1:1, in my view, is a heading *and* summary of 1:1–2:3, *as well as* the lead-in to v. 2 and following.[14] It should be noted that, after v. 2, every subsequent verse in this section begins with the *waw-consecutive* conjunction (*wa* followed by *dagesh forte*) indicating the flow

---

Genesis 1–3, DBWE 3, ed. John W. de Gruchy, trans. Douglas Stephen Bax (Minneapolis: Fortress, 1997).

10. Gen. 2:4; 6:9; 10:1; 11:10, 27; 25:12, 19; 36:1, 9; 37:2.

11. For Gen. 2:4 as a heading for what follows, see Gordon J. Wenham, *Genesis 1–15*, WBC 1 (Waco, TX: Word, 1987), 49; Victor P. Hamilton, *The Book of Genesis: Chapters 1–17*, NICOT (Grand Rapids: Eerdmans, 1990), 150–52. For the more common historical-critical view that Gen. 2:4a refers to what precedes it, see Claus Westermann, *Genesis 1–11: A Commentary*, trans. John J. Scullion (Minneapolis: Augsburg, 1984), 8, 12–17.

12. Westermann, *Genesis 1–11*, 80.

13. Cf. Wenham, *Genesis 1–15*, 10–14.

14. Readers should compare the commentaries on these issues. For a detailed defense of my view, see Craig G. Bartholomew and Bruce Ashford, *The Doctrine of Creation* (Downers Grove, IL: IVP Academic, forthcoming in 2019).

of the narrative. The common meaning of the *waw* is "and," although Hebrew scholars rightly recognize that it can have a variety of nuances such as "but" (adversative *waw*), "now," etc. However, as Walter Ong has rightly pointed out, in a literary-oral culture such as Israel, it is highly unlikely that some of the detailed nuances attributed to *waw* in Genesis 1 by contemporary scholars would ever have occurred to Israelites listening to this narrative.[15] In v. 2, the simple form of the *waw* (*we*) prefixed to a noun indicates a link with v. 1 and should be translated either as "and" or "now," but in terms of the relationship between the two verses, "the earth" is the connecting element. As we will see below, any legitimate interpretation of vv. 1–2 will need to explain the meaning(s) of "earth" in these two verses and their relationship.

Barth's and Bonhoeffer's Reading of Genesis 1:2

Karl Barth

Barth notes of Genesis 1:2 that "This verse has always constituted a particular crux interpretum—one of the most difficult in the whole Bible—and it is small comfort to learn from Gunkel that it is a 'veritable mythological treasure chamber.'"[16] Gunkel's *Creation and Chaos in the Primeval Era and the Eschaton: A Religio-Historical Study of Genesis 1 and Revelation 12* is well known and has more recently been reissued by Eerdmans.[17] Gunkel argues that Genesis 1 is not a free construction but developed from reshaping traditional material:

> Wellhausen recognized the theme of chaos as indicative of the narrator. In reality, an introduction such as this—darkness and water at the beginning of the world—belongs to mythology and should not be

---

15. Walter J. Ong, *Orality and Literacy: The Technologizing of the Word*, New Accents (New York: Routledge, 2002), 37–38.

16. Barth, *CD* III.1, 102.

17. Aaron Tugendhaft ("Bible-Babel-Baal," in *Creation and Chaos: A Reconsideration of Hermann Gunkel's Chaoskampf Hypothesis*, ed. JoAnn Scurlock and Richard H. Beal [Winona Lake, IN: Eisenbrauns, 2013], 190–98, 194) notes, "The corpus of texts that attest the mythic motif of a storm god who fights the sea has grown since the days of Gunkel and Delitzsch. Nevertheless, the predilection has been to approach these new finds with the same basic questions that motivated those German scholars a century ago."

considered as a fabrication of a writer, much less of a person such as the author of the Priestly document.[18]

Gunkel finds traces of mythology all over Genesis 1:1–2:3, but, in terms of 1:2, he discerns the *Chaoskampf* motif in *tohu* and *bohu* (formless and void), the darkness, and the waters. The *ruah* (S/spirit or wind) is a mythical conception, and its brooding resonates with the myth of the world egg. Gunkel asserts that "at Gen 1:2 . . . [*tehom*][19] is the name of chaos"[20] and evokes the struggle of Marduk with Tiamat in the Babylonian Creation Story (the Enuma Elish), the struggle that precedes creation in that story.[21]

Intriguingly, Gunkel finds in this chaos motif a basis for Old Testament eschatology. He provisionally concludes that "pre-prophetic" Israel already had an eschatology. As in the beginning, so there will be in the future a destruction of the world with a time of blessing to follow. The subtitle of Gunkel's work is important; Gunkel's thesis is that the *Chaoskampf* motif of Revelation (Rev. 12) was not only an eschatological event but happened before in the beginning, before creation. In Genesis 1, God first fought Rahab, Leviathan, and Yam—the forces of chaos—and then began to create. He concludes from his examination of Revelation that "In the end time what had happened in primal time will be repeated. The new world order will be preceded by a new chaos."[22] His particular focus is Revelation 12, and he argues that his analysis shows how the Babylonian tradition has shaped the tradition of Israel fruitfully at many places.

As with so many subsequent scholars, Gunkel notes the intertextual connection with Isaiah 45 and Genesis 1:2.[23] He maintains the Chaos myth is recalled in Isaiah 45:18b: "who formed the earth and made it (he established it; he did not create it a chaos, he formed it to be inhabited!)." Clearly there is

---

18. Hermann Gunkel, *Creation and Chaos in the Primeval Era and the Eschaton: A Religio-Historical Study of Genesis 1 and Revelation 12*, trans. K. William Whitney Jr., The Biblical Resource Series (Grand Rapids: Eerdmans, 2006), 6–7.

19. The waters.

20. Gunkel, *Creation and Chaos*, 22. For Gunkel, both myths, the Hebrew and the Babylonian, have all their major points in common. In *Creation and Chaos*, 77, he notes, "It is, therefore, our conclusion that the Babylonian Ti'amat-Marduk myth was taken up by Israel and there became a myth of YHWH."

21. Gunkel finds many allusions to this chaos combat in the Old Testament apart from Gen. 1, including Job 3:8; 9:13; 26:12–13; 40:19–41:26; Pss. 40:5; 68:31; 74:12–19; 87:4; 89:10–14; Isa. 27:1; 30:6–7; 51:9–11; 4 Ezra 6:49–52; 1 En. 60:7–9.

22. Gunkel, *Creation and Chaos*, 233.

23. Gunkel, *Creation and Chaos*, 92–93.

a verbal link ("chaos" = *tohu*) with Genesis 1:2. Gunkel asserts that, in Genesis 1, *tohu* is a technical term for chaos. He notes that Isaiah does not simply reiterate the tradition of Genesis 1:2. Isaiah does not say whether the world was a *tohu* before creation. Gunkel does note that it is apparent to us from Jewish literature, above all from Deutero-Isaiah, that the idea of chaos is not consistent with the idea of God as an independently working creator, and this implies that the chaos motif in Genesis 1:2 involves preexistent matter.

Already, Augustine noted five ways in which Genesis 1:2 could be interpreted (*Confessions* XII, 21).[24] Barth rightly rejects the idea of a primeval reality independent of and distinct from God. *Creatio ex nihilo* may not be clearly taught in Genesis 1, but the opposite view is refuted by the general tenor of the passage and the context. Barth, however, rejects the view of 1:2 as the first stage in God's act of creation—a view held by Augustine and Luther[25]—quoting Walther Zimmerli, who calls it "a desperate expedient."[26] Barth proposes a third way. He notes that v. 2 speaks only of the earth, the lower world of which man is part. For Barth, "heavens" in v. 1 refers to the created divine abode. Verse 2 describes a world in which there is nothing as God ordained it, only *chaos*. In this, he follows Gunkel in finding in v. 2 an expression of the chaos motif. Verse 2 is, for Barth, in utter antithesis to v. 1. The author knew this mythological element, and his only option was to illumine it and contest it. *Tohu* and *bohu* "bring us to the heart of the mythical world whose figures did not and could not have any precise or positive meaning for the thought and language of Israel-Judah but were simply personifications of that which is abhorrent."[27]

Barth refers to Isaiah 34:11, in which *tohu* and *bohu* occur, and argues that the condition of the earth in v. 2 is "identical with the whole horror of the final judgment."[28] *Tehom* (the waters) is in v. 2 a reference to the primeval flood, the principle utterly opposed to God's creation. Darkness should also be understood negatively.[29] For Barth, therefore,

> Our only option is to consider v. 2 as a portrait, deliberately taken from myth, of the world which according to His revelation was negated,

---

24. Augustine, *Confessions*, trans. Henry Chadwick (Oxford: Oxford University Press, 1991), 261.

25. And many others.

26. *CD* III.1, 103.

27. *CD* III.1, 104.

28. *CD* III.1, 105.

29. *CD* III.1, 106.

rejected, ignored and left behind in His actual creation, i.e., in the utterance of His Word; and to which there necessarily belongs also the "Spirit of *Elohim*" who is not known in His reality and therefore hovers and broods over it impotently because wordlessly.[30]

For Barth, v. 2 represents a world over which the Word of God has not been uttered, a monstrous *chaos*, which represents the shadow side of creation to which God says, "No!" The Spirit of God,[31] which Barth describes as "a divine power which is not that of the creative Word,"[32] hovers over the waters but cannot rectify this lack but only serves to foreground it more clearly: "it belongs to the very nature and essence of such a sphere that in it even the Spirit of *Elohim* is condemned to the complete impotence of a bird hovering or brooding over shoreless or sterile waters."[33] In this way, v. 2 alerts us to the risk God takes in creating.[34] Among other things, Barth appeals to Isaiah 45:18, which does indeed state that God did not create the earth *tohu*, the latter being the same word used in 1:2.

Dietrich Bonhoeffer

Barth's *CD* III.1 was published in 1945, so clearly Bonhoeffer could not have engaged with it. There are, in fact, few references to Barth in Bonhoeffer's *Creation and Fall*. Bonhoeffer is a major theologian of creation in his own right. In the winter semester of 1932–33, he gave a series of lectures at the University of Berlin entitled "Schöpfung und Sünde. Theologische Ausle-gung von Genesis 1–3," published as *Creation and Fall: A Theological Expo-sition of Genesis 1–3*. For our purposes, it is important to note that *Creation and Fall* represented Bonhoeffer's first attempt to do theology in direct dia-logue with Scripture. Like Barth, Bonhoeffer had no desire to move behind historical criticism but to move beyond it to hear God's living address for today. *Creation and Fall* helped Bonhoeffer see the vital importance of the Old Testament and that its denial or downplaying as Scripture by Christians has contributed to a dualistic separation of creation and redemption and

---

30. *CD* III.1, 108.

31. Barth, *CD* III.1, 107, rightly argues that the *ruah Elohim* is not just a mighty wind, but the Spirit of God.

32. *CD* III.1, 108.

33. *CD* III.1, 107.

34. *CD* III.1, 109.

of the public and the private spheres of life with very damaging practical consequences. "Because the world is God's world," Bonhoeffer writes, "it is good. God, the Creator and Lord of the world, wills a good world, a good work. The flight from the created work to bodiless spirit, or to the internal spiritual disposition [*die Gesinnung*], is prohibited. God wills to look upon God's work, to love it, call it good, and uphold it."[35] God's world is good, even where it is a fallen world, because it is God's work.[36] In many ways, Bonhoeffer spent the rest of his short life working out the implications of the doctrine of creation as a Lutheran theologian.

Interestingly, Bonhoeffer reads Genesis 1:2 quite differently from Barth. He takes Genesis 1:1 to be not a heading, but the start of creation itself. Bonhoeffer says regarding "the earth was a formless void and darkness":

> It was nevertheless our earth which came forth from God's hand and now lies ready for God, subject to God in devout worship. God is praised first by the earth that was formless and empty. God does not need us human beings to be glorified, but brings about divine worship out of the world which is without speech, which, mute and formless, rests, slumbering, in God's will.[37]

Of the darkness covering the waters, he says that it highlights the glory of God's majesty. It is like looking down from the top of a mountain to the depths below. Bonhoeffer affirms the link between *tehom* and *Tiamat* in the Babylonian myth but takes this allusion in a very different direction from Barth:

> This power and force still serve to honor the Creator now, but once torn away from the origin, from the beginning, they become tumult and rebellion. In the night, in the abyss, there exists only what is formless. Thus the formless [*wüste*], empty, dark deep, which is not able to take on form by itself, the agglomeration of formlessness [*die Zusammenballung des Gestaltlosen*], the torpid unconscious, the unformed, is both the expression of utter subjection and the unsuspected force of the formless, as it waits impatiently to be bound into form.[38]

35. Bonhoeffer, *Creation and Fall*, 46.
36. Bonhoeffer, *Creation and Fall*, 45.
37. Bonhoeffer, *Creation and Fall*, 36.
38. Bonhoeffer, *Creation and Fall*, 37.

This represents a moment in which God is thinking and planning. The hovering of the Spirit is God reflecting upon his work and the start of binding the formless into form. "The creation still rests entirely in God's hand, in God's power; it has no being of its own. Yet the praise of the Creator is completed only when the creature receives its own being from God and praises God's being by its own being. In the creation of form the Creator denies [the Creator's own self]. . . . In this form creation exists over against God in a new way, and in existing over against God it wholly belongs to God."[39]

Evaluation

Barth and Bonhoeffer offer rich theological readings that take exegesis and critical biblical study seriously. As we seek to read the Scriptures for the church, they are major models for us to explore and learn from. However, they could not be more different! Barth sees Genesis 1:2 as the antithesis of v. 1, whereas Bonhoeffer sees v. 2 as following on from v. 1 in the progressive movement of the act of creation. Bonhoeffer's reading has historical precedent in Augustine[40] and many of the church fathers. Augustine speaks of the *informitas* (formlessness) of what was created out of nothing *primo* (at first), the *materia* (matter, material, stuff) that waited to be bound in form. In his *Confessions*, Augustine says, "For you, Lord, 'made the world of formless matter.' . . . You made this next-to-nothing out of nothing."[41] Augustine argues that this "formless matter" was prior as a source but not prior in time, since creation was simultaneous. Thomas Aquinas notes that the fathers differ on this issue, and central to the differences is how "formless" is understood. He notes Augustine's view but then says, "But the other holy writers understand by formlessness, not the exclusion of all form, but the absence of that beauty and comeliness which are now apparent in the corporeal creation."[42] From this perspective, "the earth was void" or *invisible*, because the waters covered it, and *empty*, because it was unadorned.

Let me state up front that in my view Bonhoeffer is far closer to a right reading of Genesis 1:2 than Barth. Verse 2 should be understood as

39. Bonhoeffer, *Creation and Fall*, 39.

40. Augustine, *Confessions*, Books XII, xxix, and XIII, xxxiii.

41. Augustine, *Confessions*, XII, viii.

42. Thomas Aquinas, *Summa Theologica*, Christian Classics (Notre Dame: Ave Maria, 1981), Part I, Q 66, Art. 1, p. 329.

referring to the initial creation—not preexisting matter or a threat to the creation—before it went through the process of formation to become our recognizable world. As Luther rightly notes, "He [God] first creates the rudiments of heaven and earth, but these as yet unfashioned, and waste and void, with no life or growth or shape or form."[43] Indeed, it is difficult to see how "earth" could have such different meanings in two consecutive verses as required by Barth's reading. Bonhoeffer is better attuned to the *narrative shape* of Genesis 1:1–2:3. As we noted above, there is no textual reason for seeing 1:2 as an aside that is set in antithesis to v. 1. The *we* with which v. 2 begins links it into the narrative chain that extends to the end of 2:3; and there is nothing that demarcates it as the sort of aside we find in Barth's reading. Rather, it is a continuation of the narrative begun in v. 1 but now with a focus on the initial condition of the earth.

Both Barth and Bonhoeffer are right in seeing the *ruah Elohim* as a reference to the Spirit of God. Among modern interpreters, many see v. 2 as a description of the primeval chaos and translate *ruah Elohim* as "a mighty wind" (so von Rad, Speiser, Westermann).[44] Gordon Wenham opts for "the Wind of God" as a vivid image of the Spirit of God.[45] As Wenham notes, reading *Elohim* as a superlative is unlikely in this chapter, and nowhere else in the Old Testament does *ruah Elohim* mean a "mighty wind."[46] *Ruah Elohim* must refer to some attribute or action of *Elohim*. But which one?

Deuteronomy 32:11 is the only other place in the Old Testament where the Piel stem of *rhp* (hover and tremble, NRSV "swept over") is used, here of an eagle hovering over its young as a picture of God's care and guidance of Israel in the wilderness. Intriguingly, in the description of the wilderness, the word *tohu* is found in Deuteronomy 32:10, one of the two words used in Genesis 1:2 for the state of the earth. The NRSV translates, "He sustained him . . . in a howling wilderness waste." One cannot be certain, but, in my view, this image from Deuteronomy 32 fits well with Genesis 1:2. God is present by his Spirit in his courteous and living way, and the Spirit moves creatively over the formless earth in preparation for God's formative work in turning the "wilderness" into a habitable environment. There is also the

---

43. Quoted in Barth, *CD* III.1, 103; Luther, *Sermon on Genesis*, 1527, *Weimarer Ausgabe*, vol. 10, 25:24.

44. Gerhard von Rad, *Genesis*, rev. ed. (Philadelphia: Westminster, 1972); E. A. Speiser, *Genesis*, AB 1 (New Haven: Yale University Press, 1964); Westermann, *Genesis 1–11: A Commentary*.

45. Wenham, *Genesis 1–15*, 2.

46. Wenham, *Genesis 1–15*, 17.

possibility of an intertextual allusion to Genesis 1:2 in Deuteronomy 32, implying that God's formation of Israel is related to and akin to a new creation.

Eisenbrauns has recently published a notable collection of essays titled *Creation and Chaos: A Reconsideration of Hermann Gunkel's Chaoskampf Hypothesis* (2013).[47] It is clear from these essays that Gunkel's entire thesis is in flux;[48] and, in fact, nowadays it is rejected by many. In a fascinating essay in this collection, JoAnn Scurlock argues that *rhp* in Genesis 1:2 should be translated as "surveying." She translates 1:2, "With darkness over the face of the Abyss and spirit of God surveying the face of the waters."[49] She arrives at this translation through finding a functional equivalent to *rhp* in Ugaritic *rḥp*. She concludes that, "In the context of Gen 1:2, רחף [*rhp*] would specifically represent that *necessary intimate knowledge of raw materials*, which for both Mesopotamians and Hebrews must precede the formative process of creation."[50] Doubtless the debate about these issues will continue; suffice it to note that such a translation would fit well with my reading of this verse.

Barth is so concerned with creation *by word* that he sets it against what we have here in Genesis 1:1–2, namely creation *by deed*. It is thus true that in Genesis 1, *Elohim* uses the *tehom* as material for creation but not that such material preexisted or threatened creation. In a footnote, Scurlock quotes an intriguing passage from the medieval Jewish commentator Rashbam:

> Everything that exists under the sun or above was not made from nonexistence at the outset. Instead He brought forth from total and absolute nothing a very thin substance devoid of corporeality but having a power of potency, fit to assume form and to proceed from potentiality into reality. This was the primary material created by G-d. . . . He did not create anything, but He formed and made things with it, and from this (primary matter) He brought everything into existence and clothed the forms and put them into a finished condition.[51]

---

47. Edited by JoAnn Scurlock and Richard H. Beal (Winona Lake, IN: Eisenbrauns, 2013). Cf. also Debra S. Ballentine, *The Conflict Myth and the Biblical Tradition* (Oxford: Oxford University Press, 2015).

48. See, in this respect, Bernard F. Batto, "Kampf and Chaos: The Combat Myth in Israelite Tradition Revisited," in *Creation and Chaos*, ed. Scurlock and Beal, 217–36.

49. JoAnn Scurlock, "Searching for Meaning in Genesis 1:2: Purposeful Creation out of *Chaos* without *Kampf*," in *Creation and Chaos*, ed. Scurlock and Beal, 48–61, here 61.

50. Scurlock, "Searching for Meaning in Genesis 1:2," 60. Emphasis added.

51. Quoted by Scurlock, "Searching for Meaning in Genesis 1:2," 51n.10.

Barth is thus wrong in pitting the Spirit of God against the Word of God. I agree with Barth that the *ruah Elohim* is the Spirit of God but resist the view that this is a divine power *not that of the Word.* Lee Irons and Meredith Kline rightly note that, "The Spirit is hovering over the formless void to fashion it into an orderly cosmos . . . (cf. the Spirit's transforming role as replicator in the new creation—John 20:21–22; 2 Cor. 3:18)."[52] There is debate about the precise meaning of *rhp.* Scurlock argues that the verb implies purposeful movement so that "hovering" or "brooding" are inadequate translations.[53]

Barth helpfully raises the question of the relationship between Genesis 1:2 and Isaiah 45:18 but misconstrues the intertextuality at work. Isaiah 45:18 reads:

> For thus says the LORD,
> who created the heavens
>   (he is God!),
> who formed the earth and made it
>   (he established it;
> he did not create it a chaos,
>   he formed it to be inhabited!):
> I am the LORD, and there is no other.

Central to Barth's case for reading Genesis 1:2 the way he does is the phrase in Isaiah 45:18, "he did not create it a chaos [*tohu*]." However, the parallel expression to this phrase—"he [God] formed it to be inhabited!"—is instructive in how to interpret "he did not create it a chaos." The ESV, in my view, translates the meaning correctly: "he did not create it empty, he formed it to be inhabited." There is thus no contradiction between Bonhoeffer's and my reading of Genesis 1:2 and Isaiah 45:18, since from my perspective the *tohu* and *bohu* of v. 2 refer to the *prehabitable* creation, that is, the initial creation before it was ordered and formed by God.

We do not have time now to explore in detail the usage of *tohu* and *bohu* in the Old Testament. Suffice it to note that *bohu* occurs only three times and always with *tohu*: here and in Isaiah 34:11 and Jeremiah 4:23.[54]

---

52. Lee Irons and Meredith G. Kline, "The Framework View," in *The Genesis Debate: Three Views on the Days of Creation*, ed. David G. Hagopian (Mission Viejo, CA: Crux, 2001), 217–56, 240.

53. Scurlock, "Searching for Meaning in Genesis 1:2," 60.

54. The reference in Jeremiah is noteworthy. Michael Fishbane ("Jeremiah iv 23–26

Tohu occurs some twenty-two times, eleven of which are in Isaiah and a notable occurrence in Deuteronomy 32:10, in a phrase that the NRSV translates as "in a howling wilderness waste."

Michael Fishbane rightly notes the close links between Isaiah's theology of creation and Genesis 1:1–2:3.[55] However, for Fishbane, "Deutero-Isaiah provides a spiritualizing polemic against a variety of notions embedded in the creation account of Gen 1:1–2:4."[56] On this reading, a central concern of Second Isaiah in the context of Persian influence was the status of preexistent matter such as "waste and void" and "darkness." "The God of Israel is, the prophet argues in language targeted toward Genesis 1, the only god; and primal matter was utilized in a structured form: it never had the status of a restive or unformed chaos."[57] Fishbane's reading depends on Gunkel's combat motif and, as we have argued, this is an incorrect reading of Genesis 1:2. Especially in the light of recent work on Gunkel's *Chaoskampf*, such readings of Isaiah as polemically correcting Genesis 1 need to be revised. Isaiah is in line with Genesis 1 rather than polemically set against it. Isaiah does not correct Genesis 1 but draws out its implications for his own context. Furthermore, Isaiah 45:7 alerts us to the good character of darkness as created and severely undercuts any view of creation from preexisting matter. Isaiah 45:7 is quite clear that "He . . . creates darkness."

Both Barth and Bonhoeffer recognize the mythical elements in Genesis 1:2 but read them in opposite ways. It is notoriously difficult to be sure of comparative mythical allusions, as recent discussions of the combat motif discussed above demonstrate, but Bonhoeffer seems to me closer to the truth *if* one discerns mythical allusions in 1:2. They have been demythologized and made thoroughly subservient to *Elohim*. Here we may have an example of what Childs called "broken myth,"[58] referring to how the Old Testament makes use of but deconstructs mythical elements it

---

and Job iii 3–13: A Recovered Use of the Creation Pattern," *Vetus Testamentum* 21.2 [1971]: 151–67) refers to this section in Jer. (4:23–26) and Job 3:3–13 as modeled on Gen. 1 in an undoing of creation.

55. Michael Fishbane, *Biblical Interpretation in Ancient Israel* (Oxford: Clarendon, 1985), 325–26.

56. Fishbane, *Biblical Interpretation*, 325.

57. Fishbane, *Biblical Interpretation*, 325. Fishbane was preceded in this by Moshe Weinfeld, "God the Creator in Genesis 1 and in the Prophecy of Second Isaiah," *Tarbiz* 37 (1968): 105–32 [Hebrew]; and followed by Benjamin D. Sommer, *A Prophet Reads Scripture: Allusion in Isaiah 40–66* (Stanford, CA: Stanford University Press, 1998).

58. Brevard S. Childs, *Myth and Reality in the Old Testament*, SBT, First Series, No. 27 (Eugene, OR: Wipf and Stock, 2009 [London: SCM, 1962]), 31–43.

encounters that are in conflict with its perspective on reality. Indeed, on my—and Bonhoeffer's—reading, if Genesis 1:2 is utilizing the chaos motif, it breaks it far more strongly than Childs himself suggests. Childs follows Barth's and Gerhard von Rad's readings of Genesis 1:2, explaining that this passage accordingly depicts "an active chaos standing in opposition to the will of God."[59] Instead, "the primeval chaos" is the first stage in God's good creation.

Conclusion: Listening to Genesis 1:2 Today

In my view, the goal of theological interpretation must be to enable the church to hear what God is saying to us through his Word. Thus, in conclusion, we ask, what might we hear God saying to us today through this challenging text?

First, Genesis 1:2, as the first stage in God's act of creation, alerts us to the gap between it and the shape of the world by day seven, on which God rested, having seen (day six) that his work was "very good." In Bonhoeffer's evocative language, the formless earth waits impatiently for its formation! We live on the other side of that impatience. The vital point is that every aspect of the form of the creation comes from God. The Spirit moves over the waters expectantly and thoughtfully, anticipating the birth of the creation in its glorious multidimensionality. Genesis 1:2 reminds us that our extraordinary world *is* creation; this is its glory but also its humility. It is not God, and neither are we.

Second, in Genesis 1:2, the unformed creation stands, as Bonhoeffer notes, in opposition to God; but by day seven, its autonomy is far greater, and not least that of humans. This is what Bonhoeffer means by the strange expression, the Creator denies the Creator's own self. God creates a world with a degree of its own freedom and autonomy in relation to him. But it is a contingent freedom entirely the gift of God and can be taken away. This is one reason why judgment can be and is evoked in terms of uncreation, a reduction, as it were, to Genesis 1:2. Genesis 1:2 ought, therefore, to drive us to a greater commitment to honor and glorify God as the Creator; to decrease so that he might increase.

Third, Genesis 1:2 reminds us that every aspect of the formed creation is to be honored and celebrated as God's gift. We ought to be impatient

---

59. Childs, *Myth and Reality*, 43.

with our fellow Christians who subvert the inseparable relationship between creation and redemption and play down the importance of all the dimensions of the creation and the wonderful wholeness of being human. As Ola Tjørhom notes, creation is the very stuff of redemption.[60] Not to take this seriously is, as it were, to opt for Genesis 1:2 over day seven. Still good, but so very much less than God intended.

Fourth, the making of creation subservient to redemption is also to be rejected. In a fascinating chapter subtitled "The Gunkel Hypothesis Revisited," Scurlock argues that while Yahweh is credited with defeating a host of monsters in the Old Testament, "in no case . . . is the defeat of such a monster in any way foundational to the original creation of the world."[61] Scurlock proposes that, if Genesis 1 is sufficiently late to be contemporary with the Neo-Assyrian and Neo-Babylonian Empires, then

> The new choice presented by the contrast between the national gods of these two Mesopotamian empires with whom first Israel and then Judah found itself in intimate contact was between a Creator god who, by the by, was also a warrior; and a warrior god, who, by the by, was also a Creator. . . . In this light it is essential to understand the significance of the apparent omission of the *Chaoskampf* from Genesis 1's account of creation. . . . When we understand that the question is whether the primary activity of God on earth is creation or combating the forces of evil, it is painfully obvious why Gunkel made the choice that he did. . . . Genesis 1 was written with *Enūma eliš* in mind and with a view to disputation with it. The image of God presented in Genesis 1 is of an El-type Creator God with secondary, warrior-like characteristics. This is in sharp contrast to Marduk as presented in *Enūma eliš*, who is a Ba'al-type warrior god with secondary, Creator-like characteristics. Finally, the omission of the combat motif was deliberate and was designed to prove that it was God, not Marduk, who created the universe.[62]

60. Ola Tjørhom, *Embodied Faith: Reflections on a Materialist Spirituality* (Grand Rapids: Eerdmans, 2009), 36.

61. JoAnn Scurlock, "*Chaoskampf* Lost—*Chaoskampf* Regained: The Gunkel Hypothesis Revisited," in *Creation and Chaos*, ed. Scurlock and Beal, 257–68, here 259. Such a view is, of course, contested. Mitchell Dahood (*Psalms II: 51–100*, AB 17 [New York: Doubleday, 1968], 205) says of Psalm 74:13 that "the psalmist appeals to Yahweh's victory over the forces of chaos and evil before he created the universe."

62. Scurlock, "*Chaoskampf* Lost—*Chaoskampf* Regained," 264–65, 268. This point

Theologically, Genesis 1:2 thus turns out to be a rich and important text for contemporary life. Far from evoking preexistent matter or the shadow side of creation, it represents a stage in the complex formation of the creation that is ordered into existence by God with all its nuance and complexity. With Isaiah, we might say that God, indeed, did not create a chaos but *a world* to be inhabited.

---

needs far more discussion than I can provide here. In his stimulating *Creation and the Persistence of Evil: The Jewish Drama of Divine Omnipotence*, 2nd ed. (Princeton: Princeton University Press, 1994), Jon Levenson engages with the work of Yehezkel Kaufmann, *The Religion of Israel* (New York: Schocken, 1972), who took a similar view to that of Scurlock. Levenson acknowledges that the position of Genesis 1 at the outset of the Old Testament must be taken seriously. However, he thinks that the waters in Genesis 1 are likely primordial and finds evidence for a combat approach to creation in passages such as Psalm 74:12–17. For Levenson, the view of creation not resulting from combat connects Yahweh to El, whereas creation understood as combat connects him with Marduk.

CHAPTER 5

A Canonical Reading of Ecclesiastes

Christopher R. Seitz

The book of Ecclesiastes presents the modern reader with a host of questions. We will address four of these in the discussion to follow. First, who are we meant to understand as its protagonist or author? The book uses an unusual word (often translated "vanity"), and it uses it repeatedly. So any interpretation of Ecclesiastes has to think through what this theme-word means if the message of the book is to be heard properly. Second, the book repeatedly uses the word *hebel*. How best are we to translate it, given its obvious thematic importance? Third, Ecclesiastes is often contrasted with Proverbs, yet it contains a significant amount of material, particularly in its second half, which we would immediately recognize as proverbial. Is this a sign of complementarity, debate, rejection of an older kind of proverbial wisdom, or in what way do we describe this relationship between the Proverbs of Solomon and the proverbs of Qoheleth? Finally, Ecclesiastes appears in different orders in the various canons of Hebrew Scripture. How does this relationship with neighbors in the canon affect how we hear its individual message?

Authorship

Virtually all modern commentary on or introduction to the book of Ecclesiastes opens with an evaluation of the book's authorship.[1] This topic

---

1. See, for example: Tremper Longman III, *The Book of Ecclesiastes*, NICOT (Grand

---

I would like to thank Leonard Finn for his editorial assistance with this essay.

is pursued for its own sake but also in conjunction with a familiar litany of questions focused on the book's date, purported audience, relationship to other books labelled "wisdom literature," and historical setting. These questions are taken to be axiomatic entry points for the interpretation of Ecclesiastes and, according to this mindset, for every biblical book in the Old and New Testament.

But the question of authorship in the case of Ecclesiastes has a particular character that makes it like but also unlike similar questions put to Deuteronomy, Job, Isaiah, the Gospel of Mark, or the letter to the Ephesians, to choose a sample across the canon. This is because Qoheleth has traditionally been read in connection with two other works, which in some canonical lists also precede or follow it, that is, Proverbs and Song of Songs. The interpretation of Ecclesiastes and the question of its authorship are in some measure answerable within what we might call a canonical association of three individual works. And that these three works are associated with each other goes back, of course, to the superscriptions that head each work and that, in three different but in some sense kindred ways, appear to associate them with King Solomon.

One might pause to ask why the ascription is not stereotyped and clear across the three works but instead diverges. Proverbs is the most clear. The proverbs, which the book contains and to which reference is made, are Solomon's, son of David, King of Israel. The diligent reader will observe that, toward the end of the book, other kinds of ascriptions emerge, including "these also are sayings of the wise" (Prov. 24:23), "these also are proverbs of Solomon, which the men of Hezekiah king of Judah copied" (Prov. 25:1), and twin reference to "words"—of Augur and of Lemuel, constituting the final two chapters 30 and 31, respectively. Still, these appendices—if that is the correct word—do not upset much the clear attribution to Solomon that heads up the work. More on them in a moment.

The superscription to Song of Songs is equally clear, though the genre in this case is superlative song, not proverbs: "The Song of Songs, which is

---

Rapids: Eerdmans, 1998), 2–3; James L. Crenshaw, *Qoheleth: The Ironic Wink* (Columbia, SC: University of South Carolina Press, 2013), 9; Michael V. Fox, *Ecclesiastes*, JPS Bible Commentary (Philadelphia: Jewish Publication Society, 2004), ix; Iain W. Provan, *Ecclesiastes, Song of Songs*, NIV Application Commentary (Grand Rapids: Zondervan, 2001), 26–31; Choon-Leong Seow, *Ecclesiastes: A New Translation with Introduction and Commentary*, AB 18C (New York: Doubleday, 1997), 36–38; Roland E. Murphy, *Ecclesiastes*, WBC 23A (Dallas: Word, 1992), xix–xxiii, 1–2; R. N. Whybray, *Ecclesiastes: Based on the Revised Standard Version*, NCB (Grand Rapids: Eerdmans, 1989), 3–5.

Solomon's," the opening verse compactly states. In English printed Bibles, Ecclesiastes sits between these two books with their Solomonic reference: Proverbs and the Quintessential Song. The popular notion of Solomon as the author of Ecclesiastes is based upon the internal reference in Ecclesiastes 1:12 where a first person voice proclaims, "I have been king in Jerusalem," and which then proceeds to speak of great wisdom, wealth, and accomplishment—all details that comport with what we know about King Solomon in the narratives of Kings and Chronicles. The superscription is consistent with this when it speaks of the author as "son of David, king in Jerusalem" (Eccles. 1:1). So the modern question of authorship plays out against what is presumed to be the literature's own claim, on the one hand, and a setting aside of that claim, on the other, based upon indexes of lexicography (the late biblical Hebrew of the book), theories of wisdom literature and its alleged evolution, and a generally aggressive view that whatever Proverbs had to say about Wisdom, Ecclesiastes revises, reverses, or otherwise dismisses altogether. In turn, Song of Songs simply carries on under the lamplight of dubiousness regarding Solomon as author but in its case for different reasons. The superlative song is a *sui generis* hymnal whose protagonist is Every Lover.

In the light of this scholarly consensus, what is intriguing to note is that questions concerning a simple Solomonic authorship are not modern ones only.[2] In earlier versions, however, it is important to note that movement away from association with Solomon is not undertaken as a dismantling of prior settled convictions, as in modernity's skepticism. It comes, rather, as a result of close reading of a different kind, which notes that where one expects reference to Solomon, it is in fact missing. Close reading of this kind is not so much questioning Solomon's authorship as noting it is not registered in ways we should properly expect.

I want to note one chief difference, however, before examining the language of the early church fathers Origen and Gregory of Nyssa. The absence of the name Solomon in the book of Ecclesiastes is noted as only an incidental factor when modernity declares the book not his own and dates it to the postexilic period, as the terminating phase in increasingly disheartened or skeptical wisdom. Most assume the book is in fact seeking to

---

2. Origen, *The Song of Songs Commentary and Homilies*, trans. R. P. Lawson, ACW 26 (New York: Newman, 1957), 51–52; Gregory of Nyssa, *Gregory of Nyssa: Commentary on Ecclesiastes, An English Version with Supporting Studies*, ed. Stuart George Hall (New York: Walter de Gruyter, 1993), 33–34; Jerome, *St. Jerome: Commentary on Ecclesiastes*, trans. Richard J. Goodrich and David Miller, ACW 66 (New York: Newman, 2012), 33–35.

make this authorial claim, though some will note it does so with a studied indirection that requires explanation, akin to wondering about the book's epilogue now presented as third-person evaluation of what precedes.[3] That is, the fact that an epilogist can speak of Qoheleth with some evaluative distance means that he might rightly be called the book's author and the proper authorial lens through which the book is to be read.

What catches the eye of the ancients is not just the failure to mention Solomon by name, which they do note, but rather *the express decision to call him something else.* That, they believe, is the critical evaluative hint. He is Ecclesiast (from the vernacular translation of Hebrew *qohelet*). The point of view of the book, if not its actual author now reconceived in other than historicist terms, is unveiled by the decision to call him something after all: the Qoheleth.

Gregory explains the reference to "king of Israel" in the book's title through the lens of Nathaniel's exclamation in John 1:49, "You are the son of God and the king of Israel."[4] For "son of David," he has recourse to the Gospel of Matthew, which traces the messiah's lineage back to David, and kindred references across the New Testament. "The true Ecclesiastes gathers into one assembly those persons who have been scattered and frequently deceived," he writes. "Who could this be but the true King of Israel . . . ?" The point is made earlier by Origen, "an ecclesiast takes his title from his function of assembling the ecclesia."[5] To the degree that Solomon is evoked at all—Origen also notes the absence of his name and instead refers to the assembling function implied by the root *qahal*—it is in the form of a type of Christ. Origen also develops the idea of an ascending knowledge to be attained by movement across the three books associated with Solomon, by adopting different superscriptions that give clues about how this ascent is to be understood.[6] More on this important hermeneutical observation below.

Though the translation "ecclesiast" might send our ancient commentators in various directions, they correctly conclude that the word has to do with gathering. The Hebrew *qohelet* appears related to the noun, *qahal*, assembly or congregation, though, in its participial form, who or what is being gathered is not clarified. Luther's "preacher" assumed a congre-

---

3. Most notably, Michael V. Fox, "Frame-Narrative and Composition in the Book of Qohelet," *Hebrew Union College Annual* 48 (1977): 83–106; Fox, *Ecclesiastes*, 82–83.

4. Gregory of Nyssa, *Commentary on Ecclesiastes*, 34.

5. Origen, *Song of Songs*, 51–52.

6. Origen, *Song of Songs*, 46–55, esp. 53–54.

gation (listening to God's Word).[7] But the wise also gather proverbs and are all the wiser for doing so (Eccles. 12:9). The decision to render the word by a transliteration ("Qoheleth") corresponds, on the one hand, to caution (about what is being gathered) and, on the other, to the desire to give the function something like a proper name—though an engaging, thought-provoking one it would be, akin to Malachi, or Shear-jasub, or Maher-shalal-hashbaz. But in either case, the effect is clear, though its significance is in some ways better grasped by the ancients than by modern commentators wanting to interrogate a claim to Solomonic authorship. For them, to say "Qoheleth" is *not* to say "Solomon," and so one must ask what that might mean. For Origen and Gregory, it means the book's message is more decisive than any claim to association with the historical Solomon might comprehend. At one point, Gregory makes a pregnant comment about Solomon not being mentioned because the book would be read too narrowly as about him in consequence, by which he must mean, as autobiography or memoir. To read it this way would be to fail to see its greater ambition of theme and scope. That seems to be his point.

Recently, Jennie Barbour, a modern commentator, has introduced the book in a way that tracks more closely with the view of Origen and Gregory, though proceeding from distinctly modern and historical assumptions—in her case, having to do with perceptions of kingship after the exile and reflections on its demise.[8] Our Qoheleth is a kind of Every King, intentionally designed to speak comprehensively, if obliquely, about Israel's cultural memory of kingship, once it has collapsed. Rather than, by virtue of its ambition of theme, looking ahead progressively to Christ, it looks retrospectively to the whole business of kingship as a totality, from Saul and David down to the blinded Zedekiah. Barbour argues this on the basis of intertextual clues in Qoheleth that she sees as brokered via cultural memory, embedded sufficiently well in the literary deposit of Kings and Chronicles to be noted there. Her book seeks to track these and make the case for them. Qoheleth is David, Solomon, Hezekiah, and a whole host of minor, often dysfunctional, monarchial types from northern and southern experiences of kingship.

In my view, the problem with the argument is that it can account for only a relatively small portion of the literary deposit of Ecclesiastes in its

---

7. Martin Luther, "Prefaces to the Old Testament," in *Luther's Works*, American ed., vol. 35, ed. E. Theodore Bachman (Philadelphia: Fortress, 1960), 263–64.

8. Jennie Barbour, *The Story of Israel in the Book of Qohelet: Ecclesiastes as Cultural Memory*, Oxford Theology and Religion Monographs (Oxford: Oxford University Press, 2012).

final form, and so it tends to collapse the canonical text into a curious, if sometimes compelling, reception-historical moment of postexilic musing. It is on the right track in probing what kind of king this Qoheleth seems to be, and that is surely more than a thin rendering of "Solomon the Author" (then to be dismissed by critical theory). Barbour seeks to do justice to the peculiar character of the message of the book by broadening its take on kingship to encompass its entire messy and terminated history, thus leaving us with an *evocation* of Solomon and setting aside any explicit claim to his single authorial stamp, however we might conceive of that.

It would be my position that the book hews far more closely to its Solomonic base than Barbour realizes, even as it does this to bespeak a certain perspective on kingship that is far more than whatever might be held together by an appeal to Solomon as author. Here the use of the name Qoheleth is quite intentional and critical to a proper appreciation of the perspective the book is working with. Rather than ranging all over the long history of kingship via the postexilic lens of cultural memory, we might better imagine the book focusing on one critical juncture in the narrative account of Solomon's reign: the long sixty-six-verse chapter of 1 Kings 8, having to do with the dedication of the temple, including Solomon's prayer and his blessing. It is at this juncture, unsurprisingly when one bothers to look, where the term or name "Qoheleth" seems most at home. The depiction of Solomon's reign is provided in narrative form in a sustained nine-chapter unfolding (1 Kings 3–11). What the evocation of Solomon, through the lens of Qoheleth, is undertaking is a specific take on kingship that in turn is critical to the appreciation of the book of Ecclesiastes.

In 1 Kings 8, both verb and noun forms of *qahal* appear. Solomon *assembled* the elders of Israel (1 Kings 8:1); all the men of Israel were *assembled* to Solomon (8:2). The whole *assembly* is blessed by Solomon (8:14). Solomon stands in front of the altar before the whole *assembly* (8:22) and delivers a great prayer on their behalf (8:23–53), asking that they be forgiven when in time various infractions and afflictions take place. Again he blesses the *assembly* upon concluding (8:55) and offers a benediction (8:56–61). The festival of dedication of the temple takes place for fourteen days and a *vast assembly* is present (8:65).

The use of the name/function "Qoheleth" in Ecclesiastes is an evocation of this aspect of Solomon's kingship. He assembles all Israel and prays for them and blesses them. Chronicles recycles the story in pretty much the same form (1 Chron. 5–6). The reference to Qoheleth in the context of collections of proverbs and of searching them out and setting them in order (Eccles. 12:9–11), then, would not appear to hold the key to the term's use. Not an assembler or collector of wisdom or information of various kinds—the empiricist or encyclopediast—forms the primary register then, but rather one who assembles people solemnly. Here we assume that the author of Ecclesiastes is meaningfully drawing on the account about Solomon such as we can read it in Kings and Chronicles, picking out this theme and using the term Qoheleth because it is apposite there.

As has been noted, a direct link to Solomon, such as we find it in Proverbs and Song of Songs, presumably could have been made but is not. The past-tense reference to Qoheleth having been king (Eccles. 1:12), and having been wiser than all who ruled before him (Eccles. 1:16), introduces a perspective that functions very well in Ecclesiastes but less well as a direct reference to the Solomon we know from these same narratives. This is why above we speak of an evocation of an aspect of Solomon's kingship, rather than a direct reference to something like Solomonic authorship as such.

Of all the things that might have been evoked from the account of Solomon's reign, the author of Ecclesiastes has chosen to select the term that is suggestive of what we find in chapter 8 of 1 Kings. So if we ask, what is it about this scene that makes it distinctive, would we be pursuing the right question about how to read its deployment in Ecclesiastes? Here we assume the author of Ecclesiastes has chosen to focus on Solomon not for the purpose of authorial claims, but for canonical enlargement and inspired reflection (so also Psalm superscriptions and David). The parallel with the hoary figure of antiquity, Job, the legendary man of prayer, is close to hand. Job as author did not write the book, but he is its main protagonist by inspired design. In the case of Qoheleth, we have more material available for an author to draw upon than in the case of Job (Ezek. 14:14).

The assembling of all Israel is the focus of 1 Kings 8, in the context of the dedication of the temple. All Israel. A vast assembly, stretching from the mouth of Hamath to the Wadi of Egypt (8:65). A *spacially* implausible depiction, but one all the more effective for making the point of full comprehension, under God's all-seeing eye. Solomon also prays for all *temporal* eventualities Israel will encounter in times to come (thirty-two verses *in toto*). God is in heaven. But he can hear and attend and forgive "from heaven." Life "under the sun"—to use the idiom of Qoheleth—will be fraught with failings and afflictions. But Solomon's prayer is meant to encompass and enclose all that within the vast range of his prospective petitioning.

The Great Assembler is Ecclesiastes's royal protagonist. No temple of comparable significance appears on its stage, but the prayer that heralded its dedication sounds its notes. The personal experience of the protagonist King is now, in Ecclesiastes, one of sober retrospection. What he saw in the future under God's judging eye has come to pass in his own lifetime. In a sense, this is emblematic of kingship as a whole, but Barbour is wrong in her more global application not to see this from the specific, prospective, prayerful vantage point of 1 Kings 8, as guiding the reflections that now constitute the book of Ecclesiastes. In time, all things come to an end: as in the life of one great man, so in the life of kingship unfolding from him under God's eye. Ecclesiastes looks at time and life from that perspective. To everything there is a season, and a time for every purpose under heaven: a time to be born and a time to die. Everything comes under the eye of the Assembler. This is not the gaudy collecting of silver and gold (so 1 Kings 10:14–29), the everything of acquisition, but the everything of acknowledging their true worth when measured by God's final judgment in time and in space. The temporal and spatial range of 1 Kings 8, enabled by the perspective prayer especially allows, is what is germane to the perspective of our somber and aged king in Ecclesiastes.

At this point, we can even see how Gregory of Nyssa relates the Ecclesiast to Christ and the incarnation. He comes down, as Christ, to view the whole world of time and space and to experience its *habel habalim*. He is the King who can see all and see through it to God's good purpose.[9] Gregory's ability to move between the poles of the Ecclesiast as type and Ecclesiast as Christ prevents the popular portrayal of the book as grim preparation for the gospel, a *via negativa* made barely manageable by an epilogue that warns us about what we have just read: a painful absurdity of absurdities. Beyond these beware. Fear God and keep his commandments. This is mortality's duty. The harsh medicine of Qoheleth can be digested only by a return to the law and the prophets.

With this basic presupposition in place about who Qoheleth is and with what perspective we are meant to read this challenging book, we can now ask what the refrain concerning *hebel*, so critical to its sense-making and organization, might mean.

---

9. Gregory of Nyssa, *Commentary on Ecclesiastes*, 49–50.

Hebel

Whatever difficulty there may be in translating a rare Hebrew word into English is compounded when the uses of the word so disproportionally appear in a single work.[10] So it is with *hebel* in Ecclesiastes. The possibility of an artful or creatively unique usage is higher when the term is virtually a theme-word or running motif ("vanity of vanity, all is vanity"). *Hebel* may elsewhere in the Old Testament mean vapor or idol or something transitory like breath itself—speech exhaust—but the translation in Ecclesiastes must be attentive to the specific content and context in which the word is being used across this equally unusual book. The danger is in over-stipulating with a word like absurd, fleeting, or futile.[11] All of these exist within specific modern contexts, in which an agent is competent or capable but that which is being observed is flawed: it is transitory or irrational or vexing or confounding or absurd. As one modern commentator has said, the beauty of the word "vanity" is that it is no longer used reflexively in English, so it asks us to think more carefully about what vanity might mean within the unfolding depiction of Ecclesiastes as such.[12]

The real question the translation of *hebel* raises is whether what is being observed by Qoheleth is flawed, or rather, whether the observing agent as such is. If the world being observed is flawed in some way, it is hard to avoid the conclusion that God is either to blame for this or is incompetent in some way vis-à-vis the good creation he has made. "Absurd" and "futile" head in this direction, "fleeting" perhaps a bit less so, given that one aspect of creation is that our place in it is surely temporary.

10. More than half of the word's occurrences in the Old Testament are found in Ecclesiastes. Longman identifies "over thirty-five" in Ecclesiastes alone and "approximately thirty-two" elsewhere. Crenshaw suggests thirty-nine in Ecclesiastes with a textual emendation in 9:2, and Murphy finds thirty-eight or possibly thirty-seven. See Longman, *Ecclesiastes*, 61, 63; Crenshaw, *Qoheleth*, 126 n. 1; Murphy, *Ecclesiastes*, lviii.

11. As possible translations, Fox canvasses ephemerality, vanity, nothingness, incomprehensibility, deceit, nonsense, and absurd (which he favors); see Michael V. Fox, *A Time to Tear Down and a Time to Build Up: A Rereading of Ecclesiastes* (Grand Rapids: Eerdmans, 1999), 27–33; cf. Fox, *Ecclesiastes*, xix; similarly, Longman favors meaningless; see *Ecclesiastes*, 61–64.

12. See Murphy, *Ecclesiastes*, lviii–lix; cf. Seow, *Ecclesiastes*, 102; A. Lauha, "Omnia Vanitas: Die Bedeutung von hbl bei Kohelet," in *Glaube und Gerechtigkeit: In Memoriam Rafael Gyllenberg*, ed. Jarmo Kiilunen et al., SFEG 38 (Helsinki: Vammalan Kijapaino Oy, 1983), 24–25.

The proper translation of *hebel* is raised right away in chapter 1, in the context of the depiction of the created order (Eccles. 1:4–7). Indeed, one can pretty quickly determine what kind of interpretation of the book and of *hebel* will follow on the basis of how the commentator understands the opening verses. Anticipating the narrative on King Qoheleth's accomplishments to follow (1:12–18), we learn that labor cannot produce what the author calls *yitron*, "lasting profit" (1:3). All monuments to human achievement will collapse in time. But following hard on this observation, to be pursued in the concrete case of the accomplisher *par excellence*, reference is made to the created order. Is what we see restless and without any meaning? A kind of mirror of human striving of a restless and meaningless sort? Or does it bespeak this and yet show itself in contrast to human agency? Much turns on how one marks the transitions in chapter 1. Human faculties are the obvious subject of 1:8–11. Seeing, hearing, remembering; these are all fine and beautiful things. But they are also limited in range. When people declare something new, it is simply because they have not remembered an earlier version of it. (Anything truly new is only a species of something that already exists in its principal form, or a commodity freshly packaged to sell to a public itchy for change and novelty.) What about words and speaking? They happen without any obvious labor, but do they complete themselves in any satisfactory way? Of the making of many books there is no end, we will hear at the conclusion of this book, and yet the book gets spoken forth in what we have before us.

Earth, sun, wind, and water go about on their circuits. And yet they do not wear out or lose themselves in a trail of exhaust. The sun is there every morning. The wind blows but does not blow itself out. The water runs into the sea, but it does not spill over its banks in so doing, even as it never stops its filling action. There is a circuitry—some of it not clear to the human eye (where does the sun go when we do not see it?)—that keeps all in bounds. The carefully preserved and bounded world after the flood comes to mind (Gen. 8:22). Or the bulwarks against chaos provided by God that we read about in the Psalms. In some ways, this picture of created order and durability is fairly clear as the point of the opening chapter. One thing that may disturb it is the translation of 1:8: does it summarize what precedes or introduce what follows (vv. 8–11 and 12–18)? Are all things full of weariness (RSV)? That would make the ordered circuitry of creation suddenly bespeak something vain, and yet that note is absent in verses 4–7. Generations come and go, but the earth endures forever, and so the mysterious rounds of creation itself.

A better reading keeps verse 8 intact and reads it together with what follows. In contrast to the order of creation, even in its movements, are the human faculties. The ear does not "hear things up"; the eye does not "see things up"; remembering does not recall things altogether. And speech and words do not record all things. The word *debarim* in verse 8 should be translated "words" not "things." We can also think of human events or actions as encompassed by *debarim*. This makes the verse completely consistent with what is said next, including the great events and actions of our protagonist Qoheleth, who in verse 12 looks back over the circuitry of his own vast accomplishing. The greatest example of unhindered human faculty and agency has been left free to amass all that the eye, ear, mouth, and memory can produce. And yet all this human agency does not reach something like its wonted bounds, for its desire will forever exceed its grasp. (Gregory notes this carefully.)[13] The world is not absurd, futile, nothingness: it endures forever; it is bounded majesty, where effort matches perfectly what is required for godly order. And in this, it mocks the greatest of our efforts to comprehend, control, or exhaust it. In this is warranted the conclusion of the book: *habel habalim*, sometimes accompanied by "and a chasing after wind" (e.g., 1:14; 2:11, 17)—the wind that can't be caught and yet comes right back and starts over with durable regularity. The agent, and not creation or God, is what gives rise to *habel habalim*. And so a translation must be given that suits this. "Not to be grasped." "Not within our control." "Sovereign."

Here is where having the proper picture of the protagonist is also crucial. Qoheleth is the man who has seen it all, had it all, known it all, tasted and drunk it all. He, quite specifically the man who has had it all, is the one who announces *habel habalim*. It is an announcement consistent with his sober realization that he is not master but bounded agent in God's good creation.

Proverbs in Ecclesiastes

The final section of Ecclesiastes describes Qoheleth as having "set in order many proverbs" (Eccles. 12:9). One effect of this is to raise the question whether the epilogue is seeking to connect Qoheleth to the proverbs famously set in order in the Book of Proverbs, and to have us think of them as

---

13. Gregory of Nyssa, *Commentary on Ecclesiastes*, 43.

a first installment of what we read here. Or, does this refer more narrowly to what we have in the book of Ecclesiastes itself, and whatever else we might imagine Qoheleth to have taught? The question turns on how we are to understand the canonical independence of the book of Ecclesiastes, but also its relationship to the proverbial wisdom of Solomon.

One popular answer sees the contribution of Ecclesiastes as a discrete witness, as adverting to the sentence wisdom of Proverbs so as to limit it, refract it, or even reject it.[14] Where Ecclesiastes uses the proverb form, it shows us proverbial wisdom coming to its wit's end. Wisdom upside down. Leaving aside for a moment the correct evaluation of Qoheleth's use of proverbs, it is important to note that the actual species does in fact appear in the book. Those studies that have sought more narrowly to identify actual quotations of proverbs—however they finally determine that—at least remind us that the book of Ecclesiastes is not without the proverb form, however else it goes its own way as it tests and probes work, pleasure, wisdom, achievement, death, and love. Is there significance in the simple use of the form in Ecclesiastes that also helps us understand how the book is a species of wisdom? Some have likened Proverbs to a primer and Ecclesiastes to an advanced class. Basic rules and exceptions to the rules. That is, not antagonistic, but proper in the right sequence and so complementary. To miss this fact would be to set up a false comparison.

Most structural accounts of Qoheleth see the book as consisting of two parts.[15] The *hebel* refrains appear mostly in the first two chapters, slacken a bit in chapters 3–8, and then disappear until the inclusion of 12:8. Both main sections contain appeals to enjoy life, which serve as countrapuntal notes playing off against the *hebel* refrains. That they persist across both main sections, and indeed increase in length, may suggest that they literally have the final word (en route to Song of Songs, as speech gives way to *hebel*-free music).

---

14. For example, see various analyses of Ecclesiastes 7:11–14: Longman, *Ecclesiastes*, 189–92; Craig G. Bartholomew, *Ecclesiastes*, BCOTWP (Grand Rapids: Baker Academic, 2009), 250; James L. Crenshaw, *Ecclesiastes: A Commentary*, OTL (London: SCM, 1988), 138–39; Murphy, *Ecclesiastes*, 65–66; Seow, *Ecclesiastes*, 242–52.

15. See Addison G. Wright, "The Riddle of the Sphinx: The Structure of the Book of Qoheleth," *Catholic Biblical Quarterly* 30.3 (1968): 313–34; Murphy, *Ecclesiastes*, xxxix–xli; Seow, *Ecclesiastes*, 46–47. For a dissenting position, Whybray argues for a lack of uniformity to the book; see *Ecclesiastes*, 21–22. Crenshaw and Bartholomew have posited a frame and approximately twenty discrete sections; see Crenshaw, *Ecclesiastes*, 47–49; Bartholomew, *Ecclesiastes*, 82–84. Norbert Lohfink (*Qoheleth*, trans. Sean McEvenue, CC [Minneapolis: Fortress, 2003], 7–8) has proposed a chiastic structure.

It is in the latter chapters where proverbial wisdom in its more characteristic form appears. An English printed text gives helpful evidence of this in chapters 7, 10, and 11, where the maxims appear in typical two-line form. If we prescind from the question of whether the maxims have a very different content than what we find in the book of Proverbs—and I think this is not easy to show—what the form of the book may give evidence of is our protagonist wrapping things up in very much the same way that wisdom began. Are the proverbs more advanced, more ironic, more difficult to comprehend, more obscure? How might we expect otherwise, if we are reaching the "end of the matter" from the Great Assembler (Ecclesiastes 12:13)? Unmistakable as the book draws to a close is the approach of death. Just as wisdom had a beginning, to use the refrain of Proverbs, so too it has an end, or comes to its proper end. Just as the sun, winds, and water return to where they started, within a bounded universe of good, so too wisdom reaches its farthest bank. A generation comes and a generation goes, and within the span of Solomon-Qoheleth's "life," all has been heard. The major and the minor notes of life, with life itself having the final word. The sun darkens, after rain there is more rain, one's teeth and limbs weaken, and with the approach to the eternal home, one is aware that blossoms will yet blossom and the grasshopper will continue his daily trek. There is no comprehending that is not finally surrender.

The appearance of the proverb form is important as the book draws to a close. It can be likened to the wisdom poems and rebukes of the foolish that reappear on Job's lips after three long rounds on the dung-heap. He is gaining a wisdom gained only through abjection and loss. The entropy of Qoheleth follows a natural cycle known to all mortals, even the greatest of the wise and the most successful in consequence of that. Job is thrust down into this place of death out of time, ahead of time; but having found wisdom there, his days will be doubled by the same divine justice gone for such a long season, or so it seemed. In both cases, we are right to look for the message of the book in how it is structured and how it moves forward, even when this may take some hard work to grasp properly. The form of the book matches the theme that is at its heart: the difficulty of gaining wisdom, but also the essential character of the quest, whether God is to be feared and life found in him.

Qoheleth in the Canon

As mentioned at the start, the typical manner of proceeding for correct interpretation is inquiry into authorship, setting, date, and so forth. The focus, and ground assumption, is what makes the book as an individual witness unique. And in the case of Qoheleth, uniqueness and individuality are defined in relation to how this book is not like Proverbs, or how it finds its place on a grid of deteriorating confidence in wisdom, one stage beyond Job.

The interpretive instinct to read works as discrete witnesses—whether the letters of Paul, the Gospels, or books of the Old Testament—has come with salutary results in helping us appreciate the specific message each canonically marked book makes. But it also can fail to note when the canon itself makes strong suggestions for how the individuality of the witness is to be grasped within a larger field of association. I make the case for this in my commentary on Colossians within the Pauline letter collection.[16] Recently the case has been made in questioning the hyphen between Luke and Acts, when it is clear from the early reception history of Acts that it typically introduces the General Epistles and does not disturb the fourfold Gospel collection as its own canonical achievement, where John meaningfully closes off this major building block of the New Testament.[17]

Our forebears in the history of interpretation did not fail to note the unique testimony of Ecclesiastes over against kindred writings, even as the concept of wisdom literature would have made them scratch their heads. More relevant than a modern conceptual category like "wisdom" is the canonical witness itself. "He wrote the *Song of Songs*, with its accent on love, in his youth; *Proverbs*, with its emphasis on practical problems, in his maturity; and *Ecclesiastes*, with its melancholy reflections on the vanity of life, in old age" (Midrash *Shir Hashirim Rabba* 1:1, sec. 10).

Parenthetically, we know from the lists of books in Jewish and Christian circles that various fields of association existed—including one in which both Qoheleth and Song of Songs circulate within the Megilloth (or five small scrolls for reading at Jewish liturgical settings).[18] That does not

16. Christopher R. Seitz, *Colossians*, Brazos Theological Commentary on the Bible (Grand Rapids: Brazos, 2014).

17. See the robust discussion of this issue in Andrew F. Gregory and C. Kavin Rowe, eds., *Rethinking the Unity and Reception of Luke and Acts* (Columbia, SC: University of South Carolina Press, 2010).

18. For a recent survey of thought, see Julius Steinberg and Timothy Stone, eds., *The Shape of the Writings*, Siphrut 16 (Winona Lake, IN: Eisenbrauns, 2015).

prevent the kind of observation we see here, which trades on gradations in wisdom appropriate to one's aging in life. Origen's notion of ascent in spiritual apprehension—from Israel, to Jerusalem, to Christ as the Song of Life—is a different idea, but it is identical in believing that Ecclesiastes's message is to be grasped within a field of association the canon itself assists us in properly apprehending.

I want to note another rabbinic commentary on Ecclesiastes that takes as crucial to its interpretation inner-canonical association, in this case, the narratives of 1 Kings 3–11. Especially pertinent is their conclusion in Solomon's dream—or nightmare warning about disobedience—and the depictions of late-life excess and idolatry, which occasion the tragic breakup of a kingdom before it has barely gotten off the ground.

> When King Solomon of Israel was sitting on his royal throne, his heart became very proud because of his wealth, and he transgressed the decree of the Memra of the Lord; he gathered many horses, chariots, and cavalry; he collected much silver and gold; he married among foreign peoples. Immediately the anger of the Lord grew strong against him. Therefore, He sent Ashmedai king of the demons against him, who drove him from his royal throne and took his signet ring from his hand so that he would wander and go into exile in the world to chastise him. He went about in all the districts and towns of the Land of Israel. He wept, pleaded, and said, "I am Qohelet, who was previously named Solomon. I was king over Israel in Jerusalem."[19]

What we must grasp here is that this account is not some independent record of "what really happened" on the plane of historical inquiry, akin to asking whether Solomon wrote Ecclesiastes. Rather, the Targum offers a penetration into the logic of the book of Ecclesiastes, made by close reading of what are taken to be significant canonical clues. These include: (1) why the name of Solomon is replaced by Qoheleth; (2) what the true impact of the final chapter of 1 Kings 13 really is, measured against all that tragically follows in the Deuteronomistic History, which outstrips its own economy and brevity as a single chapter within the total presentation of Solomon in the nine chapters about him

---

19. Peter S. Knobel, *The Targum of Qohelet: Translated, with a Critical Introduction, Apparatus, and Notes.* In *The Aramaic Bible*, vol. 15: *The Targums* (Collegeville, MN: Liturgical Press, 1991), 1.12, at p. 22.

at the beginning of 1 Kings; and (3) the moral of the story of wisdom when it reaches its limits and goes too far, beyond the fear of the LORD, which is to calibrate its specific gravity as wisdom's true beginning and ending. "The end of the matter; all has been heard. Fear God, and keep his commandments" (Eccles. 12:13).

The conclusion of Qoheleth found in Ecclesiastes 12:9–14 is not, as Tremper Longman and others hold, an effort to bring within reasonable bounds what otherwise is unreasonable and even wrong.[20] The premise is that the work's independence is its hallmark, and so by secondary contrivance a way is found to silence its true message, which cannot be heard independently without damage. What we have seen is that whatever independence we might imagine Ecclesiastes once had—and one can be properly dubious about the premise itself and the characterization of the book that follows from it—the canonical force of association runs in the opposite direction. We cannot understand the message of this work without listening to the clues it itself provides for its interpretation. These are found in the narratives of Kings and the book of Proverbs.

Asking "what really happened" questions and "who wrote Qoheleth" without proper attention to the embedded character of this work within a field of canonical association is not to claim a superior historical reading, but a very thin version of it—one that passes over the history of the text's own life within a properly canonical field of meaning. What the Targum, rabbinic, and Christian history of interpretation teaches us is how this field of association was appreciated by readers who knew better what they were looking for when they asked what a text's meaning was. For such meaning is best grasped within the field of association being presupposed by the plain-sense presentation, and one that an author might well expect us to acknowledge and integrate into our interpretation as well.

---

20. Longman, *Ecclesiastes*, 274–84; Fox, "Frame-Narrative and Composition in the Book of Qohelet," 100–106; Crenshaw, *Qoheleth*, 93–99.

CHAPTER 6

What's "Catholic" about
the "Catholic" Epistles Collection?

Robert W. Wall

My thesis is this: the four apostolic witnesses, James, Peter, John, and Jude, are gathered in a discrete canonical collection in order to be read together by faithful readers as the interpenetrating parts of a coherent theological whole. The historical process that formed the Catholic Epistles collection, as well as the aesthetic of its final form, can be mined to help guide the church's present use of this collection as Scripture for theological under-standing, spiritual wisdom, and moral guidance.[1]

1. I have explored the theoretical foundation and theological implication of this thesis with my colleague, David R. Nienhuis, in *Reading the Epistles of James, Peter, John, and Jude as Scripture: The Shaping and Shape of a Canonical Collection* (Grand Rapids: Eerdmans, 2013); cf. the thesis-related remarks on p. 10. Several passages in the following essay draw from and even repeat verbatim certain material from this earlier work, which itself has a significant prehistory in a number of my earlier publications.

My strategies of theological interpretation borrow from the "canonical criticism" of James Sanders, especially in elevating the hermeneutical importance of the historical phenomena of the canonical process, and also from Brevard Childs, especially in elevating the hermeneutical importance of a theology of Scripture predicated by its uses as a fixed ecclesial canon. My emphases on relocating the historical-critical project from the point of composition to the point of canonization and on a rhetorical analysis of the "aesthetic excellence" of Scripture's final (or canonical) form, including the interpretive importance of a text's or collection's placement within and relationship to other Scripture, are properties of a synthesis of their pioneering work. By "aesthetic excellence" I have in mind a more functional notion of Scripture's literary form: Bible readers are drawn not only because of the sheer delight of its texts but also because their engagement with them has positive spiritual and theological effects—a claim easily secured by even a cursory investigation of the history of Scripture's reception in the church and church-related academy. For my understanding of this idea, see in particular, "The Function of the Pastoral Letters within the Pauline Canon of the New Testament: A Canonical Approach," in *The Pauline Canon*, ed. Stanley E. Porter, Pauline Studies 1 (Leiden: Brill, 2004), 27-44.

In fact, the New Testament canon consists of collections of selected writings that the ancient church gathered together, each in turn, and then canonized by the inspiration of the Holy Spirit to fix the scope and depth of its apostolic witness to God's word. The internal diversity of these different collections, more than their uniformity, adds depth and extends the scope of a textual witness to better serve those ecclesial roles assigned to and performed by the church's Scripture. Indeed, the content of any single writing within any of these collections, no matter its importance, would by itself be much too sparse to serve as the source of theological goods suitable for Christian worship and catechesis. The theological problem with any "canon within the canon" is epistemological—that is, it reduces what the Spirit has sanctified and the church has recognized as necessary for our instruction in the ways of God.

There is hardly a better example of this initial observation than the canonical collection of seven "Catholic Epistles" attributed to James, Peter, John, and Jude. Modern criticism has problematized the very idea that this is a "catholic" collection.[2] The presumed address of 2–3 John, for example, is a particular Christian congregation in antiquity and not the church catholic of every time zone, including our own. Moreover, the literary genre of 1 John is not that of an encyclical letter passed around from congregation to congregation of a church catholic, but more likely a sermon or popular tract intended for insiders of a community linked to

---

The lecture at Trinity Western University and this essay provided a new setting and opportunity to clarify and elaborate ideas I've been working on for a long time, beginning with *The New Testament as Canon: A Reader in Canonical Criticism*, with Eugene E. Lemcio, JSNTSup 76 (Sheffield: JSOT Press, 1992). This work continues; see, in particular, the "Epilogue: A Reflection," in *Muted Voices: Readings in the Catholic Epistles and Hebrews*, ed. Katherine M. Hockey, Madison N. Pierce, and Francis Watson, LNTS 565 (London: T. & T. Clark Bloomsbury, 2017), 199–211, which further suggests a somewhat new direction in my thinking on the "catholicity" of this collection.

2. There is no better bibliography of current work on the Catholic Epistles than Peter II. Davids's entry in the *Oxford Bibliographies* (Oxford University Press, 2015), http://www .oxfordbibliographies.com/view/document/obo-9780195393361/obo-9780195393361-0018 .xml. With respect to a canonical approach to the Catholic Epistles, consider now the recent entry of Darian R. Lockett, *Letters from the Pillar Apostles: The Formation of the Catholic Epistles as a Canonical Collection* (Eugene, OR: Pickwick, 2016). Lockett takes his orienting cues from my earlier work on the Catholic Epistles—but without the subsequent development of my later reflections and corrections—to extend the impress of this interpretive strategy in helpful ways.

"the beloved disciple."[3] The letter of James registers a similar conclusion among many scholars.[4]

The efforts of modern criticism to reconstruct the social world and occasion of each of these epistles—cued by their different authors/editors and respective traditions, their ideological and cultural sources, and their literary conventions and theological conceptions—have resulted in their assured independence one from the other within the Catholic Epistles collection. The corpus of Pauline Letters is typically studied together with the presumption of a common apostolic tradition, even if not a common authorship or social world; and the corpus of four Gospels is studied with the historical Jesus as their common referent. However, the Catholic Epistles are approached by scholars, and thus increasingly by clergy, as an arbitrary anthology of diverse writings, composed of different literary genres, occasioned by different social crises, composed at different moments and in different geographical regions around the Mediterranean world—which the ancient church gathered together a century or two later into a seemingly incoherent collection with no special purpose to perform within Scripture.

In this light, modern criticism has determined that the Catholic Epistles collection constitutes no real collection at all but is a grouping of literary miscellanea written for different non-Pauline addresses and brought together during the canonical process without any thought of their theological coherence or canonical function *as a per se collection*. Even if one admits that the titles given to these letters suggest that they are the enduring deposit of Jerusalem's apostolic "Pillars," as Paul calls them in

---

3. There is no critical consensus regarding the genre of 1 John. Most modern interpreters, however, agree with Raymond E. Brown's observation that this composition's form (even if not its epistolary function) is the least letter-like in the New Testament (*The Epistles of John*, AB 30 [Garden City, NY: Doubleday, 1982], 87). If an interpreter tries to pin down the identity and social location of the "anti-christ's" community, then an analysis of the letter's rhetorical design and genre tends to target a particular moment in time.

4. As Dale C. Allison notes, the growing conviction that James is some form of letter is never completely detached from the recognition that its materials facilitated its religious (and oral) use in worship and catechesis (*James: A Critical and Exegetical Commentary*, ICC [London: T. & T. Clark Bloomsbury, 2013], 71–76). This allowed, however, Allison is among a growing number of recent scholars who think James was composed to serve a broader audience than a single congregation, whether pastored by James or by someone much later. Again, I think these distinctions are practically of little value since the postbiblical canonization of an authored text universalizes its intended audience to include the entire and ongoing church catholic.

Galatians 2:9, the theological independence of any Catholic Epistle from another has become an interpretive axiom of modern criticism.[5]

Even a cursory check of over forty introductions published in English since 1980 offers a veritable kaleidoscope of critical options, with at least seventeen different collections proposed that include one or more Catholic Epistles.[6] Most of these alternative collections are rearranged by different scholars in order to feature their own methodological (historical, literary, social-scientific) or confessional interests.

The rubric "General" is sometimes applied to a collection of letters in a way that assumes a common *genre* of biblical literature: typically "General" refers to an encyclical letter that was written for a generic audience to address a nondescript problem and then circulated among various congregations of a particular region. I think there is little hard evidence for doing so. The still more expansive rubric, "Non-Pauline Letters," is used to subdivide the New Testament letters into those written by the historian's Paul and those not, sometimes even including the deutero-Paulines and the Letter to the Hebrews, which the church included among the Pauline Letters in antiquity. In every case, the effect of doing so is to isolate the genuinely Pauline Letters for careful study and to marginalize the so-called non-Pauline Letters as being of minor importance, whether in order to understand earliest Christianity or to help form today's church.

Without denying the important contributions made by this work, which mines meaning from the historical circumstances, literary constructions, and social conventions that produced each Catholic Epistle for first audiences, another approach to the Catholic Epistles concentrates interpreters on a postbiblical moment—in the "fullness of time"—when the church *completed and canonized* this sevenfold collection for the ongoing use of the church catholic as a discrete revelatory text. New findings retrieved from the social world and phenomena of canonization of this second collection of letters provide a broader and more balanced representation of the apostolic witness than that provided by the Pauline collection by itself. In my view, these findings challenge the critical consensus regarding the limited theological coherence and practical value of the Catholic Epistles collection.

---

5. See *Reading the Epistles of James, Peter, John, and Jude as Scripture*, 9.

6. On the following, see Nienhuis's introductory comments in *Reading the Epistles of James, Peter, John, and Jude as Scripture*, 3–8.

The Shaping of the Catholic Epistles into a Canonical Collection

The formation of the Catholic Epistles collection took place long after the Gospels and Pauline Letters collections had formed a proto-canon, which was placed in broad circulation by the end of the second century.[7] Irenaeus (ca. 130–200) was the first to argue for a particular content and shape of the Christian Bible. He knew and used 1 Peter and a collection of John's writings (including the Apocalypse), although far less when compared to his reliance on the Pauline Letters. Paul's influence, especially in the West, was not without problems for the church's apostolic mainstream, since his support was also claimed by non-apostolic rivals such as Valentinus and Marcion.

Irenaeus understood his task as defender of "the tradition derived from the apostles, of the very great, the very ancient, and universally known church founded and organized at Rome by the two most glorious apostles, Peter and Paul" (*Adv. Haer.* 3.3.2; *ANF* 1.415). That is, the working relationship between Paul and Jerusalem's "Pillars," represented by Peter, formed an undivided church—a point scored by Paul in Galatians 2:8–9. As Tertullian elaborated later, any apparent separation between Paul and the Jerusalem Pillars had to do with a divinely divided mission, not their common message (cf. *Praescr.* 23.9). Simply put, a biblical canon that already included Paul would have no problem including letters from the Pillar apostles since both groups were parts of an undivided whole.

Even so, while the so-called Muratorian Fragment (ca. 200) knows the epistles of Peter, John, and Jude, there is no evidence of a letter from James or of a collection of Catholic Epistles at the end of the second century. It is Origen of Alexandria (ca. 184–253) in the East who is the first to comment on all twenty-seven writings now part of the New Testament canon (even though disputing 2 Peter and 2–3 John as "authentic"). Origen is also the first to note the existence of the Letter of James and quotes from it extensively as an apostolic letter. Suggestively, he finds James useful in protecting the church from a Paulinism that has distorted the relationship between faith and works in God's economy of grace. For example, against those who appeal to Romans 4 to underwrite the heresy of *sola fideism*, Origen appeals to Jesus who challenges his Jewish opponents by saying,

---

7. On this section, see the wider discussion in *Reading the Epistles of James, Peter, John, and Jude as Scripture*, 17–39, here drawing especially on aspects of 20–28, 34–35, 38–39.

"If you are Abraham's children, you would be doing the *works* of Abraham" (John 8:39). If Jesus had used the singular "work," Origen insists, then faith alone would be required; but this "would not be conceded by those who accept the saying as authoritative, 'Faith without works is dead'" (*Com. Jn.* 20.10.66). Origen recognizes James as Scripture precisely for this reason: to correct those who would use Paul unprofitably to support a faith-only Christianity.[8]

The first historian of the canonical process, Eusebius, was also the first to note the existence of this second collection of letters, which he called "catholic."[9] He went on to observe the disputed reception of this letter collection within the early church, especially when compared with the fourteen-letter Pauline corpus and fourfold Gospel already fixed in its final form by the church and in wide circulation. Eusebius noted that the disputation over certain members of the Catholic Epistles collection was not over their catholic or "orthodox" content but over the scope of their circulation within the church, which wasn't sufficiently catholic or "global." The assumption, of course, is that a collection's canonical address extends to and is applicable for every Christian congregation. Canonization universalizes the particular circumstances of a letter's first address as applicable to the time zones of every congregation of any age.[10]

8. Although the Catholic Epistles collection came to the Latin West a generation after its canonicity was settled in the East, Augustine is the first to leave behind an accounting about why the Catholic Epistles were included in the New Testament canon. In *On Faith and Works* (ca. 413), he argues, as Origen had two hundred years earlier, that using the Catholic Epistles collection keeps readers from misusing Paul and falling into a loveless fideism. This conclusion accords with the evidence of the collection's formation from Irenaeus and Tertullian against Marcion, through Origen and on to Augustine: at every turn the insistence is that the Pauline witness must be placed in an appropriate interpretive frame provided by the Catholic Epistles collection, lest tradents contract the spiritual sickness of antinomianism.

9. The initial observation by Eusebius (ca. 263–339) of the existence of a second epistles collection (*Hist. eccl.* 2.23.25) included a more cautious assessment of the canonicity of James, 2 Peter, 2–3 John, and Jude. His ambivalence was not because of their apostolic content, but because they lacked a "catholicity" of circulation. Nonetheless, the title that Eusebius gave to the entire collection, "the Catholic Epistles," cued its ultimate inclusion in the church's canon lists (beginning in the Greek East) as a completed *collection*.

10. Even though the church collected these writings together to form a discrete canonical collection, called "catholic" for meta-theological reasons. I say for "theological reasons" because the ancient rubric given this collection has been recently problematized on literary grounds. If "catholic" refers to the geographical scope of the letters' original address, or perhaps to the encyclical intent of their literary genre, then we also have problems with the use of "catholic" to name this canonical collection. The intended audiences of 1 Peter and

The irony of Eusebius's title for this disputed collection is underscored by the Nicene Creed's assignation of "catholic" as one of four identifying marks of "one holy *catholic* and apostolic church." Daniel Castelo and I have argued that these four ecclesial marks also delineate the nature or "marks" of the church's Scripture, whose content and consequence is also one holy catholic and apostolic.[11] I take it that what Eusebius had in mind for a "catholic" collection of epistles was roughly the same as what Nicaea had in mind when marking the church "catholic": in both cases, the catholicity of canon and church turns on the orthodoxy and pluriformity of geographical reach and theological makeup.

We should not assume, however, that the idea of a "catholic" collection refers to the scope of its intended audience or the orthodoxy of its content, even though both meanings are consistently applied to the catholicity of the church's creed and canon in antiquity. As Ignatius (*Smyrn.* 6.2) and Clement (*Strom.* 7.17.107) make clear, when the church named this group of seven letters a "catholic" collection sometime during the third century, the word likely would have denoted a *whole* or *complete* apostolic witness received from the incarnate "word of life" (1 John 1:1) and thereby distinguished it from other non-apostolic rivals.

As the last piece of the New Testament canon to be formed, excepting Revelation in the East, this collection was folded into the church's still inchoate canon to *complete* it, both aesthetically and theologically. In particular, given the pervasive concern about protecting an apostolic (i.e., "catholic") reading of Jesus and Paul against their many heretical champions, the church would have received this collection to include in its biblical rule of faith as a kind of *unifying* safeguard against any theological or moral misuse of the fourfold Gospel tradition and, especially, the canonical collection of Pauline Letters. We should recall that 2 Peter tells us so in 3:15–16! *To catholicize the biblical canon required the church to add bits to it that would complete it in a way that guarantees the orthodoxy of its use, as well as the universal scope of its application.*

---

certainly 2–3 John seem to be more congregational than "catholic" in scope; and the literary genre of 1 John (and some would add James) is not that of an encyclical "epistle," but more like a sermon or treatise intended for insiders of the community of "the beloved disciple."

11. Daniel Castelo and Robert W. Wall, "Scripture and the Church: A Précis for an Alternative Analogy," *Journal of Theological Interpretation* 5.2 (2011): 197–210; the argument is developed in our *The Marks of Scripture*: *Rethinking the Nature of the Bible* (Grand Rapids: Baker Academic, forthcoming in 2019).

The Shape of the Catholic Epistles Collection

The Catholic Epistles collection is a work of aesthetic excellence, a literary shape of great beauty.[12] By aesthetic I mean that the collection's final form, which the church finally recognized and received as canonical,[13] is its most useful version for performing the normative roles of Scripture. I would further suggest that we understand the integral completeness or catholicity of this collection as an aspect of its aesthetic. The way in which the collection is put together as a sevenfold whole ensures its maximal effectiveness as an inspired auxiliary of the Spirit in Christian formation.

This is to say, then, that the sequence of the seven Catholic Epistles is not arbitrary or mechanical; it is not based upon a chronology of their composition or canonization, or some other mechanical metric such as book length. Evidence would suggest that James is the last composed but placed first. One might suppose that their ordering is indexed by Paul's mention of the Pillars in Galatians 2:9; but this then doesn't account for Jude. Moreover, the consistency of a particular sequence of Catholic Epistles in both manuscripts and canon lists at the point of canonization (at least in the East) secures the contention that the church recognized that each letter, while making its own distinctive contribution, is materially linked to the others within a precise shape. Albert Outler refers to this as "canon-logic"—that is, the theological goods of each letter are related to the other letters in precise and purposeful ways that will facilitate their collected use in teaching and training, reproving and correcting God's people for spiritual wisdom and good works.

This logical sequence of writings within the collection does not envisage a linear progression that only looks forward, one Catholic Epistle to the next. Rather its collected witness to God's word unfolds in a more dynamic way, as though the letters are co-texts that read each other both forward and backward. Not only do successive letters elaborate prior themes (reading the collection front to back), but the repetition of these themes throughout the collection form intertexts that recall prior iterations in ways that thicken their subsequent use (reading back to front).[14]

---

12. See my wider discussion in *Reading the Epistles of James, Peter, John, and Jude as Scripture*, 40–69; the remarks in this short section are drawn in part from comments found at 248–52.

13. For a theological account of canonization, see John Webster, *Holy Scripture: A Dogmatic Sketch* (Cambridge: Cambridge University Press, 2003), 58–67.

14. I have hypothesized in several recent publications that the interpreter's shift of in-

Here is the shorthand version of the collection's inner logic, which I've mapped in detail in *Reading the Epistles of James, Peter, John, and Jude*.[15] The Letter of James was canonized, perhaps even composed, sometime during the late second century to perform the role of the collection's frontispiece. By "frontispiece" I mean to suggest that James was placed first in this Pillars collection to put into play a range of core agreements and working grammar that frame the unifying theology of the entire collection. These theological commitments are then picked up and elaborated in 1 Peter, whose theological conception is completed by 2 Peter to make more robust the collection's Petrine ingredient. 2 Peter is linked to 1 John by their common concern for the authority of the church's apostolic witness, which is epitomized by 2 John and qualified by 3 John. Jude concludes the collection by forming with James the collection's bookends, which not only roots its witness in the Pillars' Jerusalem mission to Israel but then also in the holy family. This deep logic apprehends a collection held together like the links of a chain! *I commend an interpretive approach to the sevenfold CE collection, therefore, that approaches the aesthetic of the whole collection as envisaging a working grammar or logic that aids the reader in bringing to full potential the contribution it makes to Scripture's witness of God's word.*

---

terest from the author's production of individual, independent compositions to the church's decisions that fixed a collection of sacred writings for canonization was a recognition of that fixed collection's aesthetic excellence—that its different parts were now properly arranged in a final form that works well when performing the ecclesial roles given to it. The formation of a single biblical canon under the Spirit's direction also creates a holy intertext that allows for a variety of new textual relationships unrecorded by the biblical authors. To illustrate the substantive payoff of this interpretive move, see my essay, "A Canonical Approach to the Unity of Acts and Luke's Gospel," in *Rethinking the Reception and Unity of Luke-Acts*, ed. Andrew F. Gregory and C. Kavin Rowe (Columbia, SC: University of South Carolina Press, 2010), 172–91.

15. For an accessible introduction to the application of this logic on the New Testament, now see David R. Nienhuis, *A Concise Guide to Reading the New Testament: A Canonical Introduction* (Grand Rapids: Baker Academic, 2017).

The Unifying Christology of the Catholic Epistles Collection: A Case Study[16]

In his programmatic study of Scripture's Pauline canon, Brevard Childs contends that the church's theological reflection should begin with a Pauline definition of apostleship.[17] His contention is first of all based upon his observation that a collection's apostolicity was an essential category of the early church's recognition of a text's authority, designating the earliest eyewitnesses of the historical Jesus who were appointed to receive and transmit God's word disclosed in him, the Word made flesh.[18] The apostolic origins of the church's authoritative tradition, then, is an encounter—a "witness"—of the risen Messiah, which was then applied to a variety of settings in a variety of ways, including in the production of Scripture's diverse deposits of different apostolic witnesses. Childs readily observes the contested nature of Paul's claims to his apostolic office, which is thematic of several Pauline Letters (especially Gal. 1–2, 1–2 Cor., 1 Thess.). He rightly argues that Paul's apologetical use of "apostle" seeks to secure his prophetic calling as the principal carrier of God's word about the risen Messiah to the nations (cf. Titus 1:1–3; 1 Tim. 2:7). The implication is that his writings are an extension of his apostolic persona.

But Childs (and most others) say nothing of the controversy that swirled around Paul's claim to apostleship that concentrated his opponents on the precise nature of his "witness" of Jesus, especially when compared to the Jerusalem Pillars. This is a crucial subtext of the Acts of the Apostles, whose canonical performance supplies the narrative setting that frames the church's reading of the two collections of apostolic letters that follow. Clearly the message and mission of the canonical Paul of Acts are sanctified and indispensable to the church's future. And yet, just as clearly, he does not possess the résumé required for membership in the church's apostolate (see Acts 1:21–22): he was not with the historical Jesus from the beginning, in sharp contrast to the Twelve who were. A close reading of Peter's speech in Cornelius's home (Acts 10:34–43)—which emphasizes the special importance of his sacred appointment as personal witness of the risen One, in continuity with all the prophets—makes this point per-

---

16. The first half of this section draws closely on *Reading the Epistles of James, Peter, John, and Jude as Scripture*, 250–51; see, further, n. 21 below.

17. Brevard S. Childs, *The Church's Guide for Reading Paul: The Canonical Shaping of the Pauline Corpus* (Grand Rapids: Eerdmans, 2008), 81–83.

18. Childs, *The Church's Guide for Reading Paul*, 21–22.

fectly clear, especially when paired with the preceding account of Saul's Damascus Road conversion and commissioning.

One also should note Paul's sustained defense of his apostolic appointment found in Galatians, which targets those within the earliest community who apparently argued that his pseudo-apostleship derived secondhand from the Jerusalem Pillars who had schooled him in the gospel, since they knew the historical Jesus and Paul did not (cf. Gal. 1:1, 16b–24). He rather grounds his street cred in his private revelations of Jesus (Gal. 1:11–12) and also in prophetic ecstasy (Gal. 1:15–16a; 2:2) rather than in an eyewitness encounter of the historical Jesus. While Acts secures Paul's authority, which Irenaeus rightly understood, it is on the basis of his continuity with the Twelve to whom Paul was the first and most important witness.[19]

This, then, is the epistemic nub of the issue: what is the source of the church's apostolic tradition? On whose Christology do we count most? The reader of Acts recognizes that Paul's apostolic authority is rather grounded in his vision of the exalted Jesus on the Damascus Road and, according to his canonical letters, on his transformative experience that followed this encounter as a result.

The reader might reasonably suppose that Paul's witness of an envisioned Jesus is indirect, *ex post facto*, and therefore qualitatively inferior as an epistemic criterion—or else the robust defense of his apostleship in Galatians 1–2 makes little sense to me. Every gospel claim, every pastoral exhortation, every missionary act, every appeal to Scripture Paul makes in his letters is commentary on the effects that follow from his trust in Jesus's atoning death and bodily resurrection. Everything prior to that messianic moment is not a critical contingency of his hope in the new creation, even if Paul is certainly aware of the historical Jesus's biography from others (cf. Gal. 4:4). Every promise God made to Israel "according to the scriptures" now realized in faithful partnership with Jesus Christ follows from his religious experiences of the transforming effects of the cross and the empty tomb.[20]

---

19. See David P. Moessner, "Luke's 'Witness of Witnesses': Paul as Definer and Defender of the Tradition of the Apostles—'from the beginning,'" in *Paul and the Heritage of Israel: Paul's Claim upon Israel's Legacy in Luke and Acts in the Light of the Pauline Letters*, ed. David P. Moessner et al., LNTS 452 (London: T. & T. Clark Bloomsbury, 2012), 117–47.

20. The irony of referring to the Paul of Acts as an "apostle" in Acts 14:4, 14, when he fails to meet the membership qualifications of the church's apostolate set out in Acts 1:21–22, perhaps intends to stress the continuity of his kerygma and mission with the Twelve's prior mission to Israel; see my "Acts of the Apostles: Introduction, Commentary,

This discussion paves an important route into the Catholic Epistles collection by locating the source of Christological goods at a location other than in Paul: unlike Paul, the Jerusalem Pillars are eyewitnesses of the historical Jesus (1 John 1:1; 2 Pet. 1:16–18; 3:2). The epistemic claim that provides a pivot point for the entire collection and underwrites its christological conception against false claims is founded on this direct encounter and experience of the historical Jesus. The theological goods retrieved from this second collection of letters, then, are mined from memories of what the apostles actually heard, saw, and touched in close proximity to the incarnate Word. The inherent competence of their gospel proclamation to settle disputes or to define an orthodox faith against all non-apostolic rivals is predicated on their more direct and intimate access to the historical Jesus. Not only do the traditions of eyewitness memories of the historical Jesus fund a different epistemology of Christology than does the Pauline witness, it has the effect of extending the New Testament letters' interpretation of Jesus's messianic role in the divine economy beyond the cross to include his exemplary life.

With this prologue now in mind, let me quickly summarize the unifying Christology of the Catholic Epistles.[21] The Letter of James, frontispiece of the collection, describes God as "Father" who has sent the "word of truth" into the world (1:17–18) to save people (1:21) from sin (1:13–16) and death (5:19–20). This word "comes down from heaven" as a revelation of divine wisdom (1:5; 3:17) that enables believers to pass spiritual tests, rendering them perfect and complete, lacking in nothing (1:2–4). This word is "implanted" within those who are receptive (1:21) and pure (1:27); they do what the word requires (1:22–25) and are saved as a result (2:14–26). In doing so, they become servants of "the glorious Lord Jesus Christ" (2:1; cf. 1:1) who both taught and lived God's word, Torah's royal law (2:8), by

---

and Reflections," in *The New Interpreter's Bible*, vol. 10, ed. Leander E. Keck (Nashville: Abingdon, 2002), 197. The canonization of diverse apostolic witnesses, including Paul, surely recognizes the pluriform but continuous nature of Scripture's witness to Christ and the apocalypse of salvation disclosed in his earthly ministry. This witness extends to the Old Testament, whose referent is the risen Jesus (Rom. 10:4). For this reason, a canonical approach does not pit a Pauline Christology—its sources and core beliefs—against the christological conception forged by other witnesses, including the sevenfold Catholic Epistles collection and Hebrews, but rather views them together as an authoritative witness greater than the sum of its parts.

21. With a few variations, the following replicates my remarks in *Reading the Epistles of James, Peter, John, and Jude as Scripture*, 261–63.

loving his poor neighbors without prejudice and resisting their mistreatment by the rich (2:1–5; 5:1–6).

Though James never explicitly connects "the word" and "the Lord," the reception and placement of James within the Catholic Epistles collection forms the reader's intuition that this "word of truth" is instantiated in Jesus whom Peter and John saw and heard in the flesh. Within a wider canonical setting, James is read with Matthew's Gospel, which depicts Jesus as a messianic teacher of wisdom, and the Pauline witness that calls him the "wisdom from God" (1 Cor. 1:30) and refers to the gospel as "the word of truth" (2 Tim. 2:15). In fact, the words "God" and "Lord" are used almost interchangeably in this letter, such that at certain points it is difficult to tell whether we are reading about the Creator or the Christ (e.g., 1:7; 3:9; 4:10, 15; 5:4, 7, 8, 10, 11, 14, 15). Whether this high Christology is described as "implicit"[22] or just plain ambiguous, the ultimate effect for a reading of James as Scripture is the same: in the terminology of Tertullian (*Praescr.* 13), the Word who was seen in diverse manners by the patriarchs and heard at all times in the prophets was at last brought down by the power of the Father in Jesus the Christ.

The Petrine Letters fill out the christological analogy introduced by James in exceedingly rich detail, making explicit what was implied in the first Catholic Epistle. In 1 Peter, God is "the Father of our Lord Jesus Christ" (1:3) who sent him into the world as both atoning sacrifice (1:2, 18–21; 2:22–25; 3:18) and exemplar of faith (2:13, 21; 3:13–18; 4:1, 13–16). In his work and witness on God's behalf, Jesus shepherds God's people (2:25; 5:4), guarding their souls (1:5; 2:25) through the hope of the resurrection (1:3, 21) until their salvation is complete (1:7–9, 13). This work and witness is focused most particularly in his role as God's suffering servant (2:21–25) whose costly obedience liberates suffering believers, enabling them to abandon their pagan citizenship to become God's resident aliens, living according to the cultural habits and mores of their future heavenly home (1:3–9; 5:13–14). This transferal of hope (1:3, 13), the effect of their "new birth," is brought about by the power of "the living and abiding word of God" (1:23) preached by the apostles of the Lord (1:25).

Second, Peter in turn expands the christological vision further, widening the lens beyond his past suffering and death to include the earthly revelation of his power and glory in the transfiguration (2 Pet. 1:16–18),

---

22. E.g., Franz Mussner, *Der Jakobusbrief* (Freiburg: Verlag Herder, 1964), 250–54; Richard Bauckham, "James and Jesus," in *The Brother of Jesus: James the Just and His Mission,* ed. Bruce Chilton and Jacob Neusner (Louisville: Westminster John Knox, 2001), 131–35.

his *present* role as the Master (2:1) who provides empowering knowledge of salvation (1:3–11; 2:20; 3:18), and his *future* advent as Lord and Judge of creation (3:10–14). As was the case with 1 Peter, so also here: it is emphasized that this salvation is mediated to believers through the word of Christ's apostles (1:16–18) who proclaimed this good news in the past and established the epistolary means by which future believers would be continually reminded of their saving proclamation (1:12–15). Those who attend to this apostolic word are protected against the ignorant and unstable who would lead them astray (3:15–18).

The Johannine Epistles extend the christological claims of the previous three letters. As in James, so also here: Jesus is "the righteous one" (James 5:6; 1 John 2:1). As in 1 Peter, so also here: Jesus is the atoning "expiation (*hilasmōs*) for our sins" (1 Pet. 3:18; 1 John 2:2) even though "he committed no sin" (1 Pet. 2:22; 1 John 3:5). As in 2 Peter, so also here: the "word of life" (1:1–2) that has come in the flesh is witnessed to (1:1), proclaimed (1:3), and then written up (1:4; 2:13; 5:13) by the Lord's apostles. Right reception of this apostolic word is necessary to know the truth about God: since "no one has ever seen God" (4:12, 20), anyone who denies the witness of those who encountered him in the flesh will inevitably end up in epistemological error, while those who receive the apostolic witness will be properly informed in order to live their lives rightly before God. In fact, those who do not abide in this apostolic "doctrine about Christ" do not have God (2 John 9). Those who do remain in the tradition will be vindicated by the Lord when he "comes" again (1 John 2:28) on judgment day (4:17), to destroy the works of the devil (3:8) and vindicate those whose righteous lives evidence their right faith in Jesus (2:28–29; 5:4–5; cf. 2 Pet. 3:1–7).

The letter of Jude rounds out the collection's Christology with a resounding emphasis on Christ as Master and Lord of creation, before whom all owe obedience (v. 4). Jude's concluding emphasis repeats the collection's insistence on right action and the need to protect the apostolic tradition to ensure right teaching about Christ as Lord. Jude forms an *inclusio* for the Catholic Epistles collection on this same theme by speaking of Jesus in the same voice as that of his brother James: because Christ is the Word sent forth by the Creator, each of them blurs Christ and Creator under the title "Lord" (vv. 4, 5, 9, 14, 17, 21, 25; see, e.g., James 5:4, 7, 8, 10, 11, 14, 15).

Conclusion

Another element of a collection's catholicity suggests that its addition to the biblical canon completes or makes whole what is already there. I would suggest that this way of thinking about Scripture may also be applied to our ecclesial practices in a congregation's worship. One example of this application must suffice.[23] At the center of the church's traditional procla-mation of the "mystery of faith," recited as part of the eucharistic liturgy, is this familiar christological affirmation: "Christ has died, Christ is risen, Christ will come again." But this affirmation is indebted to Pauline Chris-tology (cf. 1 Tim. 3:16). While its sources remain contested, it is surely not grounded in Paul's eyewitness of the historical Jesus, but in his vision of the risen Jesus and the personal transformation he experienced as a result. On this basis, the tendency of Pauline Christology is to detach the theological goods of the historical Jesus (e.g., his teaching and moral example) from his death and resurrection, which reduces the apocalypse of God's salva-tion to the Lord's passion and *parousia*. The practical effect of this Pauline reductionism, evinced throughout the church's history, is to displace the ethics of a holy life, examined and exemplified by Jesus according to the Gospel narratives, for glib professions of saving faith focused on the cross and empty tomb.

But surely this ecclesial effect is unintended by the apostle Paul, for whom the life of righteousness (or moral rectitude) is the mark or conse-quence of genuine faith (Rom. 6). We may, therefore, allow that the addi-tion of the Catholic Epistles collection to the New Testament canon has the salutary effect on its readers of checking the church's sometimes fideistic misappropriation of Paul's gospel to fund a healthy balance between faith in Christ and Christ-like works.

In response, then, the christological agreement of the Catholic Epis-tles collection, deeply rooted in the apostolic eyewitness of the historical Jesus, concentrates the reader on his faithful life—what was seen and heard of the incarnate Word. That is, without setting aside his messianic death, resurrection, and return, Jesus's lordship is also evinced in his ministry among the poor (James), his costly service to God (1–2 Peter), and his self-sacrificial love (1–3 John). The result of this orienting con-cern is to supply a messianic model of God-likeness, which the church is

---

23. On the following, see *Reading the Epistles of James, Peter, John, and Jude as Scrip-ture,* 274–75.

called to imitate. In this sense, then, the addition of the Catholic Epistles collection to Paul shapes a more catholic or complete understanding of the church's "mystery of faith" by including the messianic life of the historical Jesus: "*Christ has lived*, Christ has died, Christ is risen, Christ will come again."

CHAPTER 7

Mixing Wine with Water: Enjoyment and Expectation through the Style of the Apocalypse

Edith M. Humphrey

The Apocalypse, along with the rest of the New Testament writings, has been subject to scholarly fads over the past century and a half, making for various assessments and interpretations. It also continues to be the object of popular interest and scrutiny, firing the imaginations (and fancies!) of those with little interest in the academic methods of biblical studies. In this essay, we will consider literary, cultural, and theological elements of the Apocalypse, as we engage in a close reading of two of its most dramatic scenes, looking in particular at their protagonists: the two witnesses (chapter 11); and the regal woman, child, and dragon (chapter 12). Northrop Frye's anatomy of literary levels or "modes" is a helpful interpretive lens through which we may discern how the visionary, in a creative and startling fashion, combines both folk story and irony with myth or divine story. We will see that the exaltation of the two witnesses and male child variously evoke a range of figures and literary forms found in the Hebrew Bible, Second Temple Jewish texts, and Greco-Roman literature. In this way, they ironically rework and conflate assorted cultural features, shaping the narrative plot and tone of the texts in complex and uncomfortable ways. And in the midst of all this is the Christ, astonishingly shown as a mere child, a humble figure, taken up to the very throne of God. We conclude that Revelation's artistry demands greater attention to its stylistically blended narrative modes, since it is a canonical text that draws readers into a distinctive, if startling, theopolitical vision.

We begin by considering the assessment of the Apocalypse at the time when the historical-critical method was just entering its heyday. For some time, John's vision was understood, following the lines of nineteenth-century scholar Franz Overbeck, as an intriguing example of *Urliteratur*, writing that was foundational to the early Christian movement, and also as *Kleinliteratur*, writing that was "popular" and came from the midst of the people, rather than from great artists. So, then, the book of Revelation was understood to be a means by which the community transmitted its inner interests, translating its oral traditions into writing "before its commingling with the world round about."[1] Along with the gospels, the Apocalypse was considered to be "low" or "folk writing," functioning "as a surrogate for oral tradition," with a "minimiz[ation] of authorial activity."[2] However, when Overbeck first suggested the naïve quality of gospel writing, he conceded that Christians *had* borrowed the form of *apokalyptik* (*sic*) from Judaism:[3] in this exceptional case, a certain Christian overture toward "formal" literature might be detected. In Overbeck's day, however, the complexity of the genre apocalypse was not fully appreciated and was identified mainly by means of bizarre imagery and eschatological urgency. In the case of the New Testament Apocalypse, many compared its "awful Greek" unfavorably against, say, the Gospel of Luke, and assumed that the seer, consumed with ecstatic visions, had written in code to buttress sectarian resistance in the light of the imminent end. As a result, the Apocalypse continued to be classed as a folk phenomenon rather than as an example of literary sophistication.

Klaus Koch called for a reevaluation of the genre of apocalypse and the New Testament Apocalypse in the 1970s, insisting that scholars cease defining and describing these only in terms of cataclysmic eschatology.[4] His pioneering work was followed by such think tanks as the SBL Apocalypse Seminar, a subgroup of the prominent Society of Biblical Literature, which published its comparative findings on various apocalypses, including the book of Revelation, in two experimental volumes: *Semeia* 14 and *Semeia* 36.[5] After so much thorough work, one might think that

1. Franz Overbeck, "Über die Anfänge der patristischen Literatur," *Historische Zeitschrift* 48.3 (1882): 417–72, here 443. Published by Oldenbourg Wissenschaftsverlag GmbH, http://www.jstor.org/stable/27593885, accessed May 2017. My translation.

2. John S. Kloppenborg, *The Formation of Q: Trajectories in Ancient Wisdom Collections* (Philadelphia: Fortress, 1987), 4.

3. Overbeck, "Über die Anfänge der patristischen Literatur," 443.

4. Klaus Koch, *The Rediscovery of Apocalyptic: A Polemical Work on a Neglected Area of Biblical Studies and Its Damaging Effect on Theology and Philosophy*, trans. Margaret Kohl, SBT 2.22 (London: SCM, 1972).

5. John J. Collins, ed., *Apocalypse: The Morphology of a Genre, Semeia* 14 (Missoula, MT: Scholars Press, 1979); and Adela Yarbro Collins, ed., *Early Christian Apocalypticism: Genre and Social Setting, Semeia* 36 (Atlanta: Scholars Press, 1986).

the fortunes of the book, so far as its reputation is concerned, would have changed. For in the 1970s and 1980s, the genre apocalypse *was* afforded a new precision in terms of genre, form, content, purpose, and wider social context. Alas, the reversal was neither immediate nor complete. Even today, the very currency of the author John with his surrounding cultures is for some commentators indicative of a derivative mind that produced only "a pastiche of mythological motifs," rather than a coherent use of sources.[6] It is assumed that "the traditional character of the imagery . . . places a limitation on our understanding of the nature of the seer's creative genius. Most of his images are not metaphors created by an individual poetic mind in isolation. . . ."[7]

Questions are raised: is creative genius measured by evidence of an individual mind in isolation? Further, why is *authorial* isolation admirable, whereas the isolation of a *community* suggests its preliterary state? And is either situation, the author's insularity or the community's insularity, likely or demonstrable in the New Testament era? We do well to heed the warnings of Kloppenborg, that the distinction of *Kleinliteratur* ("folk-literature") from *Hochliteratur* ("high" or formal literature) in biblical scholarship was predicated upon a hypothesis concerning the psychology of the early Christian movement(s): that is, scholars assumed that the earliest community, because of its emphasis upon the communal body, could not bring forth literature that required the creative reflection of a single author working out his own genius. Kloppenborg also warns us that, because reality is messy, and the history of the earliest church complex, "the genre of a written work cannot be assumed to be [merely] a . . . function of the prior oral tradition."[8] The Apocalypse in particular cannot "be conceived of as simply a process of sedimentation of oral apocalyptic tradition."[9] Separate from his concentration upon the

---

6. David E. Aune, *Revelation 6–16*, WBC 52B (Nashville: Thomas Nelson, 1998), 672.

7. Adela Yarbro Collins, *The Combat Myth in the Book of Revelation* (Missoula, MT: Scholars Press, 1976), 57.

8. Kloppenborg, *The Formation of Q*, 3–9, quotation at 7. In his discussion, Kloppenborg makes use of Erhardt Güttgemanns, *Candid Questions Concerning Gospel Form Criticism: A Methodological Sketch of the Fundamental Problematics of Form and Redaction Criticism*, trans. William G. Doty, PTMS 26 (Pittsburgh: Pickwick, 1979), 130–31, who questions the caricature of Dibelius and others concerning the "unlettered" nature of the early communities, and also the work of Albert B. Lord, *The Singer of Tales* (Cambridge: Harvard University Press, 1964), who shows on pages 129–38 that literary factors may be involved all along in movement from oral folk stories to literary works.

9. Kloppenborg, *The Formation of Q*, 6. Here Kloppenborg rightly takes issue with

hypothetical Q source, Kloppenborg's assessment is helpful: "The rigid distinction between *Hochliteratur* and *Kleinliteratur* and the attendant characterizations 'literary' and 'non-literary' must give way to a more adequate heuristic. The literature of early Christianity . . . admits of more and less sophisticated literary forms."[10]

The Case of the Apocalypse

As we read the Apocalypse, we are hard-pressed to decide whether we have to do here with something "more and less sophisticated." Does the author place himself charmingly within the drama, or is the "seer" a literary creation that enables the plot to move forward in the style of a vision? Can we characterize the Apocalypse by stressing its disarming use of sequential narrative, strung along with repeated use of "and" (*kai*); or is it better described in terms of an intricate structure and encyclopedic (Schüssler Fiorenza says "anthological"[11]) command of cultural metaphors? At times, we meet John as a willy-nilly prophet who is just one of "the brothers," but later as the transmitter of an immutable divine word that must not be altered. At times, we are in esoteric territory, and at others, we are drawn in chummily to appreciate ironic references to imperial oppression.[12] Astute readers must take great pains to attend to the details of a particular scene while also accounting for *inner*textual echoes between parts of the book. We can close our ears neither to differences between what normally passes for "high" and "low" nor to the unusual commingling of such modes.

Our "emerging awareness of the inadequacy of the idea of *Kleinliteratur*"[13] paves the way for a more helpful approach to how John incorporates and reconfigures folk traditions, mythology, and legend, whether via written or oral sources. Northrop Frye, who appeals to the Aristotelian

---

H. Thyen, who characterizes the genre as an example of *Kleinliteratur*, without regard to the fundamental literary nature of these works.

10. Kloppenborg, *The Formation of Q*, 8.

11. Elisabeth Schüssler Fiorenza, *The Book of Revelation: Justice and Judgment*, 2nd ed. (Minneapolis: Fortress, 1998), 135.

12. On this aspect, see especially Harry O. Maier, *Apocalypse Recalled: The Book of Revelation after Christendom* (Minneapolis: Fortress, 2002); and David A. deSilva, *Seeing Things John's Way: The Rhetoric of the Book of Revelation* (Louisville: Westminster John Knox, 2009).

13. Kloppenborg, *The Formation of Q*, 8.

criterion of characters who are relatively "weighty" (*spoudaios*) or "light" (*phaulos*), offers us an anatomy of literary levels, or "modes," complete with useful signals.[14] If the hero is superior in kind to other humans and environment, we have to do with myth; if superior in degree to other humans and environment, with romance or legend; if superior in degree to other humans but not of the environment, we have a hero of the "high mimetic" mode; if parallel to us and to the environment, a protagonist in the "low mimetic mode"; and if inferior, we are in the realm of irony.

Revelation is replete with striking protagonists, especially in its "most difficult and the most important" chapter 11,[15] which I read as connected integrally with chapter 12.[16] Let us try on Frye's spectacles, for they have the advantage of continuing to show us the distinctives of "high" and "low," without requiring that we buy into speculative sociological views concerning the early church. We will read chapters 11 and 12, focusing upon the disconcerting use of folk story and irony in what is otherwise a work of the highest mode, that is, a myth or divine story: and by "myth," we do not mean a story that is merely a yarn or untrue, but a story that concerns the world of the "gods" or of God himself (the definition given by Northrop Frye for this level of story). It is important to recognize that the main protagonist, the Lamb, is incomparably "higher in degree" than any other hero and the consummate master over his environment (to put it mildly!). This exercise is intended not only to heighten our appreciation for the rhetorical artistry of John, who has constructed for his readership a dizzying spectacle. Indeed, there is reason to think that John intends, by means of the way that he disorients the reader, to call us into an experience, through reading, that approximates the visionary experience that he had—we are given a vision by "proxy," so to speak. To read the book according to Frye's suggestions will also, I hope, cause us to attend to modes of narrative in a canonical book, showing that theological discourse within the Apocalypse interprets these mythical and legendary levels of story so that they speak faithfully to us of Christ—even while the stories are presented to us in

14. Northrop Frye, "Historical Criticism: Theory of Modes," in *Anatomy of Criticism: Four Essays* (Princeton: Princeton University Press, 1969), 33–67, here 33. The taxonomy that follows is a summary of Frye's description.

15. Martin Kiddle, *The Revelation of St. John* (London: Hodder & Stoughton, 1940), 174.

16. For an explanation of the intimate relationship of these two chapters, connected as part of the open and ingested *biblaridion* of 10:2, see Edith M. Humphrey, *The Ladies and the Cities: Transformation and Apocalyptic Identity in Joseph and Aseneth, 4 Ezra, the Apocalypse and The Shepherd of Hermas*, JSPSup 17 (Sheffield: Sheffield Academic, 1995), 84–118.

surprising combinations. John's Apocalypse (as we will see) incorporates legend into serious theology and thus may well provide a model by which we can understand later Christian works, such as martyrologies and saints' lives. In the colorful words of 2 Maccabees, "while wine mixed with water is sweet and delicious and enhances one's enjoyment, so also the style of the story delights the ears of those who read the work" (2 Macc. 15:39).[17]

Chapters 11 and 12 both focus upon key actors who *stand* and *move* decisively *up*, linking our world with another, always in contrast to the enemy, whose actions offer a dramatic counterpoint. Both the two witnesses and the male child recall, as we shall see, a host of stories concerning assumption and apotheosis (the transformation of a human into a god), resurrection and ascension, drawn from the Hebrew Bible, Second Temple and pseudepigraphal literature, and the Greco-Roman world. It may be too programmatic to suggest with A. Y. Collins that "the author of Revelation was consciously attempting to be international"; yet he does construct these chapters "by incorporating and fusing traditional elements from a variety of cultures."[18] John the seer is himself linked with Daniel and other Hebrew visionaries in 11:1–2, where he is commanded, "Arise!" (the literal translation of *egeire*), so that he may obey God's command. This instruction is enriched by the Christian motif of resurrection known to John and his readers, which has a rich history of varied uses, as seen in Jesus's command to the "little girl" (Mark 5:41) or in the apostle's quotation of an early creed or hymn in Ephesians 5:14. As we move on, 11:4 pictures two witnesses who "stand before the Lord," 11:7 an "ascending" beast, 11:11 the standing up of the pair, and 11:12 the command to "come up" and the assertion that they did so. Chapter 12 speaks of the dragon who "throws down" and "stands" to destroy (12:4), of a child "caught up" to God and the throne (12:5), four times of the dragon and his minions "thrown down" (12:9–10), of the dragon "coming down" (12:12), again of the dragon "thrown down"(12:13), of the enemy again "throwing down" (12:15), and of a final threatening "standing" of this antagonist. How do the action and description of these characters, seen in light of Frye's modes, confirm and upset readerly expectations?

17. Quotations of biblical literature in this essay are from the NRSV, except where otherwise rendered.

18. Collins, *Combat Myth*, 58.

The Case of the Witnesses: A Tale of Triumph

And who are the two witnesses, anyway? Sixth-century interpreter Oecumenius, though he himself interpreted them as referring to the Jewish and gentile witness of the early church, tells us that the earliest commentators saw these as Enoch and Elijah.[19] However, before Oecumenius, Tyconius (fourth c.) identified the two ecclesially and innertextually (cf. 1:12–20) as "lampstands" enriched by the two testaments,[20] and Primasius (d. 560?) related their polarizing effect to the good or bad aroma of the apostles in 2 Corinthians 2:16, redolent of an ecclesial authority to give life or death.[21] Parallels have also been drawn with Elijah and Jeremiah (Victorinus), Peter and Paul, Stephen and James the Just, John the Baptist and Jesus, the two Jameses, the high priests Ananus and Joshua,[22] and in the generous opinion of an eighteenth-century Anglican woman, the weakened Roman and Orthodox Churches, who must be revived and witness to the truth yet again![23] Sometimes, the interpreter is concerned to offer a precise identity, viewing the Apocalypse as a riddle to decode; other times, the quest is instead to uncover the models used by John for this narrative.

A variety of models and patterns are apparent in the text itself: in speaking of "olive trees," John evokes the Zecharian "sons of oil," both king and priest (Zech. 4:14); in hearing the divine voice say that these witnesses will "prophesy" and in viewing the fire coming from their mouth, we infer the role of prophet; in their apparel of sackcloth, we imagine a variety of humbled and godly characters who direct God's people to be penitent, from David and Hezekiah to Daniel; in the activities of shutting up the sky and blighting the water and earth, we are directed to Moses

---

19. *Comm. Apoc.* 11:3–6, 16; see William C. Weinrich, ed., *Revelation*, ACCS 12 (Downers Grove, IL: InterVarsity, 2005), 159–60, 169. Cf. Tertullian, *An.* 50; Hippolytus, *Antichr.* 43; but only dubiously, Irenaeus, *Adv. Haer.* 5.5.1. Parallels to the Enoch and Elijah story in Apocalypse of Elijah 4:7–18 provide another example of this understanding, especially if one sees the story as dependent upon Rev. 12. Cf. J. C. Poirier, "Jewish and Christian Tradition in the Transfiguration," *Revue biblique* 111.4 (2004): 516–30, here 527 n. 28. Poirier disagrees with Aune (*Revelation 6–16*, 588), who sees Apoc. El. as independent, or Rev. 12 and Apoc. El. 4 as both dependent on an earlier source.

20. *Comm. Apoc.* 11:4; Weinrich, *Revelation*, 160.

21. *Comm. Apoc.* 11:6; Weinrich, *Revelation*, 161.

22. For these and other interpretations, see Aune, *Revelation 6–16*, 598–603.

23. Elizabeth Stuart Bowdler, *Practical Observations on the Revelation of St. John: Written in the Year 1775* (Bath: printed by R. Cruttwell; and sold by G. G. and J. Robinson; and J. Hatchard, London, 1800), 51–57.

and Elijah.[24] These activities, coupled with the entrance of the figures into heaven (cf. 2 Kings 2:11) by means of a cloud (cf. Exod. 24:15–18), have commended Moses and Elijah as the dominant models to most contemporary interpreters. However, the seer himself clearly is conflating stories, as also he conflates contexts, since all this takes place in "the great city that is prophetically called Sodom and Egypt, where also their Lord was crucified" (11:8).

All of the "heroes" evoked find an easy place in two of Frye's modes, either the "high mimetic" or "romance/legend": those who are anointed but don sackcloth are different in degree (not kind) from others, can suffer from their environment, and so are "high-mimetic"; those who can perform miracles are different in degree both from others and their environment and so inhabit a legendary narrative. (I hasten to add that we are talking about literary modes, not making a comment upon the historical status of the biblical models.) John's vision combines the modes, with dramatic effect. The initial appearance of the witnesses in sackcloth, and their temporally limited power (1260 days, 11:3), might have prepared readers for the death and indignity that they will suffer: somehow it does not! Fire-breathing mouths that can destroy "any who would harm them" (11:5), coupled with prophetic powers to upset the environment "as they desire" (11:6), seem unlikely targets for antagonists, at least of the earthly variety. So, then, these heroes are different in degree from ordinary human beings. Moreover, the cues lead us to expect a conclusion other than ignominious death, since Moses and Elijah, who performed such miracles, are associated with noble endings. For Moses, there was a hidden resting place, though in the first century CE, another version records that the reference to his death was actually Moses's own humble demurral of the real truth, and that he was divinely assumed.[25] With Elijah, there is an undisputed and dramatic vindication

---

24. B. P. Robinson, "The Two Persecuted Prophet-Witnesses of Rev 11," *Scripture Bulletin* 19.1 (1988): 14–19, here 17, also suggests that the number forty-two may be associated with Moses (Num. 1:1; 14:34) and Elijah (the forty-two-month drought). This is possible, but the number persists throughout chapters 10–15, so it is more likely meant to elicit *half* of seven years, that is, a limited and not a "full" time.

25. So Josephus, *Antiquities* 4.8.48: "as he [Moses] was going to embrace Eleazar and Joshua, and was still discoursing with them, a cloud stood over him on the sudden, and he disappeared in a certain valley, although he wrote in the holy books that he died, which was done out of fear, lest they should venture to say that, because of his extraordinary virtue, he went to God" (trans. Whiston, http://www.sacred-texts.com/jud/josephus/). Note also

as he is snatched away in the chariot, without undergoing death like the normal run of humankind. Romance, then, is the main mode, and we anticipate a comic shape to the narrative, because of the biblical models that inform the main characters.

This is not the shape of the apocalyptic tale, however. "But when they shall have brought their testimony to a conclusion," the verbal testimony (*martyria*) of the two is transmuted into a physical martyrdom (11:7)! The beast, the *arising* beast, comes on the scene without fanfare or preparation—"we are startled . . . by the casual mention here for the first time of the notorious figure."[26] The victorious heroes are whisked into a tragedy, and, as Joe Mangina observes, their fortunes undergo "a great reversal . . . because [almost!] nothing in the narrative . . . prepares us for it,"[27] either in the area of plot or tone. The very ones who by all rights should escape death are subject to death and humiliation: we feel like the little boy in the film *The Princess Bride*, "No, Grandpa, you are telling it wrong! They *can't* die!" At the very least, we expect for these fallen heroes that there will be an elegiac remembrance to cap the chronicling of their exploits.[28] Instead of elegy, however, we are in the realm of horror, where enemies rejoice and where the cathartic effects of pity and fear take over.[29] Our divine men are demoted from romance to "high mimetic" tragic figures whose fate, described in four detailed verses (11:7–10), is poignantly reminiscent of the human condition save for one particular. They are "where also their Lord was crucified!" (11:8).

---

the cloud imagery. For an illuminating investigation of the nuances and complex tone of Josephus's writings on Moses, see James D. Tabor, "'Returning to the Divinity': Josephus's Portrayal of the Disappearances of Enoch, Elijah, and Moses," *Journal of Biblical Literature* 108.2 (1989): 225–38. See also Assumption of Moses, where no explanation of Moses's coyness is offered. Assumption of Moses is available in various English translations, including Johannes Tromp, *The Assumption of Moses: A Critical Edition with Commentary*, SVTP 10 (Leiden: Brill, 1993).

26. Felise Tavo, *Woman, Mother and Bride: An Exegetical Investigation into the "Ecclesial" Notions of the Apocalypse* (Leuven: Peeters, 2007), 207.

27. Joseph L. Mangina, *Revelation*, Brazos Theological Commentary on the Bible (Grand Rapids: Brazos, 2010), 138.

28. Frye, *Anatomy of Criticism*, 37, describes the "elegiac" quality of tragic romances, commenting on how this mode "mingles the heroic with the ironic," since it concerns the fall of a leader. For a handy chart that visualizes Frye's modes, see the work of Michael Joseph at http://comminfo.rutgers.edu/~mjoseph/argument.html.

29. Frye, *Anatomy of Criticism*, 37–38.

So comes yet another reversal. Rowland calls it "resuscitation,"[30] but it is clearly more. Aune calls it "a *rapture story*"[31] (or assumption) and a "miraculous divine rescue"[32]—but surely it is neither. This "surprising twist in the plot"[33] merits punctuation by the great fear of the crowd (11:11, 13), and the two, in response to divine command, go up in victory. They are *not* seized. Rather, they are filled with divine *pneuma*, arise, take their stand, and then ascend. The nervy seer John adopts, indeed repeats twice, the language that Luke avoids in his stories of Jesus's ascension (24:51; Acts 1:9)—the common Hellenistic term for ascent (*anabasis*). The placement of chapter 12 within a huge literary digression (chapters 10–14)[34] should have warned us that these heroes were liminal characters—"separate[d] . . . from the rest of humanity" but also "embed[ded] . . . in the world of tragic historical events," as Peter Perry demonstrates in his monograph.[35] The entire life of the witnesses, as Mangina tells us, is "render[ed] in deliberately bold, exaggerated strokes," and so is their entrance upon the glory cloud. This dramatic mimesis does not have the purpose, however, "to valorize" them "but to glorify the God of heaven,"[36] as the final verse of the passage declares, in an appropriate cadenza.

Here, then, is a story that sets up expectations, astonishes, and then surprises again. John is able boldly to retell the expected story, transmuting assumption into suffering, death, resurrection, and ascension, and also using frank exaltation language for mortals because their life pattern calls attention to the Lamb: they are arch-witnesses. They *die* even though they have been given power to avoid death, and then they follow in the double upward movement of the "standing slaughtered" Lamb who is in the midst of the throne. Ultimately, their import is not heroic status, but rather that they are measured along with all whom God will reward: the "servants, the prophets and saints and all who fear [the] name, both small and great"

---

30. Christopher C. Rowland, "The Book of Revelation: Introduction, Commentary, and Reflections," in *The New Interpreter's Bible*, vol. 12, ed. Leander E. Keck (Nashville: Abingdon, 1998), 642.

31. Aune, *Revelation 6–16*, 625.

32. Aune, *Revelation 6–16*, 625, 632.

33. James L. Resseguie, *The Revelation of John: A Narrative Commentary* (Grand Rapids: Baker Academic, 2009), 159.

34. See Humphrey, *Ladies*, esp. 111–14, and Schüssler Fiorenza, "The Composition and Structure of the Book of Revelation," in *Book of Revelation*, 159–80.

35. Peter S. Perry, *The Rhetoric of Digressions: Revelation 7:1–17 and 10:1–11:13 and Ancient Communication*, WUNT 2.268 (Tübingen: Mohr Siebeck, 2009), 240–41.

36. Mangina, *Revelation*, 138.

11:18).[37] The way up is more complex than the romantic mode suggests, but the trail has been blazed already. In this assurance, the story of the witnesses seems to come to full closure: a heroic tale of grandeur, seeming loss, and victory, full of tension, but capped by obeisance to God. Yet where has the "ascending beast" (11:7) gone? John's story is not over yet.

The Case of the Child: A Tale of Endurance

It is not over, for a voice tells us that "the third woe is coming very soon" (11:14). Then, we hear the seventh angel sound his trumpet and are immediately accosted by a dual vision that relates many other ups and downs. The signs in heaven of the queenly woman and the dragon put the reader beyond the high mimetic or romantic modes and squarely in the mode of myth, as defined by Frye. These figures are far beyond us and beyond the human environment, in kind and not merely in degree. The in-depth work of A. Y. Collins shows how the story of the woman/dragon/child finds its parallel in several world mythologies (Babylonian, Persian, Egyptian, Greek, Accadian, Hittite, Ugaritic, and Phrygian), but most particularly in the Apollo-Python-Leto myth.[38] Conveniently, Frye typifies a "comic" (i.e., triumphant) narrative in the mythical mode as "Apollyon" and describes it as a story concerning "how a [divine] hero is accepted by a society of gods."[39] Indeed, "in Christian literature it is the theme of salvation, or, in a more concentrated form, of assumption."[40] Revelation 12 actually tells us two stories, one of a woman (with her child[ren]) and a dragon on earth, the other of the dragon and the heavenly hosts, intersplicing them in such a way that we infer that they are interconnected. The plot emerges in this way: the battle in heaven is waged (12:7–9) while the divine child of the woman is threatened by the dragon, after a "wonderfully tense moment,"[41] rescued and (meeting the reader's expectations) welcomed into

37. This and the preceding paragraph rework material that appeared earlier in Edith M. Humphrey, "Which Way Is Up? Revival, Resurrection, Assumption, and Ascension in the Rhetoric of Paul and John the Seer," in *Essays in Honour of Frederik Wisse: Scholar, Churchman, Mentor*, ed. Warren Kappeler (*ARC: The Journal of the Faculty of Religious Studies*, McGill University, Volume 33, 2005), 328–39, at 335–36.

38. Collins, *Combat Myth*, 57–65.

39. Frye, *Anatomy of Criticism*, 43.

40. Frye, *Anatomy of Criticism*, 43.

41. Mangina, *Revelation*, 151.

the heavens to the very throne of God (12:5). The sequel portion of this double narrative (12:13–17) retains, for all its drama, some "idyllic" elements associated with the upbeat mode of myth, as when wings are given to the woman, or the earth opens its mouth to help out.

But the vision will not let us rest easy in the realm of comic mythology. Indeed, the informed reader will not have been easy with this mode from the beginning of the chapter. Perhaps the typing of God's people after a pagan goddess has caused discomfort, despite the possible parallels that the astute could draw with such Old Testament notaries as Joseph, that merciful and rescued servant who at the end is bowed down to by familial sun, moon, and stars (Gen. 37:9–10; 45–46). But more disorienting is the strange retold story of the child, whom we recognize immediately as the Messiah, "who is to rule all the nations" (12:5; cf. Ps. 2:8–9). We have already met the same majestic figure, full grown, as the standing slaughtered Lamb (chapter 5)—but in chapter 12, his death is bypassed, elided, even evaded! Some may suggest that John is hampered by his source: he has chosen to tell the Christian story in terms of pagan mythology, and so must follow the pattern. The trouble is, the foundational myth, as shown by Collins, *highlights* the hero's death and revival (e.g., Baal and Osiris).[42] In picturing the flow of the story, Collins must introduce this key element into her chart by means of scare quotes, speaking about "the Champion's 'Death'" in verse 5b as parallel to the foundational story. It is true that, in the Greek myth, Apollo does not die, and the story is more about the threatened mother who labors long for the birth of her child and who is threatened by Python. But this version also does not include the rapture of the divine child at all, so why add the rapture motif in the Apocalypse version, while at the same time highlighting the Leto story where no death of the hero occurs? Perhaps John would have been better served by such stories as that of the infant Dionysus, devoured by the Titans, who dies prior to the rescue of his heart by Hestia, and his rebirth as a god.

Commentators work long and hard to make John's mythological tale include what it does not include, but the explanations do not satisfy: the story, they say, is about the infant Jesus's escape from Herod[43] (but, then, why a rapture rather than sending the child away with the mother?); the

---

42. Collins, *Combat Myth*, 61–63, ensuing quotation at 61.

43. The opinion of Oecumenius, *Comm. Apoc.* 12:3–6, is replicated today by Grant R. Osborne, who asserts that "the primary parallel is of course Herod's 'slaughter of the innocent' children at Bethlehem" (*Revelation*, BECNT [Grand Rapids: Baker, 2002], 462).

story's birth signifies the crucifixion, not the nativity[44] (but how can a rescue intimate death on the cross?); "apparently the essential truths of the vision could best be served by brevity"[45] (but is not the crucifixion essential?); "what is born is not a real baby,"[46] rather "the revelation of Jesus Christ to the contemplative soul"[47] (but does the contemplative soul "rule the nations with a rod of iron"?); and, extremely improbably, this story is an *"explicit mention of the Rapture of the Church."*[48] No, none of these will do. As Schroeder remarks, "John is a symbolic thinker who consistently resists literal interpretation and strict chronological constraints."[49] Again, Joe Mangina is sensitive to the disruptive nature of this story, speaking about the "almost comical anticlimax" of the baby's rapture.[50]

In the imaginations of those who knew their classical stories, the Apollo-Python-Leto myth has been enriched or amplified by legends concerning rapture and apotheosized characters in the romantic mode (to revert to Frye's typology). Coming on the heels of chapter 11, the rapture language may bring to mind such biblical figures as Enoch, Elijah, Moses, and perhaps also Ezra, Baruch, Phineas, and Tabitha (depending on when the latter stories first saw the light of day).[51] But in the classical world, there are other candidates—Dionysus, Heracles, Aristaeus, Asclepius, Aeneas, Romulus, and (more politically!) Empedocles, Alexander, and a number

44. So, many commentators, e.g., Wilfrid J. Harrington, O.P., *Revelation*, SP 16 (Collegeville, MN: Liturgical Press, 1993), 130; Brian K. Blount, *Revelation: A Commentary* (Louisville: Westminster John Knox, 2009), 231.

45. Robert H. Mounce, *The Book of Revelation*, rev. ed., NICNT (Grand Rapids: Eerdmans, 1998), 234; also Ben Witherington III, *Revelation* (Cambridge: Cambridge University Press, 2003), 169, who calls the story "a merism" that implies the whole Jesus event. More interestingly, Gerhard A. Krodel, *Revelation*, ACNT (Minneapolis: Augsburg Fortress, 1989), 240, suggests that the vision follows a creedal statement seen also in 1 Tim. 3:16 (manifest in the flesh, vindicated in Spirit)—but this is very speculative and ignores the fact that "revealed in flesh" may as well refer to the crucifixion as the incarnation.

46. John Ben-Daniel, "Towards the Mystical Interpretation of Revelation 12," *Revue biblique* 114.4 (2007): 594–614, 607.

47. Ben-Daniel, "Towards the Mystical Interpretation of Revelation 12," 612. See also the ancient writer Andrew of Caesarea: "the 'male child' is the people of the church" (*Comm. Apoc.* 12:5; trans. Weinrich, *Revelation*, 182).

48. Michael J. Svigel, "The Apocalypse of John and the Rapture of the Church: A Reevaluation," *Trinity Journal* 22.1 (2001): 23–74, 74; italics in original.

49. Joy A. Schroeder, "Female Figures and Figures of Evil," *Word and World* 15.2 (1995): 178.

50. Mangina, *Revelation*, 151.

51. For references to these, see Aune, *Revelation 6–16*, 626.

of Roman emperors. Most of these heroes undergo rapture and apotheosis at the end of a heroic life of exploits. Perhaps as an overlay, some readers would also call to mind stories that linger on the border between mythology and heroic legend, that is, those bizarre attempted apotheoses of infants by the fond goddesses Isis, Demeter, and Thetis.[52] But in these cases, the immortality of the infants must be conferred by means of fire, that is, the burning away of the body and all that is corruptible. Understandably, the children are rightly snatched away from the well-meaning goddesses by their human mothers.[53]

All these legends and mythological scenes complicate what John shows us in his twin stories of childbirth and war. The seer applies assumption language in a sophisticated and almost playful (though ultimately serious) manner: thus he wages his own theopolitical warfare. He seems to adopt the imperial and pagan perspectives uncritically and then to expose them as inadequate. You want an emperor? A king who will rule all the nations? A human being who is invincible? You want a man so bound for greatness that his end is apotheosis? Well, it is *not* Caesar—John, as well as Psalm 2, holds national heroes in derision. *Here* is the one who will rule the nations with iron, a mere child, a humble figure. If anyone has the power to escape death, it is this one! If any is worthy of apotheosis, it is this one, this promised child taken up to the very throne of God.[54]

Even as he tells this marvelous tale, John must surely have expected that his "ideal" reader, who knows the traditional story about Jesus, would recognize that this version is somewhat skewed. We are like the hero in the film *A Beautiful Mind*, when he recognizes that what he is seeing cannot be real, or like the heroine Orual in C. S. Lewis's *Till We Have Faces*, who

---

52. For references to these stories, see James G. Frazer, *Adonis, Attis, Osiris: Studies in the History of Oriental Religion* (London: Macmillan, 1906), 92, also nn. 1–2 on the same page.

53. We may be tempted to think also of the medieval story of the infant John the Baptist rescued from Herod by the angel Uriel, but the origins of the story remain irretrievable. (Though see an early version of it in the Protevangelium of James 12.3.) If this is at all a possibility, it would make necessary a reappraisal of what has been considered a quixotic interpretation by J. Massyngberde Ford, who posited a revelation derived from Baptist circles as underlying our book (*Revelation*, AB 38 [Garden City, NY: Doubleday, 1975]).

54. In popular lore in antiquity, as well, children who died prematurely were spoken about as snatched from life (*harpazō*), a fate congruent with their purity and connected with the idea of assumption. Dionysus, Aesculapius, and Heracles all were babies snatched as infants and granted apotheosis.

hears a botched version of her own story.[55] Yes, we know almost immediately that this story of the Messiah has been altered: for the Messiah, whom we have already recognized in Revelation 5, was indeed *defined* by the slaughtering and standing: he is the "standing slaughtered Lamb." He was not rescued, though legions of angels stand at his service. Moreover, in John's *vision* (12:1–6), the child is rescued, but in the *oracle* that interprets the vision (12:11–12), we hear neither of apotheosis nor iron rule. Instead, the voice proclaims that the Lamb's "rule" of vulnerability, won by his blood, is a death shared by the martyrs. Like child, like mother: her wings take her to her own tribulation in the desert, to a time prepared for her by God! It is the Lamb's humiliation and *not* his exaltation that issues in the Dragon's downfall, and the faithful people must expect to follow this pattern.[56] It is by death, and then resurrection, that victory is won: rejected are the pagan stories where the shell of human flesh is burnt away to release the soul; exposed as inadequate and unable to yield any ultimate victory are also the Jewish stories of assumption.

The mode and tone, then, vary in chapter 12, as they do in chapter 11. We begin in myth with the heavenly woman and dragon, move liminally into legend with the apotheosis of the child, move back to myth in the description of the heavenly war, and mingle hymnody with elegiac in the declaration concerning Christ's death and the witness of the martyrs, who "did not cling to life even in the face of death" (12:11). Unlike the story of the witnesses in chapter 11, this chapter does not reach closure but remains disturbingly open: "The dragon was angry . . . and went off to make war on the rest of her children, those who keep the commandments of God and hold the testimony of Jesus. Then the dragon took his stand on the sand of the seashore" (12:17–18). In this way, the mythological mode, while it is retained, dips down to include the readers ("those who . . . hold the testimony of Jesus"). Thus, we as knowing readers, both ancient and modern, are encouraged to pattern ourselves as resistant heroes, high-mimetic in character, and to receive a story that we perhaps wish had stayed farther away—in the mythical or legendary realm. The child may be a match for this enemy, and the two witnesses may have been revived and honored after the dragon made war upon them—but what will the rage of the antagonist mean for *us*?

---

55. C. S. Lewis, *Till We Have Faces: A Myth Retold* (New York: Harcourt, Brace & Company, 1984).

56. This and the previous paragraph rework material found originally in Humphrey, "Which Way Is Up?," 335.

John is not unaware of our discomfort. Indeed, careful readers will remember that he is digesting the contents of a bitter-sweet scroll that he was compelled to swallow at the beginning of this extended sequence,[57] in chapter 10. The interpreting oracle in chapter 12 also captures our discomfort: "*Rejoice* then, you heavens and those who dwell in them! *But woe* to the earth and the sea, for the devil has come down to you with great wrath, because he knows that his time is short!" (12:12, italics added). The pill that John asks us to swallow is bitter: but he has presented it in a fashion that makes it edible. Indeed, it may be absorbed by the imagination if not by the intellect. For we know ourselves to be, in one sense, in heaven—thus, we can rejoice. Yet we know fully well that we cohabit with the dragon, with all that this dangerous existence entails. The logic of John's vision is convoluted: the dragon has been vanquished, banished from heaven to earth, and *because of that*, we expect to suffer.

By means of reconfigured mythology and legend, however, John can commend this to our imaginations and to our wills. In the retelling of rapture stories, so that they become narratives of suffering, death, resurrection, and ascension, and in the poignant mistelling of the Savior's story (divinized as an infant, and not experienced in death), he mixes for us wine and water. In giving us stories of closure and open-endedness, he gives us both joy and sobriety. As Ben Witherington puts it, "all sources are fair game. . . . Here, then, we have an example of 'plundering the Egyptians.'"[58] However, Witherington only partially traces John's method. He notes that "John has freely drawn on elements of these [stories], *adding certain elements to conform the story to the Christian narrative*."[59] What he does not notice is that John is even more daring in his authorial activity. John deals with open as well as closed stories, disarming as well as confirming. Certainly he edifies; but he also enthralls, engages, and astonishes us. Indeed, sometimes he ironically allows the stories to contradict our Christian metanarrative and so invites us, the faithful community, to do the necessary correction: it is *we* who are asked to drink the cup and to digest it! In the end, the fare that we receive is neither a hallucinogenic brew of mutually contradictory myths, nor a neverland of legend and romance, but a full-blown and divine picture of our complex world. It is not too trivial,

---

57. See Humphrey, *The Ladies*, 84–118, where I argue, adapting the structure of Schüssler Fiorenza, that chapters 10 through 15:4 contain a single sequence with a few interruptions.

58. Witherington, *Revelation*, 164.

59. Witherington, *Revelation*, 165, my emphasis.

I think, to speak of a combined impact like this as providing "enjoyment" for the reader, though it is enjoyment of a deep and contemplative nature. With John we acknowledge, to be sure, a world punctuated by irony and marred by tragedy. But this is also a world embraced by the One who has trampled down death by death and who invites his followers to hold to this testimony. In these surprising ways, John shows his faithful readers that they are a people who, in the dreariness and sorrow of the wilderness, are being prepared for that same One, who will unite a new heaven and his new earth.

PART 3

Interpreting by Reading in Faithful Company

CHAPTER 8

Reading the Exodus Story with Melito and Origen

Hans Boersma

The Exodus: Allegory as Arbitrary Reading?

Can patristic allegorical interpretation still be of use to us today? This is a weighty question, since by definition "allegorizing" may seem to imply misinterpretation of the biblical text. The etymology of the term "allegory" speaks for itself: *allos* (other) and *agoreuein* (to speak), "to speak other"— other, that is, than what the words themselves appear to say. By what right would one "speak other" than what the words themselves convey? And how does such a practice of allegorizing not turn into an arbitrary imposition of our own preconceived notions onto the biblical text? By way of response to these questions, I will turn to the exodus from Egypt, in particular the institution of the Passover at the beginning of the exodus narrative in Exodus 12. I will take for my guides, in the reading of this segment of Scripture, two early Christian interpreters of the passage, Melito of Sardis (d. ca. 180) and Origen of Alexandria (ca. 185–ca. 254). In their readings of Exodus 12, we come face-to-face with questions regarding the validity of allegorical exegesis. I will make the argument that Christology is so central to both writers that they were convinced that Christ (and, by implication, the church) is already present within the history described in Exodus 12. That is to say, Christ and the church constitute the New Testament mystery that is sacramentally already present within the Old Testament text.

This chapter is a slightly condensed and stylistically reformatted version of Hans Boersma, "Other Reading: Melito of Sardis and Origen on the Passover of Exodus 12," in *Scripture as Real Presence: Sacramental Exegesis in the Early Church* (Grand Rapids: Baker Academic, 2017), 81–104; used by permission.

As modern readers, we tend to be anxious about exegesis becoming a free-floating, arbitrary endeavor—free from boundaries, guidelines, and the possibility of verification. Interestingly, within the early church the accusation of arbitrariness was never voiced—not even by those staunchly opposed to the allegedly nonhistorical approaches of Origen and others from what is sometimes called the Alexandrian school of interpretation.[1] The main reason no one in the early church worried about arbitrariness in typological or allegorical exegesis is that they regarded the Bible as the book of the church. We often think of biblical exegesis as lying within the purview of the academy and of liturgy as the domain of the church; not so the church fathers. For them, the way we read the Bible has everything to do with how it functions in the church. Exodus 12, for Melito and Origen, speaks not just of historical realities of long ago; it speaks of the liturgical gathering of the church, as well as of the confession that the church holds dear. *Lex orandi, lex credendi* is the catchphrase expressing this conviction: the rule of prayer (the liturgy) is closely linked to the rule of faith (what we believe). Our interpretation of the Bible (and our doctrine) is intimately tied up with our worship practices.[2] This means that the exegesis of Scripture did have concrete boundaries, guidelines, and points of verification, and these were given by the church's liturgy and confession. It is because exegesis wasn't a self-governing endeavor, but instead functioned within an ecclesial setting, that no one expressed the fear that typology and allegorizing might run amok.

Typology in Scripture

The church fathers were convinced that the Bible itself anticipated their ecclesial, theological readings. For them, what justified their interpretation of the Scriptures was the way in which the New Testament authors had approached the Old Testament, and before that, the way in which,

---

1. Antiochene interpreters such as Diodore and Chrysostom did object to Alexandrian exegetes imposing an "other" meaning on the text that they regarded as foreign to it. But the Antiochenes recognized that this imposition wasn't a matter of personal whim, something random or arbitrary.

2. Cf. Christopher A. Hall, "Creedal Hermeneutics: How the Creeds Can Help Us Read the Bible," in *Serving God's Community: Studies in Honor of W. Ward Gasque*, ed. Susan S. Phillips and Soo-Inn Tann (Vancouver: Regent College Publishing; Singapore: Graceworks, 2014), 109–26.

within the Old Testament, earlier passages had been read by later authors. This comes to the fore with particular clarity in the way in which the Passover account of Exodus 12 (along with the rest of the narrative of the exodus from Egypt) functions within the later biblical witness. Before we turn to Melito and Origen, therefore, I want to look at how the Passover narrative functions in the Bible itself. I am taking my cue from Jean Daniélou's excellent 1950 publication, *From Shadows to Reality: Studies in the Biblical Typology of the Fathers.*[3] Daniélou's basic argument is that we can properly understand the fathers only by regarding their interpretation as an extension of the typology that the Scriptures themselves employ. Daniélou puts it as follows: "The Fathers have rightly insisted at all times that the types of the Exodus are fulfilled in the life of Christ and the Church, and in this they have but followed the teaching of the New Testament, which shows that these types are fulfilled in Christ."[4] So the typological lines, according to Daniélou, run from Exodus, via the Prophets, to Christ and the church; and this typological development, he argues, is anchored in the Bible itself.

How is this the case? Daniélou shows how already the Prophets announce a new, future exodus, one that has each of the main features of the first exodus: a crossing of the sea, a desert journey, living water pouring from rocks, a cloud, and a new covenant.[5] Daniélou turns to Hosea 2:14–15:

> Therefore, behold, I will allure her,
>> and bring her into the wilderness,
>> and speak tenderly to her.
>
> . . . .
> And there she shall answer as in the days of her youth,
>> as at the time when she came out of the land of Egypt.

Later, in chapter 12, Hosea promises that Israel will again live in tabernacles:

> I will again make you dwell in tents,
>> as in the days of the appointed feast. (Hos. 12:9)

3. Jean Daniélou, *From Shadows to Reality: Studies in the Biblical Typology of the Fathers*, trans. Wulstan Hibberd (London: Burns & Oates, 1960).

4. Daniélou, *From Shadows to Reality*, 153.

5. Daniélou, *From Shadows to Reality*, 155–57. Biblical quotations in this chapter are from the English Standard Version unless otherwise indicated.

For Hosea, Israel's original exodus serves as a type that corresponds to the antitype of her anticipated restoration. Isaiah does much the same thing. Daniélou quotes Isaiah 11:15–16 to make this point:

> And the LORD will utterly destroy
>   the tongue of the Sea of Egypt,
> and will wave his hand over the River
>   with his scorching breath,
> . . . .
> And there will be a highway from Assyria
>   for the remnant that remains of his people,
> as there was for Israel
>   when they came up from the land of Egypt. (cf. Isa. 10:26)

The exodus theme is unmistakable. According to Isaiah 4:5, on the day of Israel's redemption, "the LORD will create over the whole site of Mount Zion and over her assemblies a cloud by day, and smoke and the shining of a flaming fire by night." Again, the fire and the cloud are reminiscent of the exodus (Exod. 13:21; Ps. 77 [78]:14). Finally, according to Isaiah 10:26, God will wield against his enemies "a whip, as when he struck Midian at the rock of Oreb. And his staff will be over the sea, and he will lift it as he did in Egypt." These early chapters of Isaiah consistently anticipate a redemption that will be in line with the exodus from Egypt.

The later chapters of Isaiah seem, to Daniélou, to be even more insistent in the way they recall the exodus from Egypt. Isaiah 43:16–19 exclaims:

> Thus says the LORD,
>   who makes a way in the sea,
>   a path in the mighty waters.
> . . . .
> "Remember not the former things,
>   nor consider the things of old.
> Behold, I am doing a new thing;
> . . . .
> I will make a way in the wilderness
>   and rivers in the desert."

There will be a pillar of fire and a cloud as in the exodus; water will again come from the rock (Isa. 48:21); and, unlike the first exodus, this new one will not be a hasty flight but will take the form of a triumphal march:

> For you shall not go out in haste,
>   and you shall not go in flight,
> for the LORD will go before you,
>   and the God of Israel will be your rear guard. (Isa. 52:12)

According to Jeremiah, the grandeur of the new exodus will far out-shine the old: "Therefore, behold, the days are coming, declares the LORD, when they shall no longer say, 'As the LORD lives who brought up the people of Israel out of the land of Egypt,' but 'As the LORD lives who brought up and led the offspring of the house of Israel out of the north country and out of all the countries where he had driven them.' Then they shall dwell in their own land" (Jer. 23:7–8). In the same way, the new covenant will be greater than the old, according to the famed prophecy of Jeremiah 31 (which states that the new covenant will not be "like the covenant that I made with their fathers on the day when I took them by the hand to bring them out of the land of Egypt" [Jer. 31:32]). Thus, while typology is based on similarities between the original type and the later antitype, there are also significant differences: the glory of the new exodus will be much greater than that of the initial one.

The New Testament, the Gospel of Matthew in particular, picks up on this exodus theme of the Prophets and—as Daniélou makes clear—shows it as being fulfilled in Christ.[6] Jesus Christ, returning from Egypt after Herod's death, fulfills the prophecy of Hosea, "Out of Egypt I called my son" (Hos. 11:1; cf. Matt. 2:15). John the Baptist serves as the "voice of one crying in the wilderness: 'Prepare the way of the Lord" (Matt. 3:3; cf. Isa. 40:3). After his baptism, which functions as his own Red Sea crossing, Jesus, much like Israel, is "led up by the Spirit into the wilderness" (Matt. 4:1). There he fasts for forty days and forty nights (Matt. 4:2), a number corresponding to the forty years of the wilderness journey and the forty days of Moses's fast. The three temptations in the desert echo the temptations of Israel in the wilderness. The evangelist presents Jesus as the new Moses, with his Sermon on the Mount serving as the new law. Jesus distributes bread as Moses distributed manna (Matt. 14:19); and Jesus sends out seventy disciples much as Moses chose seventy elders (Luke 10:1; Num. 11:16).

---

6. Daniélou, *From Shadows to Reality*, 157–60.

Something similar, Daniélou explains, takes place in John's Gospel, which he argues functions "as a kind of Paschal catechetical instruction, to show to those baptized on the night of Holy Saturday that the Sacraments they then received were divine interventions which continued the great acts (the *magnalia*) of Yahweh at the time of the exodus and also at the time of the Passion and resurrection of Christ."[7] In other words, Daniélou sees the setting of Saint John's Gospel as a liturgical one—connected to the baptism of catechumens—and he argues that John locates the catechumens typologically in line with the exodus and with the suffering and resurrection of Christ. Daniélou points to the Word appearing in various forms in John's Gospel: as the Shekinah, the glory of God (John 1:14); as the bronze snake lifted up in the desert (3:14); as the manna coming down from heaven (6:31–51); as the water gushing from the rock (7:37–38); as the pillar of fire (8:12); and as the Passover lamb whose blood washes away the sins of the world (1:29; 19:36).[8] In each of these cases, the Gospel writer presents Jesus as the reality foreshadowed in the Old Testament exodus narrative.

Daniélou elaborates on the Old Testament backdrop of other New Testament books in similar fashion,[9] and he concludes with the comment:

> A deep impression forms itself on our mind after reading these many texts. It was the clear intention of the New Testament writers to show the mystery of Christ as at once continuing and surpassing the outstanding events in the story of Israel at the time of Moses. God had revealed his might in redeeming the chosen people. But the human race remained subject to another captivity more exacting and spiritual in nature. The Prophets had foretold that the might of God would be seen in a new redemption, on a far greater scale, which would inaugurate the New Covenant. The burden of the New Testament writers is to show that all this has been fulfilled in Jesus Christ.[10]

In biblical typology, the exodus plays a major role, and the linear pattern that emerges runs from the historical exodus itself, via the Prophets—who announce a new exodus—to Christ and the church.

---

7. Daniélou, *From Shadows to Reality*, 161.
8. Daniélou, *From Shadows to Reality*, 161.
9. Daniélou, *From Shadows to Reality*, 163–65.
10. Daniélou, *From Shadows to Reality*, 165.

The way in which the exodus theme is developed throughout Scripture can serve as a paradigm for patristic spiritual interpretation and explains why it is that the church fathers allegorized without worrying that their exegesis might turn arbitrary. Take the well-known example of the narrative of the bronze snake in Numbers 21. The people complain to Moses about the lack of food and drink (21:5), and in response the Lord sends venomous snakes (21:6). So the people repent, and Moses prays for them (21:7–8). We then read: "The LORD said to Moses, 'Make a fiery serpent and set it on a pole, and everyone who is bitten, when he sees it, shall live.' So Moses made a bronze serpent and set it on a pole. And if a serpent bit anyone, he would look at the bronze serpent and live" (21:8–9). Most of us know the Gospel of John quite well, and it doesn't strike us as odd or arbitrary to find here a christological reference: "As Moses lifted up the serpent in the wilderness, so must the Son of Man be lifted up, that whoever believes in him may have eternal life" (John 3:14–15). The fathers—and Daniélou shows this with references to Tertullian, Cyril of Jerusalem, and Gregory of Nyssa—eagerly appropriated this connection between Numbers 21 and John 3.[11] Neither John the Evangelist nor the church fathers appear to have had the kind of historical consciousness that made them shrink back from a christological reading of Numbers 21. Surely, though, John's use of the story of the bronze snake must raise some historical-exegetical eyebrows. It can hardly have been the historically intended meaning of the book of Numbers to make a prophetic announcement about the coming Messiah. Clearly, Saint John moves well beyond authorial intent in his treatment of this passage.

Assuming that John's Gospel and the church fathers were right about seeing the bronze snake as a type of Christ—or, we might say, if John read Numbers 21 allegorically[12]—this raises an important question: Could we perhaps do something similar with other elements in the exodus narrative?[13] The fathers thought they could and should. Moses praying with his

---

11. Daniélou, *From Shadows to Reality*, 167–68.

12. I am deliberately intermingling the categories of typology and allegory. Whatever distinctions we may impose, the church fathers did not differentiate between the two. I discuss the distinction in further detail below.

13. Richard Longenecker argues that we should not replicate the New Testament authors' allegorizing because, unlike the biblical authors, we are not inspired by the Holy Spirit (*Biblical Exegesis in the Apostolic Period*, 2nd ed. [Grand Rapids: Eerdmans, 1999], 193–98). This argument seems to me unpersuasive. It supposes that, thanks to the Spirit's leading, the biblical authors in their teaching were kept from error despite their odd interpretive

arms outstretched (Exod. 17:11–13) was, many of the fathers maintained, a type of Christ.[14] Joshua leading the people into the promised land became a type of Christ's redemption. The wood that Moses threw into the bitter water so that it became sweet (Exod. 15:25) turned into a type of the cross, which transforms the waters of baptism.[15] And the twelve springs and seventy palm trees at Elim (Exod. 15:27) stood for the twelve apostles and the seventy disciples (Luke 10:1). What is it that convinced the early church's interpreters to do all this? At bottom, this exegesis is grounded in one underlying conviction: as God's people, we are implicated directly in the exodus that takes place in Christ. We ourselves are taking the exodus journey. Since, according to the Prophets, the new exodus would be similar in character to the first, the church fathers felt compelled to look for similarities between the old exodus and the new.[16]

Thus, speaking of the twelve springs and seventy palm trees, Daniélou perceptively observes:

> This numerical correspondence will probably strike us at first sight as rather artificial. But can we be quite sure of this? We are not to expect in "twelve fountains" a hydrographical exactitude. We can consider what light Jewish tradition will afford. From this we learn that the Red Sea opened in twelve divisions to allow the twelve tribes to pass (Ps 136:13). The Koran shows us another tradition, that Moses caused twelve springs to gush forth from the rock (*Koran*, VII, 160). It seems that we must emphasize the connection of the twelve springs with the twelve tribes, as did the Rabbis, who saw in the twelve springs a type of the twelve tribes. . . . And as we said above, it seems quite clear that the choice of the twelve Apostles by Christ had its relation to the twelve tribes.[17]

---

method. Cf. Peter J. Leithart, *Deep Exegesis: The Mystery of Reading Scripture* (Waco, TX: Baylor University Press, 2009), 32–34, 36–37.

14. Daniélou, *From Shadows to Reality*, 168–69.

15. Daniélou, *From Shadows to Reality*, 171–72.

16. Henri de Lubac (*Medieval Exegesis: The Four Senses of Scripture*, trans. E. M. Macierowski, vol. 2 [Grand Rapids: Eerdmans, 2000], 87–88) points out that medieval theologians often distinguished between "allegory of deed" (*allegoria facti*) and "allegory of word" (*allegoria dicti*). What makes Scripture's allegorizing different from Hellenistic allegorizing, according to de Lubac, is the fact that it is grounded not only in words but also in the underlying historical events themselves.

17. Daniélou, *From Shadows to Reality*, 173.

Far from being arbitrary, each of these exegetical choices—perceiving the cross in Moses's outstretched arms, as well as in the wood that sweetened the waters, discerning Jesus in Joshua, recognizing the apostles and disciples in the twelve springs and the seventy palm trees—results from the church fathers' conviction that in Christ they had embarked on a new exodus. It is Christology, therefore (or, to put it differently, it is the new exodus), that shaped their readings and kept these from turning into random allegorical impositions. The fathers' readings of Moses's outstretched arms, of the wood sweetening the waters, of Joshua conquering Canaan, and of the waters and trees of Elim were in no way different from John's reading of the narrative of the bronze snake. Their allegorical exegesis simply followed the biblical example of trying to locate Christ's redemption in the Old Testament texts.

The fathers based their exegesis on the way in which the Prophets and the New Testament speak of God initiating a new exodus. The implication is that the early church's preachers believed that a new exodus was taking place in Christ and in the liturgical life of the church. This may be a novel claim to some of us, especially those of us who worship in a nonsacramental (or nonliturgical) context. But we cannot avoid this link between the exodus and the liturgy when we take the church's early exegesis seriously. As we will see, both Melito and Origen were convinced that it is through the liturgy that God allows us to join in the new exodus, which is the great archetype anticipated by Israel's rescue in the book of Exodus.

If the liturgy genuinely makes us join the exodus journey, then this fills the liturgy with tremendous significance. We see this liturgical prominence reflected in the patristic exegesis of the Red Sea crossing and of the eating of the manna: they are types of the sacraments of baptism and Eucharist. Initiation of new believers into the church was centered on these two sacramental acts. In light of the famous passage of 1 Corinthians 10—"All were baptized into Moses in the cloud and in the sea, and all ate the same spiritual food, and all drank the same spiritual drink. For they drank from the spiritual Rock that followed them, and the Rock was Christ" (10:2–4)—the fathers saw in the exodus event the sacramental initiation of new believers into the church.[18]

It would take us too far afield to go through each of the individual church fathers, but Daniélou shows that this exegetical approach was a common feature of the patristic tradition. Numerous church fathers saw

---

18. Daniélou, *From Shadows to Reality*, 176.

references to baptism and Eucharist in the exodus narrative.[19] The overall picture that emerges from reading these early interpreters is the following: baptism, which took place on the night of Holy Saturday, recalled the departure from Egypt and from the realm of sin; in the rite of initiation, the proselyte passed through each of the stages that the Israelites had also gone through. The Pauline passage of 1 Corinthians 10 provided a basis for this link between the baptizand and the Israelites.[20] As a result, a broad-ranging allegorical network emerged: Egypt became the world of the human passions; the waters of the Red Sea were seen as the means of salvation; Pharaoh and his soldiers were interpreted as the devil and his companions; the pillar of light became Christ, and the pillar of cloud the Holy Spirit; the blood of the lamb was identified with the blood of Christ that put the demons to flight; the three-day journey into the wilderness turned into the Paschal triduum (Good Friday, Holy Saturday, and Resurrection Sunday); the manna was the Eucharist; and the water from the rock was understood either as the cup of salvation in line with 1 Corinthians 10 or as baptism, following John 7:37.[21]

One specific example may be worth highlighting, that of Theodoret of Cyrus (ca. 393–ca. 458/466), an Antiochene interpreter often regarded as fairly open to nonhistorical modes of interpretation. His exegesis serves as a word of caution against distinguishing too sharply between Antiochenes and Alexandrians, as if the former sharply rejected allegorizing while the latter advocated for it. Theodoret's interpretation shows little hesitance in making use of what we may term "christological/ecclesial allegorizing."[22] The Red Sea, Theodoret explains, "is the type of the baptismal font, the cloud of the Holy Spirit, and Moses of Christ our Saviour; the staff is a type of the Cross; Pharaoh of the devil and the Egyptians of the fallen angels; manna of the divine food and the water from the rock of the Saviour's Blood. Just as they enjoyed a wonderful refreshment coming from a miraculous source, after they had passed through the Red Sea, so we, after the saving waters of Baptism, share in the divine mysteries."[23] Theodoret

19. Daniélou, *From Shadows to Reality*, 177–201.

20. Daniélou, *From Shadows to Reality*, 176.

21. Daniélou, *From Shadows to Reality*, 177–201.

22. Theodoret wasn't shy to "promote figurative (τροπικῶς) and at times allegorical (ἀλληγορικόν) interpretation—seen most acutely in his *Commentary on the Song of Songs.*" Richard J. Perhai, *Antiochene Theōria in the Writings of Theodore of Mopsuestia and Theodoret of Cyrus* (Minneapolis: Fortress, 2015), 70.

23. As quoted in Daniélou, *From Shadows to Reality*, 194.

reads the exodus allegorically as referring to the church and her sacraments. Daniélou rightly comments: "This passage brings out better than any other the value of the liturgical comparison."[24] The church fathers were convinced that in the liturgy—in baptism and Eucharist—they were taken up into the sacramental mystery of Christ himself. By implication, they were also taken up into the new exodus. Thus, there was nothing arbitrary about scrutinizing the exodus narrative for christological and ecclesiological references. The typological or allegorical reading of the exodus passages was rooted in biblical precedent and in liturgical celebration.

Melito of Sardis, *On Pascha*

So far I have used Daniélou's broad treatment of the church fathers to illustrate that Christology governed their typological exegesis. Christ was the great archetype, and as such his person, his words, and his deeds determined the search for Old Testament types that might correspond in some way to the marvelous newness of the Christ event. Needless to say, this approach assumes great confidence in God's providential guidance of the events of history.[25] The early church discerned similarities between type and antitype because they were convinced that at different points throughout salvation history the character of God comes to expression in similar ways. On this understanding, God's action in and through Christ determines the way in which we interpret his earlier dealings with humanity as well. In the light of Christ, it is no longer possible to read the Old Testament in the same way as before. This conviction, more than anything else, determined the church fathers' reading of the Old Testament. They were persuaded, rightly I believe, that they simply followed the Bible's own understanding of God's dealings with his people.

With this background, I will now turn to the Passover celebration and to the church's appropriation of the Exodus 12 narrative. The liturgical setting of the interpretation of Scripture is particularly clear in Melito of Sardis's homily *On Pascha*. Melito likely preached the sermon, which dates from about CE 160–70, as a means of introducing the eucharistic celebration. It was in the celebration of the Eucharist that the Scriptures

24. Daniélou, *From Shadows to Reality*, 194.
25. Cf. Matthew Levering, *Participatory Biblical Exegesis: A Theology of Biblical Interpretation* (Notre Dame: Notre Dame University Press, 2008).

came to their fulfillment, according to Melito. This notion—that the reality of the Scriptures was present here, in the liturgy—means that each of the elements of the liturgy took on great significance. For example, many regarded the very time slot of the Easter celebration as a matter of crucial importance. Since Easter was the Christian celebration of the Passover, Melito argued that it had to be celebrated on the same day that the Jewish Passover was celebrated: the evening of the fourteenth day of the first month (Nisan).[26] As a result, Melito and other Asian Christians who celebrated Easter on this precise date became known as "Quartodecimans" or "Fourteeners."[27] Other churches, including the church of Rome, celebrated Easter on the Sunday following the Passover celebration, which meant a break with the precise regulation of Exodus 12, as well as with Jewish tradition.

This disagreement turned into a high-stakes controversy in the late second century. Saint Irenaeus, the bishop of Lyons in central France, wrote a letter to Pope Victor in Rome to try to convince him to allow the Asian churches freedom in what he considered a nonessential liturgical matter. We may find it difficult to appreciate that this issue led to such a sharp, protracted controversy. But we need to recognize that at stake was the church's ability to say that the exodus from Egypt was the *church's* exodus—that we ourselves are the ones making the exodus journey. The celebration on the fourteenth of Nisan, for Melito and other Asian Christians, gave expression to the typological reading of the exodus event. Melito, in *On Pascha*, places himself squarely in the tradition of the Quartodecimans, and so his typology moves from the church's liturgy back to the Jewish Passover in order to appropriate for the church the Passover celebration of Exodus 12.

Melito speaks of the historical Passover celebration of Exodus 12 as "type" (*typos*) and of the fulfillment in Christ as "reality" or "truth" (*alētheia*): "For there was once a type, but now the reality has appeared."[28] Melito also uses the terminology of "mystery" (*mystērion*).

---

26. This is in line with the instruction of Exod. 12:2–3. I have published a sermon on this passage in *Sacramental Preaching: Sermons on the Hidden Presence of Christ* (Grand Rapids: Baker Academic, 2016), 15–26.

27. See Alistair Stewart-Sykes, "Introduction," in Melito of Sardis, *On Pascha: With the Fragments of Melito and Other Material Related to the Quartodecimans*, trans. and ed. Alistair Stewart-Sykes, Popular Patristic Series 20 (Crestwood, NY: St. Vladimir's Seminary Press, 2001), 1–2.

28. Melito, *On Pascha* 4 (p. 38). Throughout, I use Stewart-Sykes's translation. For the

He begins by saying, "The Scripture of the exodus of the Hebrews has been read, and the words of the mystery have been declared."[29] Repeatedly, he speaks of the "mystery" of the Pascha.[30] The term "mystery" would become quite prominent in the later Christian tradition. It has its roots in Scripture itself, especially the Pauline letters. In Ephesians 5, Saint Paul speaks of the bodily union between husband and wife and then comments, "This is a profound mystery" (*mystērion*), adding that he is "saying that it refers to Christ and the church" (Eph. 5:32). The Latin text of the Vulgate renders the word *mystērion* as *sacramentum*. Indeed, throughout the subsequent tradition, the term "mystery" has held sacramental significance. The word didn't have quite the same connotations that it has for us today. Certainly, it did not refer to a puzzle of sorts, whose secret we can uncover by means of clever investigation, a connotation that comes through when we talk about mystery novels, for example. For the patristic and medieval mindset, the word meant something slightly—but significantly—different. "Mystery" referred to realities behind the appearances observable by the senses. That is to say, although our hands, eyes, ears, nose, and tongue are able to access reality, they cannot *fully* grasp it. They cannot *comprehend* it. The twentieth-century patristics scholar Henri de Lubac explains: "In Latin *mysterium* serves as the double for *sacramentum*. For Saint Augustine, the Bible is essentially the 'writing of the mysteries,' and its books are the 'books of the divine sacraments.' The two words are often simply synonyms."[31]

Further, de Lubac argues that when at times medieval theologians did distinguish between *sacramentum* and *mysterium*, they typically saw the former as the sacramental sign and the latter as the spiritual reality:

> They are sometimes distinguished as the two terms of a relation or as the two poles of an alternating movement. Then *sacramentum* designates rather the exterior component, the "envelope," as Saint Augustine says: "Christ has been preached by the prophets almost

---

Greek text, see Melito of Sardis, *On Pascha and Fragments*, trans. and ed. Stuart George Hall (Oxford: Clarendon, 1979).

29. Melito, *On Pascha* 1 (p. 37).

30. Melito, *On Pascha* 2 (p. 37), 15 (p. 40), 31 (p. 45), 33 (p. 45), 34 (p. 45), 46 (p. 48), 58 (p. 52), 59 (p. 52), 61 (p. 53), 65 (p. 54). Cf. John Hainsworth, "The Force of the Mystery: Anamnesis and Exegesis in Melito's *Peri Pascha*," *St. Vladimir's Theological Quarterly* 46.2–3 (2002): 107–46.

31. De Lubac, *Medieval Exegesis*, 20.

everywhere with a wrapping of sacrament." This is the sign or the
letter as bearer of the sign: "the signs of things are in the sacraments."
Whether thing or person, fact or rite, it is the "type," the correlative
of the mystery, just as the "figure" or "image" is the correlative of
the "truth": "the sacrament comes before the truth of the thing." It
is the *sacrum* [sacred thing] rather than the *arcanum* [hidden thing].
The mystery is this *arcanum* itself. It is the interior component, the
reality hidden under the letter and signified by the sign, the truth
that the figure indicates; in other words, the object of faith itself.[32]

This quotation may be somewhat lengthy and dense, but it captures ex-
actly how, for the church fathers, exegesis was sacramental. The "exterior"
of the letter, while indispensable, had a purpose that lay beyond itself.
Its purpose was the "interior" of the Spirit. The type or figure of the Old
Testament had as its *telos* the hidden reality of Christ, revealed in the New
Testament.

The sacramental character implied in the notion of mystery comes
through already in Melito's use of the term. When in the above discussion I
mentioned the biblical origins of typology, we saw that it was based on the
similarities of divine action across history. Typology identifies a historical
progression from the exodus, via the Prophets, to the christological reality
in the New Testament. Daniélou accentuates this horizontal, historical,
forward-looking character of typology, and he is certainly right to do so.
But he overemphasizes it.[33] This comes to the fore in Daniélou's populariz-
ing of the distinction between allegory and typology. On his understanding
of patristic exegesis, it is the Alexandrians (followers of Origen) who especially used allegory. Allegory was derived from Philo; it was moralizing; it
looked for eternal realities; it was upward-looking; it ignored history; and
as a result it was arbitrary in its interpretation of the Bible. By contrast, the
Antiochene typological approach, according to Daniélou and others, was
biblical rather than pagan in origin; it was christological rather than mor-
alistic; it was forward-looking; it looked for historical progression rather
than for links with eternal realities; and as a result it avoided arbitrariness.

De Lubac, Daniélou's own teacher, demonstrated decisively that
his student's opposition between allegory and typology was alien to the

32. De Lubac, *Medieval Exegesis*, 21.
33. See Hans Boersma, *Nouvelle Théologie and Sacramental Ontology: A Return to Mystery* (Oxford: Oxford University Press, 2009), 168–80.

church fathers.[34] Most patristics scholarship today has abandoned any sharp distinction between allegory and typology, and I am largely sympathetic to this new consensus.[35] And we see evidence for it in Melito. Without doubt, Melito's typology is historical, in that it moves from the Passover of Exodus 12 to the suffering of Christ. But the typology involves more than *just* a historical or chronological move. The forward move from type to antitype or from shadow to reality is for Melito at the same time an upward move, from temporal, earthly types to eternal, heavenly realities.[36]

Paragraph 2 of *On Pascha* may serve to illustrate this. Here Melito comments: "Therefore, well-beloved, understand, how the mystery (*mystērion*) of the Pascha is both new and old, eternal and provisional, perishable and imperishable, mortal and immortal." Notice that Melito is able to shift effortlessly from horizontal language ("new and old") to vertical language ("eternal and provisional, perishable and imperishable, mortal and immortal"). And he keeps up this vertical language throughout. The reason is that we have in Melito not just a (nominalist) succession of unrelated, fragmented historical incidents.[37] The progression from the Passover to the suffering of Christ and so to the eucharistic celebration is not just a historical progression of separate moments in time. Rather, these events have an *internal* relationship to each other. And it is this internal relationship to later events that turns the Passover of Exodus 12 into a "mystery."

Melito makes this particularly clear at the height of his exposition, immediately prior to his explanation of typology. Addressing the angel of death directly, in paragraph 32 he asks: "Tell me, angel, what turned you away? The slaughter of the sheep or the life of the Lord? The death of the sheep or the type of the Lord? The blood of the sheep or the spirit of the Lord?" Notice how he pulls type and antitype apart here, as he asks the central question: what was the origin of the salvation of the Hebrews?

---

34. Henri de Lubac, "Typology and Allegorization," in *Theological Fragments*, trans. Rebecca Howell Balinski (San Francisco: Ignatius, 1989), 129–64.

35. See also the discussion in Peter W. Martens, "Revisiting the Allegory/Typology Distinction: The Case of Origen," *Journal of Early Christian Studies* 16.3 (2008): 283–317.

36. Cf. Henry M. Knapp, "Melito's Use of Scripture in *Peri Pascha*: Second-Century Typology," *Vigiliae Christianae* 54.4 (2000): 343–74, at 374. Unfortunately, Knapp continues to build on Daniélou's outmoded distinction between typology and allegory.

37. Nominalism (from the Latin *nomen*, meaning "name") holds that sensible objects (such as dogs) do not participate in intelligible universals (such as the canine species); we simply assign "names" to individual objects on the basis of their apparent similarities. Realism, by contrast, insists that the similarities arise from the objects' participation in eternal forms or universals.

Was it the blood of the sheep or that of Christ? His answer is unequivocal: "It is clear that you turned away seeing the mystery (*mystērion*) of the Lord in the sheep and the life of the Lord in the slaughter of the sheep and the type of the Lord in the death of the sheep. Therefore you struck not Israel down, but made Egypt alone childless."[38] The reality of Christ—the historically later event—was mystically or sacramentally present already in the Passover celebration of the Hebrews. The two historical events slide inside one another; and it is the eternal, immortal character of the christological archetype that infuses the temporal and provisional Passover of Exodus 12 with its saving power. Paragraph 69 is equally explicit. Speaking of Christ, Melito comments: "This is the Pascha of our salvation: this is the one who in many people endured many things. This is the one who was murdered in Abel, tied up in Isaac, exiled in Jacob, sold in Joseph, exposed in Moses, slaughtered in the lamb, hunted down in David, dishonored in the prophets."[39] The sufferings of each of these Old Testament figures were "mysteries," according to Melito, of the sufferings of Christ. The archetype—Christ himself—suffered *in* the suffering of the earlier types.[40] The Old Testament types contain a mysterious, inner depth that the language of historical progression cannot capture.

Melito clarifies his approach by referring to the "writing of a parable" (*graphē parabolēs*) in language and the use of a "model" or "preliminary sketch" (*typos prokentēmatos*) in sculpting.[41] He compares the law to a parable that alludes to the reality of the gospel narrative, and he likens the Jewish people as a preliminary sketch to the church as the repository of reality.[42] And so he comments: "When the thing comes about of which the sketch was a type, that which was to be, of which the type bore the likeness, then the type is destroyed, it has become useless, it yields up the image to what is truly real. What was once valuable becomes worthless, when what is of true value appears."[43]

As a small but important aside, as we transition from Melito to Origen, I should note that Melito employs etymology in defense of his christo-

---

38. Melito, *On Pascha* 33 (p. 45).

39. For a discussion of the Akedah in Melito, see Robert L. Wilken, "Melito, the Jewish Community at Sardis, and the Sacrifice of Isaac," *Theological Studies* 37.1 (1976): 53–69.

40. Melito, *On Pascha* 59 (pp. 52–53).

41. Melito, *On Pascha* 35–36 (p. 46); 39–40 (p. 47). I have slightly changed the translation.

42. Melito, *On Pascha* 40 (p. 47).

43. Melito, *On Pascha* 37 (p. 46).

logical reading of the Passover. We see this in paragraph 46: "What is the Pascha? It is called by its name because of what constitutes it."[44] The word "Pascha" (*pascha*), maintains Melito, comes from the word "suffering" (*paschein*). Among the church fathers, etymology was a common strategy in trying to identify the christological or ecclesial meaning of the Old Testament. This approach had already been used by Philo, and the church fathers' love of words and their meaning predisposed them to follow Philo in order to find the spiritual, christological meaning of the text by means of etymology.[45]

Origen, *Treatise on the Passover*

The etymology that Melito assumed—the move from *pascha* to *paschein*—is an interesting one, especially in light of the way in which Origen deals with it in his *Treatise on the Passover*, a book to which we now turn. Origen wrote his *Peri Pascha* around 245, approximately eighty years after Melito's work by the same title. Origen's book is in many ways quite different from that of Melito. The flowery rhetoric of Melito's sermon gives way to a rather straightforward two-part treatise. Origen presents his main argument in the first part: he wants to correct a misunderstanding of how the typology of the Passover works. In the second part, he presents the spiritual interpretation of Exodus 12—although, since he has done a great deal of work in terms of typological interpretation already in part 1, the second part turns out to be rather brief.[46]

In part 1, as he corrects a misunderstanding of the "mechanics" (if we may use that term) of the typology of the Passover, Origen makes a small but, in his eyes, important distinction. He rejects the notion that the Passover was a figure or type of Christ's passion. Now, we just saw that this view, rejected here by Origen, was exactly that of Melito. And Hippolytus of Rome (ca. 170–ca. 236) too had typologically connected the Passover to Christ's passion, and it may well be that Origen writes

---

44. Melito, *On Pascha* 46 (p. 49).

45. See Annewies van den Hoek, "Etymologizing in a Christian Context: The Techniques of Clement of Alexandria and Origen," *Studia Philonica Annual* 16 (2004): 122–68.

46. Origen, "Treatise on the Passover (*Peri Pascha*)," in *Treatise on the Passover* and *Dialogue of Origen with Heraclides and His Fellow Bishops on the Father, the Son, and the Soul*, trans. and ed. Robert J. Daly, ACW 54 (New York: Paulist, 1992), 39.9–50.8 (pp. 27–56).

directly to counter Hippolytus's view.[47] Origen insists that instead of being a type of Christ's *suffering*, the Passover is a type of Christ *himself* and of his "passing over" to the Father, and that as a result the Passover functions also as a type of *our* "passing over" to the Father. The church, after all, is included in Christ.[48] Careful textual critic that he was, Origen recognized that the interpretation that Melito and others had put forward errs because it fails to take into account the Hebrew original. "Most of the brethren," comments Origen, "indeed perhaps all, think that the Passover (πάσχα [*pascha*]) takes its name from the passion (πάθος [*pathos*]) of the Savior."[49] He then correctly points out, however, that the Greek *pascha* is simply the Hellenized form of the Hebrew *pesakh*, which means "passage" or "Passover," and which, when translated into Greek, would have to be rendered by the word *diabasis*.[50]

For Origen, this was more than just a lexical matter. He rejected the typological link between the Passover and Christ's suffering in part because he stood in a different tradition than that of Hippolytus, Melito, and the Quartodecimans. Melito's Asian tradition tended to be more literal or historical in its exegesis than the Alexandrian tradition of Origen. We have already seen that we need to be careful about positing absolute contrasts in terms of ancient schools of biblical interpretation. We cannot state simply that the Asian tradition was typological while the Alexandrian tradition was allegorical. Still, it is probably significant that Melito, from within the Asian tradition, insisted on the Jewish Passover being the typological counterpart to the passion of Christ. Origen's lineage was a different one and went back, via Clement of Alexandria (ca. 150–ca. 215), to the Jewish Platonic philosopher Philo (ca. 20 BC–ca. AD 50). Origen's predecessor, Clement, had recognized that the term *pascha* had to do not with suffering but with passage. And, in this, Clement had followed Philo: for Philo the Passover had been an allegory describing the passage of the soul from the material world into the eternal, spiritual world.[51]

---

47. Daly, "Introduction," in Origen, *Treatise on the Passover*, 6.

48. Daly, "Introduction," 6–7.

49. Origen, *Treatise on the Passover* 1 (p. 27). Here and in what follows, transliterations of Origen's treatise into English between square brackets are mine.

50. Origen, *Treatise on the Passover* 1 (p. 27). Cf. Daly, "Introduction," 6; Manlio Simonetti, *Biblical Interpretation in the Early Church: An Historical Introduction to Patristic Exegesis*, ed. Anders Bergquist and Markus Bockmuehl, trans. John A. Hughes (Edinburgh: T. & T. Clark, 1994), 26–27.

51. Daly, "Introduction," 8.

As a result, Origen presents several arguments against the Jewish Passover being a type of Christ's suffering. First, he argues that, while in the Passover, saints used to sacrifice a lamb, Christ instead was sacrificed by "criminals and sinners."[52] This contrast would seem to rule out a direct typological link between the Passover and the suffering of Christ. Second, this means, according to Origen, that it is Christians (the saints) who eat the true Passover lamb when they consume the body of Christ. The Passover typologically foreshadows not the suffering of Christ but the church's eschatological participation in Christ. This participation occurs, John David Dawson points out, in the very practice of one's allegorical reading of the exodus narrative: Origen "identifies the consuming of the lamb with the allegorical reading of Scripture which is contrasted with various deficient modes of reading."[53] In our reading of the Scripture, we eat Christ's flesh and drink his blood (John 6:53). So, according to Origen, the antitype of the Passover is not just Christ's suffering but Christ himself in his act of passing over, along with our participation in this passing over to the heavenly realm as we read the Scriptures in a spiritual rather than a physical manner.[54]

John O'Keefe and R. R. Reno, in their book *Sanctified Vision*, explain how Origen wants us to read the Passover narrative christologically: "Having blocked a false reading of Israel's Passover as verbally connected to Jesus' passion, Origen turns toward what he envisions as a fuller and more fruitful interpretation of the relationship between the Passover and the saving work of Jesus Christ. This fuller reading forces us to connect the narrative moments of dedication, roasting, eating, and celebration to the manner of our participation in Christ's life, teaching, death, and resurrection."[55] So, according to Origen, the antitype of the Passover is not just Christ's suffering but Christ himself in his act of passing over. In particular, as Origen makes clear later on in his treatise, it is the Passover *lamb* that is a type of Christ.[56] The hermeneutical issue for Origen, then, becomes how we relate to Christ

52. Origen, *Treatise on the Passover* 12 (p. 34).

53. John David Dawson, *Christian Figural Reading and the Fashioning of Identity* (Berkeley: University of California Press, 2002), 72.

54. Origen, *Treatise on the Passover* 13–14 (pp. 34–35). As a third argument, Origen notes that Christ himself makes the bronze snake of Numbers 21—not the Passover—the type of his suffering (John 3:14). *Treatise on the Passover* 14–15 (pp. 35–36).

55. John J. O'Keefe and R. R. Reno, *Sanctified Vision: An Introduction to Early Christian Interpretation of the Bible* (Baltimore: Johns Hopkins University Press, 2005), 52.

56. Origen, *Treatise on the Passover* 42 (pp. 50–51).

as our Passover lamb—and he answers this by suggesting an allegorical interpretation of the exodus narrative.

However one may evaluate Origen's arguments here, it is important to notice that he presents a detailed exegetical argument against the Quartodecimans. He rejects the view of Melito and Hippolytus on exegetical (partially linguistic) grounds, and he attaches significant liturgical and theological consequences to his rejection of the Asian tradition.[57] This is important because it is especially Origen—and the tradition following the Alexandrian theologian—who has been much lampooned for his so-called arbitrary allegorical exegesis. There is nothing arbitrary about what Origen does here. He presents a careful, rational argument for choosing one particular typological reading of the Passover over another. One may well disagree with his particular choice, or even reject his allegorical approach altogether (though obviously I am not inclined to do the latter myself). But any such disagreement cannot take the form of a claim that allegory is an arbitrary de-historicizing of the biblical text.[58] Such a position simply betrays lack of familiarity with Origen's work.

Origen is quite aware that the interpretive move from the historical to the spiritual is a delicate process. The important point in this process, in connection with the Passover, is absolutely evident to him: "That the Passover still takes place today, that the sheep (πρόβατον [probaton]) is sacrificed and the people come up out of Egypt, this is what the Apostle is teaching when he says: 'For Christ, our paschal lamb, has been sacrificed. Let us, therefore, celebrate the festival, not with the old leaven, the leaven of malice and evil, but with the unleavened bread of sincerity and truth' (1 Cor. 5.7–8). If 'our Passover has been sacrificed,' Jesus Christ, those who sacrifice Christ come up out of Egypt, cross the Red Sea, and will see Pharaoh engulfed."[59] Origen's key argument is that the Old Testament historical events surrounding the exodus still take place today. They take place in believers' identification with Christ as they recognize him in their spiritual reading of the narrative. This means that despite the particular exegetical

57. Alistair Stewart-Sykes argues that it "is quite possible that Hippolytus's community had a Quartodeciman past" (*The Lamb's High Feast: Melito, "Peri Pascha," and the Quartodeciman Paschal Liturgy at Sardis* [Leiden: Brill, 1998], 194).

58. I am not arguing that Origen doesn't at times downplay the historicity of the text. He does, as I make clear in Hans Boersma, "Joshua as Sacrament: Spiritual Interpretation in Origen," *Crux* 48.3 (2012): 23–40.

59. Origen, *Treatise on the Passover* 3 (p. 28). Here and elsewhere I have replaced Daly's use of italics, in rendering Origen's biblical quotations, with quotation marks.

disagreement that Origen may have with Melito, the two interpreters agree on the underlying point, namely, that the Old and New Testament events ought to be identified with each other. The Old Testament Passover in some way sacramentally or mystically contains the New Testament reality of the Christ event. The two theologians agree that we ourselves are the ones taking the exodus journey.

Origen makes several fascinating textual observations as he makes his exegetical case that we may rightly perceive today's ecclesial situation *within* the ancient text. He notes, for instance, the distinction between "beginning" and "first" in Exodus 12:1–2: "This month shall be for you the beginning of months; it shall be the first month of the year for you."[60] When we look simply for the historical meaning, we may note that the Passover was celebrated in the first month of the year, the month of Nisan. "As far as the history goes," says Origen, "this month is indeed the 'first month.'"[61] But he then adds (and here he moves to the spiritual meaning) that when Christ came, he showed the true Passover, the true "passage," and to describe *this* spiritual reality the text uses the term "beginning" rather than "first." As Origen explains: "And for the one in the passage, 'the beginning of months' is when the month of passing over out of Egypt comes around, which is also the beginning of another birth for him."[62] Origen argues that this spiritual "beginning" or new birth takes place through the water of baptism. This spiritual meaning of the text—based on the distinction between the words "beginning" and "first"—is relevant, according to Origen, only for the perfect. It is only "for you," the text says; that is to say, it is only for Moses and Aaron.[63]

In similar fashion, when Exodus 12:9 states, "Do not eat any of it raw or boiled in water, but roasted," Origen discerns here three different approaches to the Scriptures. If people simply follow the literal meaning of the Scripture, it is like eating the flesh of the Savior raw. This is a Jewish, literalist approach to interpretation.[64] Heretics, on the other hand, add water and so boil the flesh with water. It is only Christians who roast the flesh of the Scriptures with fire—the fire of the Holy Spirit.[65] Roasting the

60. Origen, *Treatise on the Passover* 4 (p. 29). I am following the translation used in Origen's *Treatise on the Passover*.

61. Origen, *Treatise on the Passover* 4 (p. 29).

62. Origen, *Treatise on the Passover* 4 (p. 29).

63. Origen, *Treatise on the Passover* 5 (p. 29).

64. Origen, *Treatise on the Passover* 28–29 (p. 42).

65. Origen, *Treatise on the Passover* 26–27 (pp. 41–42). Cf. Origen, *Treatise on the Passover*, p. 98 n. 33.

flesh of Scripture with the fire of the Spirit, maintains Origen, refers to a spiritual reading of the text.

When he finally devotes a separate section of his book (part 2) to the spiritual meaning of the Passover, Origen begins by speaking of "mystery" (the same language we have already encountered in Melito): "Since the sacred ceremony and sacrifice of the Passover was already carried out in mystery (μυστηριωδῶς [mystēriōdōs]) in the time of Moses . . . we now raise the question whether . . . it is also carried out in a different manner in our own time, the time of fulfillment—'upon whom the end of the ages has come' (1 Cor 10:11)."[66] The Passover was not just a historical event; at its heart it already contained the New Testament mystery. And so Origen explicitly distinguishes here between the historical meaning and the anagogical (upward-leading) or spiritual meaning of Exodus 12. The former refers simply to the original event; the latter speaks of the "passage" of Christians, mystically present already within the events narrated within the book of Exodus.[67] The result is an exegetical approach that is sacramental in character: the very reading of the Scriptures, in an allegorical mode, is our participation in the Passover event of Exodus 12. As Dawson puts it: "Indeed, Origen will argue that Scripture is itself a sacrament like the Eucharist. Christ the lamb is still the Word, that Word is found in Scripture, and eating the Word refers to the interpretation of Scripture. . . . The ancient Passover continues to be celebrated, then, in the allegorical reading of Scripture, which is not a disembodiment through interpretation but instead a consumption of a body through reading."[68] It is the distinction between historical and spiritual meaning, therefore, that allows Origen to speak of Christ as the true Passover lamb and also to discuss the "passage" of those who are included in Christ.

Conclusion

Melito recognized that the angel of death turned away from the houses of the Hebrews not because of the blood of the sheep but because of the blood of Christ. For Melito, the reality of Christ was really present in the Passover event. Similarly, Origen maintained that "the Passover still takes

66. Origen, *Treatise on the Passover* 39 (p. 49).
67. Origen, *Treatise on the Passover* 39 (p. 49).
68. Dawson, *Christian Figural Reading*, 71.

place today." Apparently, the church's liturgical celebration is for Origen already present in the Passover event and vice versa. Both authors are convinced that the Passover event is something in which we today participate. We ourselves celebrate the Passover, and we ourselves take the journey out of Egypt. The reason for both authors is simply this: the Old Testament history is a mystery, or a sacrament, in which the New Testament realities of Christ and the church are already present. We have a place—a real place rather than one arbitrarily imposed—within the narratives of the Old Testament.

I began this essay by asking two questions: By what right would one "speak other" than what the words themselves convey? And how does such a practice of allegorizing not turn into an arbitrary imposition of our own preconceived ideas onto the biblical text? Again, it has not been my purpose to provide a full or adequate response to these questions. At the same time, I am hoping that by turning to patristic exegesis of Exodus 12, I have given some insight at least into how these early Christian readers would have responded to our questions.

My hunch is that both Melito and Origen would have responded by saying something like the following:

> We don't care too much what you call the kind of scriptural reading that we are engaged in. You may call it typology, allegory, *theōria*, anagogy, spiritual reading—it really doesn't matter that much. Each of these terms is suitable to express what we're trying to do. Our reading is indeed "other" than what the words themselves convey in the sense that we look to the words on the "surface" of the text as merely sacraments: words that contain in themselves the greater reality of the Christ event. The words are the outward sacrament; Christ is the inward reality of grace. History and spirit, sacrament and reality, are indeed different things. So typology or allegory does look for something "other." But if by "other" you mean something completely different, something unrelated, then, no, we're not "speaking other" than what the words themselves convey. We're simply exposing the deeper, underlying meaning that is inherent in the text itself.
>
> It's hard for us to wrap our minds around the suspicion that we whimsically impose random notions onto the text. Never have we encountered that concern before. If it's true that we simply uncover a hidden meaning that is present already in the text—if there is a *real presence* of Christ and his church in the ancient narratives—then this

cannot possibly be an arbitrary thing: we can find only what's already there!

Furthermore, arbitrariness is something that you get by removing the biblical text from its proper surroundings of the believing community, away from its liturgical setting and its confession of faith. The context within which a christological reading of the text makes sense is that of the church. Therefore, the "right" by which we move from history to spirit, from temporal to eternal realities, has everything to do with the Bible being the church's Bible. And that implies, we believe, that in an important sense the Bible belongs *not* to the academy.

Such, I think, would be the response of Melito and Origen to our modern-day suspicions of allegorical interpretation—a response that I believe makes sufficiently clear why it is that still today they serve as faithful guides in our reading of the biblical text.[69]

69. I would like to thank John Behr, John Boersma, Phillip Hussey, Tracy Russell, and Matthew Thomas for their helpful comments on an earlier draft of this essay.

CHAPTER 9

Reading Paul's Letter to the Romans with Aquinas and Calvin

Charles Raith II

How might the forward-looking discipline of ecumenism and the backward-looking discipline of historical theology become integrated in a way that deepens the theological commitments of our Christian communities? In terms of ecumenism, since the birth of the modern ecumenical movement with the 1910 World Mission Conference in Edinburgh, dialogue between divided communities has often proceeded, especially since the 1960s, under a progressivist assumption that emphasizes discontinuity between the past and the present and perceives unity as a product of human social development (rather than unity resulting from remining past theological claims).[1] In terms of historical theology, the term "historical" in historical theology may suggest the study of something strictly past, and, indeed, often in the field of historical theology whatever conclusions historical theologians might assert about a certain theologian or episode of theology remain confined to that particular theological era. Thus, by and large, one discipline looks strictly forward with possibly a glance to the past, while the other looks strictly backward with possibly a glance to the present. Yet by confining themselves in this way, both disciplines dilute the possibilities each might contribute to enriching the Christian community. As an alternative, I propose here a work of what I call (for better or worse) ecumenical *ressourcement*, which will be undertaken in this essay by analyzing the biblical commentaries on Paul's Letter to the Romans from Thomas Aquinas and John Calvin and making claims about

---

1. For a recent overview of the modern ecumenical movement, with an analysis of these progressive assumptions, see R. David Nelson and Charles Raith II, *Ecumenism: A Guide for the Perplexed* (London: Continuum, 2017).

the future theological relationship between Catholic and Reformed communities. But first a further note on ecumenical *ressourcement*.

Ecumenical *Ressourcement*

There is no question that in the past sixty years ecumenical advancements have been made that have far exceeded anyone's expectation when the modern ecumenical movement got into full swing with the 1910 World Missionary Conference in Edinburgh. The various dialogues that have occurred between historically divided Christian communities alone have produced a voluminous body of helpful literature on a spectrum of divisive topics.[2] But as we move further into the twenty-first century, with our divisions still very much in place, fresh reflection on how ecumenism is to proceed is needed in order to make true advancements toward ecclesial unity. But how can unity be advanced without falling into the two traps of either historically relativizing our traditional sources in theology—a common "progressive" approach to ecumenism—or simply repeating previous theological conclusions on issues that divide our communities—a common "conservative" reaction to this progressive approach? While these are obviously broad-stroke descriptions, modern ecumenism has demonstrated that these two seemingly opposite approaches converge at a common end point: an ecumenical winter.[3] The "progressive" approach gives the appearance of moving us forward but often by advancing a reductionist or revisionist form of Christianity that bears little substantial (even if a linguistic) resemblance to the faith that has been passed down from the beginning—that is, the Christian *paradosis* ("tradition"; cf. 2 Thess. 2:15). The "conservative" approach gives the

2. Joseph A. Burgess and Jeffrey Gros, eds., *Growing Consensus: Church Dialogues in the United States, 1962–1991*, Ecumenical Documents 5 (Mahwah, NJ: Paulist, 1995); Jeffrey Gros, Harding Meyer, and William G. Rusch, *Growth in Agreement II: Reports and Agreed Statements of Ecumenical Conversations on a World Level, 1982–1998* (Grand Rapids: Eerdmans, 2000); Jeffrey Gros, Thomas F. Best, and Lorelei F. Fuchs, *Growth in Agreement III: International Dialogue Texts and Agreed Statements, 1998–2005* (Geneva: WCC; Grand Rapids: Eerdmans, 2007).

3. In terms of "ecumenical winter," see Christopher Asprey, "The Universal Church and the Ecumenical Movement," in *Ecumenism Today: The Universal Church in the 21st Century*, ed. Francesca Aran Murphy and Christopher Asprey (Burlington, VT: Ashgate, 2008), 3; Ola Tjørhom, "An 'Ecumenical Winter'? Challenges in Contemporary Catholic Ecumenism," *Heythrop Journal* 49.5 (2008): 841–59.

appearance of holding fast to the *paradosis* by reasserting previous conclusions but often runs the risk of quenching the Spirit's ongoing work of renewing the church—of moving us deeper into our eschatological calling—and may actually perpetuate what Jaroslav Pelikan described as "traditionalism" rather than the true *living* "tradition."[4] In G. R. Evans's words, the *active* reception of the Christian tradition "is a continuing activity. It has not been enough simply to go on expressing the faith in exactly the same words century after century. . . . There has never been a time when things could be said to be finally agreed, although paradoxically, the faith has always been seen as a settled thing, a secure place for mind and heart to rest."[5] Here we find the tension between permanence and change, stability and development. The two approaches broadly outlined above, however, collapse into one or the other, with neither able to produce genuine ecumenical advances.

If fruitful advancements in Christian unity are to be made, we cannot focus on divisive issues that are not worth fighting over or are not relevant for today; nor can we simply approach the issues in the same ways as before. One alternative approach—and certainly not the only one—that navigates between these ecumenical dead ends is what I call "ecumenical *ressourcement*."[6] Ecumenical *ressourcement* is not so much concerned with asking new kinds of questions of older sources—for example, what does Aquinas or Calvin have to contribute to our present arguments over same-sex marriage—as it is with asking old questions of old sources in new ways. The issue of same-sex marriage was not a driving force that spawned our present ecclesial divisions, even if this issue is dividing Christians—

---

4. Jaroslav Pelikan, *The Vindication of Tradition* (New Haven: Yale University Press, 1983). The point here is that simply reasserting past formulaic conclusions to historically divisive issues—e.g., justification is *sola fide* (faith alone)—without considering the underlying polemics that gave rise to those formulations, or how a different setting may allow differently nuanced formulations, could reflect a failure to participate in the ongoing renewing work of the Spirit healing our Christian divisions.

5. G. R. Evans, *The Reception of the Faith: Reinterpreting the Gospel for Today* (London: SPCK, 1997), viii–ix.

6. The term "ressourcement" is an intentional appropriation of the term as used by the early twentieth-century movement known as *nouvelle théologie*; for details on this movement, see Hans Boersma, *Nouvelle Théologie and Sacramental Ontology: A Return to Mystery* (Oxford: Oxford University Press, 2009); Jürgen Mettepenningen, *Nouvelle Théologie—New Theology: Inheritor of Modernism, Precursor of Vatican II* (London: T. & T. Clark, 2010). I briefly employed this term in Charles Raith II, *Aquinas and Calvin on Romans: God's Justification and Our Participation* (Oxford: Oxford University Press, 2014), 218–19.

including those within the same ecclesial body—today.[7] Historically, at least between Catholics and Protestants, divisions were driven by issues such as merit, justification, the relationship between divine and human causality, the role of the church as mediator of grace, and theological sources. And standing behind how these issues came to be understood in Catholic and Reformed traditions are theologians such as Thomas Aquinas and John Calvin, both of whom significantly shaped how these communities came to understand and live out these realities.

The *ressourcement* of "ecumenical *ressourcement*" is a desire to revisit our sources but to do so in a different light, now five hundred years removed from the immediate, heated polemics of the sixteenth century. But the new light does not flow from a triumphalist progressivism that assumes we have moved beyond the theological proposals of these supposedly outmoded sources. The authoritative sources are instead taken as just that: as authoritative. To move forward will require us to be backward-looking, not simply because the heritage should be respected, but because the heritage has the *first* voice, and a voice to which we remain accountable today. Each of our ecclesial bodies believes (one would think) that God has been involved in guiding Christians toward an understanding of Christianity that shapes our present communities; otherwise, I suppose, we would find ourselves in a different community. And if Gamaliel's principle has any validity—"if this plan or this undertaking is of human origin, it will fail; but if it is of God, you will not be able to overthrow them" (Acts 5:38-39, NRSV)—we all have to acknowledge that God has to some degree been directing each of our communities, given the coexistence of Catholics and Protestants for nearly five hundred years with no signs of an alternative anytime soon.[8] Our sources are therefore not reducible to mere artifacts of our traditions; we believe that they truly, albeit partially, communicate God's living truth. Thus, if ecumenical progress is to be rooted in God's living truth, it must include both in word and substance God's speaking in times past.

---

7. Michael Root and James J. Buckley, eds., *The Morally Divided Body: Ethical Disagreement and the Disunity of the Church* (Eugene, OR: Cascade, 2012).

8. I am not suggesting God has guided us to our present, divided state, which I take to be the result of human sin. But not all is sin, and there may be ways in the future for ecclesial bodies to embrace the good that God has granted to their communities while moving toward a greater manifestation of the unity to which all our communities are called. This will enable the full possibility of sharing goods with one another for our mutual upbuilding in the faith.

Yet because these sources are past voices, we need the work of solid historical theology to help us hear them properly, and in ways that they themselves would recognize, before we then employ these sources in contemporary theological discourse.[9] Only in this way will the source itself, rather than our use of it, be authoritative. Otherwise, we may be left with nothing more than exercising our own authority over ourselves. Moreover, good historical theology not only helps us understand the positive content and contribution of our sources; it also attunes us to the underlying concerns and polemics that shaped those sources. We discover how certain theological formulations were put forth not simply as "the way it is," but rather the way it was understood *over against other competing formulations.*[10] The positive theological formulations become the more intelligible when the competing proposal is understood.[11] Such historical sensitivity makes us aware that a simple repetition of previous conclusions may not be necessary in a context in which the *problematic* formulations are no longer being asserted. This is not to say that the positive content of the sources can be reduced to nothing more than an alternative to other proposals, as if the positive content is merely a reflection of a will-to-power dynamic. After all, the positive content also proclaims for our communities what we consider to be true. Yet this truth arose within a polemical setting in which the intelligibility of what is affirmed in some sense depends upon what is rejected. Remove the rejected proposals from the theological landscape, and the positive proposals lose some of their purpose and meaning.

Thus, sensitivity to the historical polemics underlying the claims of our traditions allows former conclusions to be reopened and engaged in new ways, but always with the hope of moving into *deeper*—as opposed to reductionist or simply alternative—perspectives.[12] The "ecumenical"

---

9. For an informative approach to the work of historical theology, see Robert L. Wilken, "Historical Theology," in *A New Handbook of Christian Theology*, ed. Donald W. Musser and Joseph Price (Nashville: Abingdon, 1992), 225–30.

10. Christian orthodoxy has most fruitfully arisen within polemical contexts, whether the birth of Christianity in the first century, Christology in the fourth century, soteriology and ecclesiology in the sixteenth century, or moral theology in the twentieth and twenty-first centuries.

11. For a good example of this, see David E. Wilhite, *The Gospel According to the Heretics: Discovering Orthodoxy through Early Christological Conflicts* (Grand Rapids: Baker Academic, 2015).

12. The reader might discern that I am here appropriating for ecumenical purposes the work that has been done on the topic of "doctrinal development." While engaging the thought of John Henry Newman, John T. Noonan, Lewis Ayres, and Khaled Anatolios,

aspect of ecumenical *ressourcement* adds the dimension of being open to appropriating sources and formulations we may not usually think of as "our own," and doing so in ways that might yield new (or renewed) conclusions to decisive issues. The result may at times go so far as to affirm theological propositions that our original sources thought untenable. But if this is ever the case, the propositions will only be affirmed in a manner that maintains the integrity of the underlying *purpose* or *substance* of the original formulation. This will also mean taking seriously the original concerns that led the sources to reject the supposed problematic propositions in the first place.[13]

The Relationship between Aquinas and Calvin as Theological Sources

For ecumenical *ressourcement* to be successful, part of the project will include having a better understanding of the theological relationship between sources we do not typically think of as common to our heritages. This has the potential for creating space to appropriate ideas that might once have been thought inimical to our own theological tradition, with the hope that these ideas might help us overcome obstacles to ecumenical rapprochement in ways that avoid undermining or relativizing that heritage.

Matthew Levering writes, "Development is not repetition or even (necessarily) a simple logical extension. Instead doctrinal development genuinely goes beyond earlier insights—for example, by asking and answering new questions while retaining previous *definitive* doctrine on the subject and correcting *nondefinitive* teaching" (*Engaging the Doctrine of Revelation: The Mediation of the Gospel through Church and Scripture* [Grand Rapids: Baker Academic, 2014], 174, italics original) (all italics in this and subsequent footnotes are original unless otherwise indicated). Cf. John Henry Newman, *An Essay on the Development of Doctrine* (Notre Dame: University of Notre Dame Press, 1989); John T. Noonan Jr., *A Church That Can and Cannot Change: The Development of Catholic Moral Teaching* (Notre Dame: University of Notre Dame Press, 2005); Lewis Ayres, *Nicaea and Its Legacy: An Approach to Fourth-Century Trinitarian Theology* (Oxford: Oxford University Press, 2004); Khaled Anatolios, *Retrieving Nicaea: The Development and Meaning of Trinitarian Doctrine* (Grand Rapids: Baker Academic, 2011).

13. To give one brief example: Reformed theology—and I speak as one who identifies with this theological heritage—has traditionally rejected any notion that human beings can "merit" their salvation. But when we discover that Calvin, for example, rejected the notion of "merit" due in large part to the underlying competitive-causal schema of divine-human causality (on which see below), we can ask: could Reformed theology accept a form of meritorious soteriology that appropriated a different underlying causal relationship between divine and human activity, with a resulting soteriology that, while possibly moving it closer to its Catholic brethren, more importantly deepens its own theological concerns?

While Augustine has long been recognized as a common source for both Catholic and Reformed traditions—some have gone so far as to reduce the Reformation to a battle over who is more Augustinian—the case has been thought to be quite different when it comes to Thomas Aquinas. Historically, the relationship between Aquinas and Calvin has been assumed to be one of conflict. Calvin was thought to have actually read Aquinas's work, such that he had good knowledge of his theology,[14] and intentionally rejected him as part of his overall denunciation of the "frivolous" and "Pelagianistic" teachings of the "schoolmen."[15] This is nowhere more evident than in the McNeill-Battles volume of Calvin's *Institutes*, the most widely read and cited English edition of the *Institutes*, in which Aquinas is cited at length as the target of Calvin's criticism.[16]

As it turns out, Calvin had very little knowledge of Aquinas firsthand, and what knowledge he did have likely came through secondary sources that were part of the Occamist school of thought, in which Aquinas was presented in a more Pelagianistic manner than his own thought warranted.[17] Richard Muller has been at the forefront of rethinking Calvin's

---

14. The editors of the *Opera Selecta*, for example, state confidently that Calvin "without a doubt" read Aquinas's books firsthand and had his books "before his eyes" (*Opera Selecta*, ed. Petrus Barth and Guilelmus Niesl [Eugene, OR: Wipf and Stock, 2010], IV.vii). See further François Wendel, *Calvin: The Origins and Development of His Religious Thought*, trans. Philip Mairet (New York: Harper & Row, 1963), 126–27.

15. Particularly problematic for Calvin was what he considered to be the presence of a rampant Pelagianism in the schoolmen's theology; see, e.g., *Inst.* 3.11.15; 3.25.11. In broad strokes, what this "Pelagianism" meant for Calvin was a theology that overemphasized human effort in obtaining salvation at the expense of the work of God in Christ *on behalf of* human beings. To be sure, Calvin's criticisms of scholastic theology are part of a larger challenge posed to scholasticism by sixteenth-century humanist-oriented Christians. For Erasmus, see Allan K. Jenkins and Patrick Preston, *Biblical Scholarship and the Church: A Sixteenth-Century Crisis of Authority* (Aldershot: Ashgate, 2007); for Luther, see Erika Rummel, *The Humanist-Scholastic Debate in the Renaissance & Reformation*, Harvard Historical Studies 120 (Cambridge: Harvard University Press, 1995).

16. A few examples where Aquinas is cited as the target of Calvin's criticisms, but in fact the position attacked by Calvin is at odds with Aquinas as well, are *Inst.* 3.2.8 on "formed" and "unformed" faith; *Inst.* 3.14.11 on justification; and *Inst.* 3.22.2 on foreknowledge and merit.

17. On Aquinas among the Occamists, see John L. Farthing, *Thomas Aquinas and Gabriel Biel: Interpretations of St. Thomas Aquinas in German Nominalism on the Eve of the Reformation* (Durham, NC: Duke University Press, 1988); Denis R. Janz, *Luther and Late Medieval Thomism: A Study in Theological Anthropology* (Waterloo, ON: Wilfrid Laurier University Press, 1983).

relationship to "luminaries" like Aquinas, positing the thesis that, due to the theological polemics of the sixteenth century, the positive relationship between Calvin and his "genuine" medieval forerunners became "obscured."[18] Calvin's attacks on the scholastics are actually aimed at his French contemporaries—the theologians of the Sorbonne (*théologiens Sorboniques*)—and their extreme nominalist views rather than at thinkers like Aquinas and Bonaventure.[19] This is true even when Calvin *thinks* he is attacking Aquinas. Calvin mentions Aquinas in any substantial capacity only twice in his corpus (only four times in total), and in the *one* place Calvin engages Aquinas at any length—*Institutes* 3.22.9—Calvin reads Aquinas on predestination in a "semi-Pelagian" manner,[20] which is consistent with how Aquinas would have been presented within the Occamist school of thought.[21] In the end, when a thorough investigation is made into the actual content of Aquinas's and Calvin's theology understood in their historical context, as I attempted to do in comparing their commentaries on the book of Romans, it turns out that most, if not all, of Calvin's warnings in his commentary about the theology of the schoolmen do not apply to Aquinas's positions, while Calvin's principal positive affirmations are embraced by Aquinas as well.[22]

To give a few examples of this point, Calvin claims at the beginning of his commentary on Romans that the principal issue of the entire epistle is: "We are justified by faith" (see Rom. 5:19).[23] Note that Calvin does *not*

18. Richard A. Muller, *The Unaccommodated Calvin: Studies in the Foundation of a Theological Tradition* (Oxford: Oxford University Press, 2000), 41; see also Alexander Ganoczy, *The Young Calvin*, trans. David Foxgrover and Wade Provo (Philadelphia: Westminster, 1987), 173–78; Armand Aime LaVallee, "Calvin's Criticism of Scholastic Theology" (PhD diss., Harvard University, 1967), 237–41.

19. Richard A. Muller, "Scholasticism in Calvin: Relation and Disjunction," in *Calvinus Sincerioris Religionis Vindex: Calvin as Protector of the Purer Religion*, ed. Wilhelm H. Neuser and Brian G. Armstrong (Kirksville, MO: Sixteenth Century Journal Publishers, 1997), 264.

20. On the problematic use of the term "semi-Pelagianism," see Rebecca Harden Weaver, "Introduction," in *Grace for Grace: The Debates after Augustine & Pelagius*, ed. Alexander Y. Hwang, Brian J. Matz, and Augustine Casiday (Washington, DC: The Catholic University of America Press, 2014), xiv–xvii.

21. James L. Halverson, *Peter Aureol on Predestination: A Challenge to Late Medieval Thought*, Studies in the History of Christian Thought 83 (Leiden: Brill, 1988), chapter 3; Charles Raith II, "Calvin's Critique of Merit, and Why Aquinas (Mostly) Agrees," *Pro Ecclesia* 20.2 (2010): 135–66.

22. Raith II, *Aquinas and Calvin on Romans*, 8–9.

23. This first example can be found in extended form in Raith II, *Aquinas and Calvin on Romans*, 25–35, esp. 32; and 48–53, esp. 51–52.

make justification per se the central disputation of Romans; on this reading, the emphasis shifts to disputes regarding the *manner* of our justification (e.g., being "declared" justified versus being "transformed" into a just person). For Calvin, these disputes hinge on and are subordinate to the central disputation of the letter, which is the topic of faith, and principally the role of faith in obtaining justification as opposed to other means (for example, merit).[24] The "main and cardinal point" regarding the disputation on faith is "we are justified by faith through the mercy of God alone [*sola Dei misericordia, per fidem nos iustificari*]" (27.64–66). It is of note that the *sola* refers not to faith but rather to the mercy of God. This is not to deny Calvin's use of *sola fide* on other occasions, but it does highlight the fact that Calvin sees the central issue surrounding the disputation on faith in Romans to be the relationship between God's strict and lofty just judgment and God's forgiving and accepting mercy. If justification—the meeting of God's just judgment—comes by *faith*, then justification rests solely in God's mercy and not in the merit of works.[25] If justification were by works, a person's works would need to meet God's lofty just judgment. This, however, is impossible for sinners and saints alike. The gospel teaches that believers can rest in God's mercy, having their consciences assured that they are at peace with God knowing that Christ's justice, as we shall see, has met the high and lofty justice of God on our behalf. His justice is imputed to us when we become united to him by faith.

Aquinas would have no problems with affirming Calvin's "main and cardinal point": we are justified by faith through the mercy of God alone. In his commentary on Romans, Aquinas demonstrates that no works of the law procure one's justification, neither in terms of perfectly keeping the law nor in terms of God's foreknowledge of our merits. Aquinas clearly explains how the cause of the justice by which one is justified before God is rooted in grace alone; justification comes solely on account of the mercy

---

24. Calvin's *Antidote* to the Faculty of Paris, in the brief section addressing "Justification by Works," contains no less than nine references to Romans (Calvin, *Articles by the Theological Faculty of Paris, with Antidotes*, in *Tracts Relating to the Reformation*, trans. Henry Beveridge [Edinburgh: Calvin Translation Society, 1844], 1:80–82). A. N. S. Lane observes that in all but one case—twelve in all—Calvin places *sola fide* as the alternative to works (*Justification by Faith in Catholic-Evangelical Dialogue: An Evangelical Assessment* [London: T. & T. Clark, 2002], 186 n. 191).

25. Elsewhere Calvin admits that the phrase "faith alone" is nowhere to be found in Scripture, but he argues that, if justification depends neither on the law nor on ourselves, it must rely on God's mercy alone, and if mercy alone, then for Calvin faith alone (69.1–5).

of God forgiving our sins due to the salvific sacrificial work of Christ on our behalf; and we receive justification by grace alone through faith and not works of the law.[26] God alone, and not the law, is the one who is both just and the justifier of those who believe in Christ Jesus. "My just one" (Rom. 1:17) is the one justified by *God*, not the law, and the just one is reputed just before God due to Christ's work on the just one's behalf.[27]

The justice by which one is justified is an alien justice, being granted to the sinner through the mercy of God alone. And for both Aquinas and Calvin, Christ's sacrificial work is the source of justification. Christ liberated sinners from the captivity of death and purified them of their guilt of sin. Calvin emphasizes that Christ satisfies God's judgment, and Aquinas emphasizes that Christ satisfies the debt of death incurred through sin. But both agree that one's initial pardon and ongoing pardon are rooted in the full and final sacrificial work of Christ. Calvin's understanding of the "Papist" teaching in which works of satisfaction *accompany* Christ's sacrificial work finds no place in Aquinas's account. For Aquinas, believers appropriate the blood of Christ by faith,[28] and this not solely at the moment of initial justification but rather for ongoing offenses and deeper conformity to the Son as an adopted son. Thus, if Calvin believes the principal disputation of Romans is that individuals are justified by faith on account of the mercy of God alone, there is profound agreement between Aquinas's and Calvin's interpretation of Romans. In *Institutes* 3.14.11, Calvin admits that he has no quarrel with the "sounder schoolmen" regarding the beginning of justification—those who claim that sinners are freely delivered from condemnation and obtain justification by the forgiveness of sins and not by meritorious works of the law—and Aquinas indeed fits the description of these "sounder schoolmen." The unmeritorious nature of justification becomes even clearer in their commentaries on Romans 8:23-20, when addressing the topic of predestination and election: for both Aquinas and Calvin, no works are considered by God in his eternal decision to justify this sinner rather than another; it is due solely to God's hidden will.

Another example is found in how Calvin and his "opponents" understand the relationship between divine and human causality in the production of meritorious works.[29] Calvin assumes that his opponents couch

26. Thomas Aquinas, *Super epistolam ad Romanos lectura* (Rome: Marietti, 1953), §212–16; abbreviated *Comm. Rom.* throughout this essay.
27. Aquinas, *Comm. Rom.* §104.
28. Aquinas, *Comm. Rom.* §310.
29. The remainder of this section can be found in expanded form in Raith II, "Calvin's

meritorious works within a competitive-causal schema relating human and divine activity. In this competitive schema, human action is in some sense causally autonomous or independent of divine activity. God and humans become two agents on the same causal plane—two actors on the same causal stage—with each doing his or her "part." When these distinct contributing elements occur, the desired result is obtained. This is true even in grace. Calvin thinks the opponents link merit with what human beings do with grace, as if grace were a mere quality given to human nature that enables human beings to act in certain ways, with such action occurring in practically autonomous ways distinct from direct divine causality. Grace is like "priming the pump," with humans finishing the job: "Perhaps the grace of God moves the will only far enough to make it inclined toward good, but does not arouse an effective volition in it."[30] In either state—in grace or out of grace—human beings are understood to be causal agents of a work in some sense distinct from God being a causal agent—the principal causal agent—of the very same work.[31]

We find that Calvin's assumption of such a competitive-causal framework in fact shapes the polemics in his commentary on Romans. To give but one among many examples: while commenting on Romans 4, Calvin claims that Abraham "had no ground for glorying" because he had no merit by which he could be justified. Instead of glorying, Calvin stresses that an individual is unable "to bring anything *of one's own* except the acknowledgement of his misery."[32] Calvin again stresses that Paul does not want believers to be "indolent" in good works, but rather "he forbids them being mercenary-minded by *demanding* something from God as their *right*

Critique of Merit," esp. 140–60, here drawing from 140–42 and 158–60; used by permission; the next two paragraphs are also found, more fully at points, in my *After Merit: John Calvin's Theology of Works and Rewards*, Refo500 Academic Studies 34 (Göttingen: Vandenhoeck & Ruprecht, 2016), 69–70, 71–72.

30. John Calvin, *The Bondage and Liberation of the Will: A Defense of the Orthodox Doctrine of Human Choice against Pighius*, ed. A. N. S. Lane, trans. G. I. Davies, Texts and Studies in Reformation and Post-Reformation Thought (Grand Rapids: Baker, 1996), 3.316, p. 123; abbreviated *BLW* hereafter.

31. Note Thomas P. Flint's comment on Molinism: "Whether the person uses the grace for the purpose that God intended is *not* up to God, for it is a doctrine of faith that grace leaves a person free" (in his "Two Accounts of Providence," in *Divine and Human Action: Essays in the Metaphysics of Theism*, ed. Thomas V. Morris [Ithaca, NY: Cornell University Press, 1988], 161).

32. John Calvin, *Commentarius in Epistolam Pauli ad Romanos*, ed. T. H. L. Parker (Leiden: Brill, 1981), 81.56; italics added. Abbreviated *Romans* hereafter.

[*iure*]."[33] Abraham demanded nothing from God, for he brought nothing "of his own" before God; his justice rests solely on God's grace. It is clear that the notion of "demanding" something from God as one's right only makes sense if the object of one's "right" is understood as being distinct from God's gift.[34] When Calvin later rejects the notion that one "merits something by his own achievements [*suis meritis aliquid promeretur*],"[35] "his own achievements" is being understood separately from divine healing and elevation.[36] Calvin rebukes those who "teach pitiable folks to procure salvation for themselves by works."[37] Clearly this "procuring" and "for themselves" is understood to occur either by human effort alone or in such a way that God and human beings each bring something to the table that somehow results in salvation.

Calvin's presupposition of a competitive-causal schema in his polemic against merit is not without basis. By the sixteenth century, as Steve Long notes, an acceptable view of human action maintained that human free action stood outside divine governance and causality.[38] But as Long goes

33. Calvin, *Romans*, 82.93–95; italics added.

34. This is especially true since Calvin elsewhere affirms that one receives grace for works done in grace (*BLW* 6.397 [pp. 234–35]). See also *Inst*. 2.3.11. To be sure, Calvin rejects the notion of "meriting grace," which is the notion that subsequent grace is "paid" on account of "using the earlier (grace) well" (*BLW* 5.353 [p. 175]). But he affirms with Augustine the notion of "grace in exchange for grace, because God constantly adds to his kindness to the elect by giving them new gifts" (*BLW* 5.353 [p. 175]; cf. Augustine, *On Grace and Free Will*, *NPNF*[1] 5:451–52); on Calvin's use of the fathers in *The Bondage and Liberation of the Will*, see A. N. S. Lane, "Calvin and the Fathers in *Bondage and Liberation of the Will*," in *Calvinus Sincerioris Religionis Vindex*, 67–96.

35. Calvin, *Romans*, 82.93.

36. Calvin's comments on 1 John 3:9 are illuminating. Note in particular how he speaks of "their own" as something distinct from acting by the grace of the Spirit: "It cannot seem absurd that men merit nothing; and yet good works, which flow from the grace of the Spirit, do not cease to be so deemed, because they are *voluntary*. They even have reward [*mercedem*], for they are by grace ascribed to men *just as if they were their own* [*perinde ac si ipsorum essent*]" (*Comm. Ep. John* 3:9 [in *Ioannis Calvini Opera quae supersunt omnia*, 59 vols., ed. J. Baum et al. Corpus Reformatorum, vols. 29–87 (Brunswick: C. A. Schwetschke & Son, 1863–1900), 55.336–37]; abbreviated *CO* hereafter).

37. *Comm. Ep. John* 3:9 [*CO* 55.336–37].

38. Steve A. Long, *Natura Pura: On the Recovery of Nature in the Doctrine of Grace* (Minneapolis: Fortress, 2010), 37–41. The seeds of this position had been sown many years before; see the comment from Thomas Bradwardine regarding his days as a student: "In the philosophical faculty I seldom heard a reference to grace. . . . What I heard day in and day out was that we are masters of our own free acts, that ours is the choice to act well or badly"; cited in Heiko A. Oberman, *Forerunners of the Reformation: The Shape of Late Medieval Thought* (Cambridge: James Clarke & Co., 1967), 135.

on to show, this position is quite contrary to Aquinas's. For Aquinas, in performing exterior acts, both the operative and cooperative dimensions of God's *habitual* grace and *auxilium* must be present for the actual performance of the meritorious act.[39] Cooperative aspects of grace, such as "strengthening" our will in order to "attain" to the act and granting the "capability" to actually perform these acts,[40] do not leave behind operative grace, but rather presuppose a movement of operative grace.[41] Joseph Wawrykow summarizes the operative and cooperative dimensions of habitual grace and actual grace as such:

> As *operans*, habitual grace changes the orientation of the sinner, granting the justified the new being and virtues which raise the sinner to the spiritual sphere and re-direct the soul to God; as *co-operans*, habitual grace works with the will, inclining the will and strengthening its performance as it wills the acts appropriate to the new being in God. As *operans*, actual grace changes the will, replacing its former will of its sinful ends by moving it to the new will of its proper end, of God; as *cooperans*, actual grace works with the justified, strengthening the human person in the deeds which in fact bring the person to God.[42]

Cooperation in Aquinas, unlike in Calvin's opponents, is not understood as the human agent acting in practically autonomous terms apart from the direct causal movement of the divine will; there is no sense of God contributing his part and *then* the human beings acting meritoriously. In the meritorious work, Aquinas considers the *same act* as having causal roots in both grace and human will. Aquinas agrees with Calvin's claim that God's grace "assists, increases, and strengthens that power which he has

---

39. There has been some debate surrounding the notion of a distinct "actual" grace (i.e., the *auxilium Dei*) in Aquinas's thought. In this section, I largely follow Joseph P. Wawrykow's analysis in his *God's Grace & Human Action: Merit in the Theology of Thomas Aquinas* (Notre Dame: University of Notre Dame Press, 2016), who follows Bernard Lonergan and affirms a distinct actual grace in Aquinas. In *ST* I-II, q. 111, a. 2, Aquinas posits a habitual grace that is both *operans* and *cooperans*, and a different kind of sanctifying grace, which later theologians designate as "actual" that is also *operans* and *cooperans* (Wawrykow, *God's Grace & Human Action*, 51).

40. Aquinas, *ST* I-II, q. 111, a. 2.

41. Aquinas, *ST* I-II, q. 111, a. 2, ad. 3.

42. Wawrykow, *God's Grace & Human Action*, 51; see also 176.

granted us, both for the completion of each particular work and for final perseverance through life."[43] When Calvin affirms merit, if the meritorious act consists of human acting "while being acted upon" by God—that is, "we will as he guides our heart, we endeavor as he rouses us, we succeed in our endeavor as he gives us strength, so that we are animate and living tools, while he is the leader and the finisher of the work"—this is precisely Aquinas's view that he expounds using both habitual grace and the *auxilium* of God in operative and cooperative terms.[44] All the more, Aquinas maintains that God's grace is the "principal" cause and that human willing is the "subsequent cause."[45] The principal agent in the meritorious act is God's grace, and this means for Aquinas that the action is attributed "more" to God than to human free will.[46] In fact, Aquinas acknowledges that although it is true that the act in a sense "depends on man's will or exertion," it is "offensive to pious ears" to speak of the act in this way. Rather, the act should be considered according to the words of the Apostle at Romans 9:16, "It does not depend on the one who wills or the one who runs, but on God who has mercy."[47] We find no room in Aquinas for "boasting" in one's meritorious work due to the centrality of God's grace as the principal cause of all meritorious activity. Aquinas is no less concerned to affirm Augustine's statement than Calvin is to affirm that merit is "grace in exchange for grace."[48]

43. Calvin, *BLW* 3.317 (p. 123).

44. When Calvin states of Abraham that he brings nothing "of his" except the acknowledgement of his own misery that seeks for mercy, Aquinas agrees that there can be no concept of "one's own" or "of his" if this implies something apart from divine causality. Even Abraham's "acknowledgement of misery," as Calvin states it, would need to be rooted in divine causality, since Aquinas attributed all "preparation" of grace to the *auxilium Dei*" (*ST* I-II, q. 109, a. 6).

45. Aquinas's ability to view the same act under its two distinct causal principles— divine and human—will become important in the next section for understanding the "worth" of the act. The issue of causality, whether competitive or noncompetitive, is intimately related to the issue of worth.

46. Aquinas, *Comm. Rom.* §778.

47. Aquinas, *Comm. Rom.* §778.

48. Calvin, *BLW* 5:353 (p. 175); cf. Augustine, *On Grace and Free Will* (*NPNF*[1] 5:451–52).

Aquinas's Contribution to Calvin's Reading of Romans

At this point, the "space" noted above has been created to see Aquinas as other than a default antagonist to the Reformed heritage. But this step alone is not enough in implementing the goals of ecumenical *ressource-ment*. As someone situated within the Reformed tradition, I now must ask the more difficult and riskier question: in what ways might Aquinas contribute to deepening the insights of Calvin's reading of Romans—a person whose reading I consider authoritative and formidably influential upon the Reformed tradition?[49] While numerous theological topics may be suggested as candidates for consideration, I believe that Aquinas's understanding of soteriological participation has the greatest potential for deepening Calvin's insights.

Calvin's interpretation of Romans reflects nonparticipatory elements of his theology that cause his reading of Romans to fall short of its full potential. Two examples of the nonparticipatory elements are (1) the fact that believers are still damnworthy in themselves and yet pardoned and accepted in Christ and (2) the belief that their good works are unworthy of reward but are rewarded because God pardons their taintedness in Christ and accepts them "as if" they were good. These nonparticipatory judgments lead Calvin to diverge from Aquinas in his interpretation of how Paul's teaching unfolds in Romans, and their divergent interpretations culminate in their approaches to Romans 8:1, where Paul declares, "There is therefore now no condemnation for those who are in Christ Jesus."

In terms of how Aquinas and Calvin see Paul's argument developing up to Romans 8, Aquinas's reading of Romans presents Paul's argument like a movie unfolding the story of Christ's grace on the soul of human beings. In Aquinas's commentary, we see the dynamism of Christ's grace moving the graced human being from the state of sin to the culminating state of glory with God eternal. The topic of justification is central to Aquinas's entire commentary. But since justification for Aquinas is the transformation of the sinner into a just person, he presents Paul's argument as moving from the transformation of initial justification, which removes original and actual sin, to the ongoing transforming "life of justice," which consists in

---

49. For a sober even if slightly exaggerated assessment of Calvin's relative place within the Reformed theological tradition, see Richard A. Muller, "Demoting Calvin: The Issue of Calvin and the Reformed Tradition," in *John Calvin, Myth and Reality: Images and Impact of Geneva's Reformer*, Papers of the 2009 Calvin Studies Society Colloquium, ed. Amy Nelson Burnett (Eugene, OR: Cascade, 2011), 3–17.

partaking in the sanctifying gifts, and leads to and culminates in the beatific vision of God.[50] For Aquinas, in Romans 1–8, Paul first discusses the *necessity* of Christ's grace for salvation; he then in turn addresses the goods we obtain through grace, unfolds the evils from which we are liberated by grace (such as original sin and actual sins), and concludes with how the work of Christ's grace enables liberation from all damnation. And all of this culminates in the life of glory with God for eternity.

The dynamic movement of Aquinas's reading of Romans serves to illuminate the nonparticipatory structure of Calvin's approach. Calvin's commentary does not unfold like the dynamics of a movie depicting the drama of grace's work on the soul; instead, it is like a picture hanging on a wall that can be observed from different angles. For Calvin, Paul takes the snapshot in Romans 1–3; it is here that Paul teaches on justification as the forgiveness and Christ's imputed righteousness. Throughout the rest of the letter, Paul continues to refer *back* to this snapshot. In Romans 4, Paul provides Abraham as an example of what has been said in Romans 1–3; Romans 5 "amplifies" what has been said in Romans 1–3; Romans 6 and 7 describe the sanctified life within the context of Romans 1–3, which serves to illustrate why justification can only be by faith; and Romans 8 returns to the teaching of Romans 1–3 to "console" believers. When Aquinas's and Calvin's interpretations as a whole are considered, we find that Aquinas reads Romans as emphasizing Christ's work of salvation *in* and *through* the believer, while Calvin reads Romans as emphasizing Christ's work *for* and *to* the believer. These emphases further illuminate Aquinas's and Calvin's participatory and nonparticipatory approaches to Paul's teaching in Romans.

Calvin's nonparticipatory judgments throughout Romans 1–7 leave Calvin struggling to fit Paul's teaching in Romans 8 into his theological paradigm. There is some irony to this conclusion, since in an attempt to emphasize participation in Calvin's soteriology some contemporary Calvin scholars have highlighted his commentary on Romans 8 as most clearly evidencing his deep participatory framework. And while it is true that Calvin does have a notion of participation that surpasses a number of his

---

50. A. N. Williams captures this "seamless" movement when commenting on Aquinas's teaching on charity: "The notion of perpetual growth [in charity] . . . inherently suggests the seamless continuity of grace and glory, for it claims that there is a single development in the human person, which has a terminus a quo but no terminus ad quem. Each human being thus possesses one life, which is nothing other than a never-ending process of growth towards God" (*The Ground of Union: Deification in Aquinas and Palamas* [Oxford: Oxford University Press, 1999], 79).

contemporary opponents, his commentary on Romans 8, especially when placed beside Aquinas's commentary, evidences the *limited* role participation plays in his theology. Calvin's commentary on Romans 8 is actually a low point in his analysis of Romans. Here he struggles to root the reason a believer has no condemnation in something outside of us, namely Christ's justice imputed, rather than in the believer's quality of being a just person. For Calvin, a person is never transformed so as to stand as just before God because that person is actually just; a believer always remains condemnable in himself. But he stands with no condemnation based on Christ's justice outside of him and imputed to him. But in order to fit Romans 8 into this understanding of justification and sanctification, Calvin has Paul making an abrupt shift from addressing sanctification in Romans 6 and 7 to addressing, once again, justification in Romans 8. Paul's statement, "There is therefore now no condemnation for those who are in Christ Jesus" (8:1), is rooted not in the believer actually no longer being condemnable, but rather in forgiveness of sin and Christ's justice imputed. Then, within Romans 8, Calvin relegates Paul's lengthy discourse on living in the Spirit to being merely a "sign" that we have Christ's justice imputed. Our participation in Christ's suffering, which Paul mentions in 8:17, is not intrinsic to obtaining eternal life, but merely an indicator that we have eternal life due to Christ's imputed justice. And when Paul speaks in 8:4 of the justice of the law being fulfilled "in us," Calvin has Paul saying that the justice of the law is fulfilled by Christ *on behalf of us* and is subsequently imputed to us. All of these exegetical maneuverings are a direct result of the nonparticipatory judgments Calvin had laid down throughout Romans 1–7.

Aquinas has much less trouble with Romans 8, given that he believes that the believer has been transformed into a just person, although the believer continues to wrestle with the remaining fallenness of the flesh. Therefore, Paul's claim that there is no condemnation for those in Christ and his emphasis on walking in the Spirit both flow naturally in Aquinas's commentary, since justification transforms a person into a just person, and a person increases in being just as that person lives a life in the Spirit. Suffering with Christ is an intrinsic part of obtaining eternal life, since a person is conformed to Christ—that is, they increase in being a just person—through participation in Christ's sufferings. And this conformity to Christ culminates in being fully just when the believer reaches glory with God eternal. All of these judgments result in a reading that is not only more participatory but arguably one that also fits better within the trajectory of Paul's argument in Romans.

Conclusion

The argument of this essay is that Aquinas and Calvin are better seen as friends than foes in reading Romans. But as friends, they seek the betterment of one another's understanding of the triune God's work of salvation in and through the person and work of Jesus Christ as explicated in Paul's letter to the Romans. Obviously they cannot do this themselves. But what I have attempted to do is facilitate what this betterment might look like. To be sure, this essay has been one-sided, asking only the question of Aquinas's contribution to Calvin's reading. The question the Catholic reader of Romans might consider is how Calvin's reading of Romans contributes to a traditional Catholic reading (to the extent that one exists). Sources other than Aquinas and Calvin may also be considered. But whatever sources are considered, if ecumenical progress is to be made, the sources must have had a substantial influence in shaping one another's ecclesial tradition.

When considering Aquinas's contribution to Calvin's reading, I attempted what I outlined above as ecumenical *ressourcement*. Calvin's positive proposals in Romans were forged within Reformation-era polemics. His concerns were largely valid. Making God's foreknowledge of merit a basis for his act of justification, on the one hand, and conceiving meritorious works within a competitive-causal framework between divine and human action on the other, undermine the participatory soteriology presented in Scripture. Calvin's positive proposals sought to counter these problems. But to avoid the errors, Calvin himself asserted proposals that did not go far enough in appreciating the depths of participation in Paul's soteriology. When I turned to Aquinas, I sought contributions that avoided Calvin's negative concerns while deepening his positive insights. The result, I argue, is a deepening of Calvin's theology, not a reduction of or simply an alternative to it. Thus, the conclusions proposed here remain within the Reformed tradition of theological reflection, though with development entailed. To be sure, this development may leave the conclusions looking more "Catholic" to some. But this is a secondary concern. The primary issue is whether the development better accounts for the gospel of Jesus Christ as presented in Scripture. I believe it does.

CHAPTER 10

Reading the Old Testament with Dietrich Bonhoeffer

Jens Zimmermann

Introduction:
Bonhoeffer's Christological, Incarnational Hermeneutics

Bonhoeffer's reading of the Old Testament has to be assessed within his overall biblical hermeneutic, which is best summarized as a sacramental view of scriptural interpretation. Bonhoeffer shares Luther's belief that the church is founded on Christ, the living Word of God, whose presence is mediated to believers through the sacraments of baptism, the Eucharist, and the sermon, conceived by Bonhoeffer as *sacramentum verbi*, the sacrament of the Word.[1] For Bonhoeffer, the primary purpose of reading the Bible is to encounter the presence of God in Christ, and, in conjunction with the Eucharist, this happens most clearly in the preaching of the Word during worship.[2] Like Luther and Calvin, Bonhoeffer insists on the importance of the sermon as the interpretive making present of God's

---

1. "Passing by the sermon means: passing by Christ. The word is something real; there is a *sacramentum verbi* (*sacramentum audibile*)"; see "Expansions of the Lecture on Homiletics," in *Theological Education at Finkenwalde: 1935–1937, DBWE* 14:514 n. 108. We know from these recorded students' notes on Bonhoeffer's homiletics classes in Finkenwalde that he used this term; and even if he had not, his lectures and writings on the topic of preaching make clear that he viewed the sermon as the presencing of God in the church. Note: all subsequent Bonhoeffer citations are from the critical editions in German (*Dietrich Bonhoeffer Werke = DBW*) and English (*Dietrich Bonhoeffer Works, English Edition = DBWE*), which are cited in the bibliography and will be indicated by their volume title and number, and page reference. Translations from the German edition are my own. Titles once given are not repeated.

2. "The sermon and the sacrament of the church are the locus for the presence of Jesus Christ" (*Nachfolge, DBW* 4:215).

word.[3] He regards biblical exegesis as subservient to preaching, for God addresses his people through the interpretation of scriptural texts aimed at proclamatory preaching.[4] Bonhoeffer is adamant that the sermon offers the same kind of real Christic presence as the Lord's Supper.[5] This insistence goes back to Bonhoeffer's Christology lectures on the "present Christ" (*der gegenwärtige Christus*)[6] and is retained all the way to his *Ethics* fragments.[7] Bonhoeffer does not deny that one can read the Bible profitably as a cultural or literary artifact, but for him, in the end, "the Bible is nothing else but the book of the church,"[8] and since the church is the body of Christ, the Bible, the Old and New Testaments, have to be read christologically.

What exactly christological reading of the Old Testament entails will occupy us later, but suffice it to say that for Bonhoeffer the church "reads the entire Holy Scripture as the book of the end, of the new, of Christ."[9] To appreciate Bonhoeffer's biblical hermeneutic, one has to take his emphasis on "the *entire* Holy Scripture" as seriously as he does. "The Scripture," he maintains, "is a complex unity, and every word, every sentence, contains such a diversity of relationships to the whole that it is impossible always

---

3. John Calvin, *Institutes of the Christian Religion*, LCC (Philadelphia: Westminster, 1960), III.ii.6.

4. "Christ attests himself only in *interpretation*, not in the mere biblical word [*Nur in Auslegung ist Christuszeugnis, nicht im reinen Bibelwort*]," in *Illegale Theologenausbildung: Finkenwalde 1935–1937, DBW* 14:508. All italicizing original unless otherwise indicated.

5. "Not different gradations of God's presence . . . not different levels of reality [*Wirklichkeit*]. The word, in sermon and Lord's supper, wants to go to the congregation. The same measure of reality [*Wirklichkeit*] in sermon and the Lord's supper" ("Lecture on Homiletics. Student Notes," in *DBW* 14:508). See also Bonhoeffer's statement in *Discipleship* that "the body of Christ takes on visible form not only in the preaching of the word but also in *baptism and the Lord's Supper*, both of which emanate from the true humanity of our Lord Jesus Christ" (*Discipleship, DBWE* 4:228).

6. "As the crucified and risen one, Jesus is at the same time the Christ who is present now . . . Christ in his person is indeed present in the church as person. Thus the presence of Christ is there in the church" (*Berlin, 1932–1933, DBWE* 12:312–13). Christ is present not as some kind of power, or as a moral idea we retrieve from history, but as person whose ontological *pro-me* structure defines his presence in the church: "The presence of Christ as the *pro-me* is his real being-for-me" (*DBWE* 12:315).

7. "The mandate given to the church is proclamation. . . . The Word that came from heaven in Jesus Christ wants to return in the form of human speech. The mandate of the church is the divine word. In this word God himself wants to be present" (Ethik, *DBW* 6:399–400).

8. *Schöpfung und Fall: Theologische Auslegung von Genesis 1–3, DBW* 3:22.

9. *DBW* 3:22.

to keep track of the whole when listening to an individual part of it." Yet nothing less is required, because "the Scripture is a corpus, a living whole."[10] This whole Bible is to be read "from Christ toward Christ."[11] This christological interpretation of Scripture is subservient to its main purpose of presencing Christ in the sermon.[12] In the sermon, the incarnate, crucified, and risen Christ appears clothed in human words, and Christ the eternal word stands behind and supports the sermon.[13] The sermon is therefore not essentially a teaching word, an expression of piety, or an address propelled by human intention. Rather, the preached word derives from the divine Word, which requires no artificial human support for its effect or validity, because the divine Word "supports and carries the entire world and in the sermon lays the groundwork for a new world."[14]

What is this new world? In his *Ethics*, Bonhoeffer explains that this new world refers to the new humanity inaugurated by Christ: "In Jesus Christ is the new humanity, is the community of God."[15] Bonhoeffer's christological biblical hermeneutic is thus eschatologically weighted toward the new humanity and new creation. Yet this eschatological direction does not take the church out of the world but reminds the congregation of its responsibility in and for the world. The reason for the "this-worldliness" of the church is Bonhoeffer's particular emphasis on the notion of *Stellvertretung*, or "vicarious representation." He explains this concept in the following crucial passage from the *Ethics*, which we quote in full because it presents us with the overall framework of Bonhoeffer's christological hermeneutic for biblical interpretation, including the Old Testament:

> The Christian community stands in the place in which the whole world should stand. In this respect it serves the world as vicarious representative; it is there for the world's sake. On the other hand, the place where the church-community stands is the place where the world fulfills its own destiny; the church-community is the "new creation," the

---

10. *Life Together* and *Prayerbook of the Bible, DBWE* 5:61.

11. *DBW* 3:22.

12. The neologism "presencing" is meant to capture Bonhoeffer's "*vergegenwärtigen*," to make something present.

13. "The word is itself the content = the historical Christ who bears all humanity along with all its punishment and its suffering," in *Theological Education at Finkenwalde: 1935–1937, DBWE* 14:512.

14. *DBW* 14:507.

15. *DBW* 6:407.

"new creature," the goal of God's ways on earth. In this dual vicarious representation, the church-community is in complete community with its Lord; it follows in discipleship the one who was the Christ precisely in being there completely for the world and not for himself.[16]

Bonhoeffer had already formulated this foundational idea of *Stellvertretung* in his doctoral dissertation *Sanctorum Communio*,[17] developed it more pastorally in *Discipleship*,[18] and continues to emphasize the church's responsibility toward the world in *Ethics*.

We emphasize this continuity of Bonhoeffer's theological development because it allows us to read his much discussed theological turn in his prison letters in light of his earlier theology. Recognizing this continuous, albeit never simply linear, development is crucial for understanding Bonhoeffer's increasing interest in the Old Testament during this time. In Bonhoeffer's earlier works, his statements on "vicarious representation" had always implied the church's responsibility for the world. Yet in his work on ethics and especially in his prison correspondence, the former focus on the inner-ecclesial dimension of *Stellvertretung*, without diminishing the importance of this element, gave way to a focus on the political or public dimension of this christological concept. As the editors of the *Letters and Papers from Prison* point out, Bonhoeffer's "call for theological renewal was primarily a call to *metanoia* in the church that would result in vicarious solidarity with the world in its need."[19] This solidarity with the world, based on the christological notion of "vicarious representation," is understandably filtered through Bonhoeffer's own political involvement to overthrow the Nazi regime; of more theological interest is that this solidarity is expressed movingly in poems, using the Old Testament figures of Jonah and Moses. There is no warrant to believe, as a number of Bonhoeffer interpreters have done, that Bonhoeffer's prison theology is a departure from his earlier emphasis on the church. Rather, his growing emphasis on a "this-worldly" Christianity further develops his original insight that only

---

16. *Ethics, DBWE* 6:404-5.

17. For example, "in the Christian principle of vicarious representation, the new humanity is summed up and sustained. In [this principle] consists the material uniqueness of the foundational Christian relation" (*Sanctorum Communio, DBW* 1:99-100).

18. "So in following Christ, this suffering falls upon [the church-community], and it bears the suffering while being borne by Christ. The community of Jesus Christ vicariously represents the world before God by following Christ under the cross" (*DBWE* 4:90).

19. J. W. de Gruchy, "Editor's Introduction to the English Edition," in *DBWE* 8:27.

in recognizing all of creation's existence through Christ and for his sake are "the world and human beings truly taken seriously."[20]

Bonhoeffer's increasing interest in the Old Testament during his last years indicates, as the Swedish Lutheran theologian Gustaf Wingren aptly put it, the deepening of his "creation-faith"; that is, Bonhoeffer further deconstructed an implicit dualism in German Protestant theology between nature and grace that resulted in restricting any knowledge about God and morality to divine revelation in Christ. Wingren acknowledges that this revelational focus had helped dialectical theologians like Karl Barth to counter the emphasis on creational orders, which Lutheran theologians had used to support nationalist and anti-Semitic theology. Yet this gain was paid for dearly with the unbiblical surrender of natural life. According to Wingren, Protestants forgot that God is also present in the midst of mundane human activities such as eating and drinking. Moreover, in marked difference to patristic and even Luther's own theology, modern Protestants had overlooked that a basic natural morality, based on a creature's essential physical and social needs, precedes explicitly Christian ethics.[21] Wingren believed that Bonhoeffer was keenly aware of this quasi-gnostic and nihilistic view of creation, and, in seeking to overcome it, he was naturally drawn to the Old Testament as a worldly theater for God's presence. Within this context, writes Wingren, it is thus "of the greatest interest that Bonhoeffer professed to prefer reading the Old Testament rather than the New for edification. He was looking for belief in creation."[22] The whole tenor of Bonhoeffer's *Ethics* fragments, especially his effort to retrieve natural ethics for Protestant theology, substantiates Wingren's reading. Bonhoeffer's thoughts about "this-worldly" or "religionless" Christianity and his increasing appreciation for the Old Testament are part of the same development, namely the deepening of his overall hermeneutic in working out the implications of the incarnation. We can thus conclude that Bonhoeffer's Old Testament hermeneutic mirrors the dynamic of his theological development, which does not present a systematic theology but nevertheless a coherent theology, unified by an emphasis on the incarnation. In the following pages, we will delineate how this incarnational hermeneutic shapes Bonhoeffer's reading of the Old Testament. To this end, we will first

20. *DBW* 6:363.

21. Gustaf Wingren, *Creation and Gospel: The New Situation in European Theology* (Toronto: Edwin Mellen, 1979), 79.

22. Wingren, *Creation and Gospel*, 54.

look at the general contours of Bonhoeffer's biblical interpretation before turning to his reading of the Old Testament.

Letting the Bible Speak:
Bonhoeffer on Theological Exegesis and Historical Criticism

Mainsteam academic scholarship, from the mid-nineteenth to the mid-twentieth century, was largely defined by the "historical-critical method," a supposedly neutral, scientific, and philological approach to the biblical text, which was interested mostly in genetic questions regarding a text's historical origins, development, and transmission.[23] Increasingly, however, biblical scholars are questioning the value of this label and its purported distance from and superiority to supposedly precritical, theologically motivated exegesis.[24] As a number of critics have pointed out, all biblical scholarship, both ancient and modern, makes use of grammatical tools, linguistic analysis, and historical comparative readings. In what, then, does the real difference between historical criticism and supposedly precritical readings consist? The difference is not captured by a simplistic opposition of scientific, critical reading to merely subjective interpretation driven by theological interests. The concept of "historical criticism" functions as a "rhetorical figure" of evaluative power, suggesting the implied superiority of modern approaches while masking ideological lenses and

---

23. For definitions of historical criticism, see John Barton, "Historical-critical Approaches," in *The Cambridge Companion to Biblical Interpretation*, ed. John Barton (Cambridge: Cambridge University Press, 1998), 9–20, here 9: "Historical critics . . . are interested in *genetic* questions about the biblical text. They ask when and by whom books were written; what was their intended readership; and . . . what were the stages by which they came into being. . . . Often the finished product seems to be of less interest to such critics than the underlying sources." See also Richard E. Burnett, "Historical Criticism," in *Dictionary for Theological Interpretation of the Bible*, ed. Kevin J. Vanhoozer et al. (Grand Rapids: Baker Academic, 2005), 290–93, here 290: "Historical criticism seeks to answer a basic question: to what historical circumstances does this text refer, and out of what historical circumstances did it emerge?"

24. John Barton wrote in 1998 that historical criticism is now "under a cloud" and experiencing a "paradigm shift" toward text-immanent interpretation ("Historical-critical Approaches," 9). For a more recent assessment, see Francis Watson, "Does Historical Criticism Exist? A Contribution to Debate on the Theological Interpretation of Scripture," *Theological Theology: Essays in Honour of John Webster*, ed. R. David Nelson, Darren Sarisky, and Justin Stratis (London: T. & T. Clark Bloomsbury, 2015), 307–18, esp. 310–11.

operative theological assumptions that often diminish the polysemy and applications of texts.[25] Increasingly, biblical scholars interested in theological exegesis refuse to be marginalized and press for a public conversation on the legitimacy of theological interpretation.[26] In effect, this return to theological interpretation was revived in Bonhoeffer's time by Karl Barth, who launched his famous *Romans* commentary as an attempt "to read the Bible differently from what we have been taught in the universities under the dominion of 1890s." Anticipating the question, "different how?" Barth responds, "I want to answer: more objective, more content-driven, more substantial [*wesentlicher*], with more attention and love for the Bible's own meaning."[27]

It was time, Barth argued, to move beyond the period of cultural Protestantism, during which the Bible had been admired as a "classic document of religious piety."[28] By "religious piety," Barth refers to the spirituality of liberal Protestantism, exemplified by Schleiermacher's understanding of the biblical text as a historical-linguistic husk whose kernel of spirituality was detachable from its time-bound expression. Once this timeless piety was established and Jesus was tamed as its messenger and moral exemplar, one could dissect the text with historical-critical tools and throw out any or all passages deemed offensive to the cultured modern mind. As time wore on, however, the essential problem with this approach became clearer: the liberal Protestant's assumption of a universal spiritual content dependent entirely on the subjective proclivities of the readers. This problem showed up in two ways. The first was that the Bible no longer had really anything new to say. As witness to a timeless moral code of humanity, tolerance, and inner piety, the Bible was rendered sterile and failed to address questions put to it by a new generation. While academic theologians were busy pulverizing the Bible into a million historically situated fragments, ironically this focus on redaction and concrete *Sitz im Leben* no longer spoke to contemporary *Leben*, that is, to the life questions of "younger pastors, theology students, and laypeo-

---

25. Watson, "Does Historical Criticism Exist?," 317. David Steinmetz has demonstrated this reductive effect for the fourfold method of medieval exegesis; see "The Superiority of Pre-Critical Exegesis," *Theology Today* 37.1 (1980): 27–38.

26. Watson, "Does Historical Criticism Exist?," 317–18.

27. Karl Barth, "Entwürfe Zum Vorwort," in *Der Römerbrief*, Erste Fassung, 1919, ed. Karl Schmidt (Zürich: Theologischer Verlag Zürich, 1985), 581–82. All translations from this text are my own.

28. Barth, *Römerbrief* (1919), 582.

ple."[29] The second result of the domesticated Bible was that, as cultural Protestantism's assumed traditional Christian values disappeared from society, theologians proved insufficiently inoculated against the Bible's appropriation by German nationalism and racial ideology. The critically dissected and disconnected fragments left over by academic work on the Scriptures could not speak a prophetic word against nationalist and anti-Semitic misappropriations of the Bible.

Barth had no intention of abjuring historical-critical tools, and he acknowledged "the faithful and successful work" produced with their aid.[30] His contention was, however, that the basic rationalistic presuppositions underlying the historical-critical school prevent the Bible from speaking for itself, and thus this supposedly objective method is, in the final analysis, not object oriented enough. In his preface, Barth judges the approach to be "inattentive and loveless with respect to the Bible's meaning."[31] This book should be allowed "to speak itself what it contains and wants to say."[32] What the Bible "wants to say" is a truth that goes beyond the historical framework of its texts. Barth fully acknowledges that the apostle Paul spoke as a product of his time to a particular audience. Yet "much more important than this truth is another, namely that he speaks as prophet and apostle of God's kingdom to all human beings of all times."[33] While the historical-critical method plays an important preparatory role in sharpening our awareness of historical distance and difference, the much more important task is to hear what the Bible tells us about God. We should never have to choose, says Barth, between historical-critical reading and hearing "the Spirit of the Bible, which is the eternal Spirit."[34] Historical-critical work is not an end but a means. We must "see *through* [*hindurch*] the method," to understanding what moved the biblical writers.[35] In essence, Barth stresses here the fundamental hermeneutical point

---

29. Barth, *Römerbrief* (1919), 582.

30. Barth, *Römerbrief* (1919), 582.

31. Barth, *Römerbrief* (1919), 582.

32. Barth, *Römerbrief* (1919), 582.

33. Barth, "Vorwort zur ersten Auflage," *Römerbrief* (1919), 582.

34. Barth, *Römerbrief* (1919), 582.

35. Barth, *Römerbrief* (1919), 582. In his second preface to the second version of the commentary, Barth denies accusations that he is an enemy of historical criticism (*historische Kritik*); he writes not against historical criticism but against the presumption that it explains the text sufficiently. The supposedly neutral attempt to establish what the text says, is at best "the first primitive attempt at such an explanation, namely the establishing of what is written there, with the help of transpositions and transcriptions of the Greek words and word

that explanation and understanding cannot be separated. Thus, pretending merely to explicate a text with scientific detachment constitutes in reality a partial and poor interpretation that operates on hidden theological and philosophical assumptions, and often those that do not rise above the level of Sunday-school instruction.

We have spent so much time on Barth, because Bonhoeffer was greatly influenced by him and shared the Swiss theologian's concern that the Bible should be allowed to speak on its own terms, and that it should address "theology and church in our time."[36] For Bonhoeffer, too, the Bible forms the basis for the church's recognition of God's will,[37] to discern the church's address of cultural and social issues.[38] Already in 1924, in a seminar paper for Reinhold Seeberg, Bonhoeffer reiterates Barth's judgment on the insufficiency of the historical-critical method. Since its principles are derived from a scientific method that in turn arose from "a mechanistic worldview," the explanations given by means of this approach are like deconstructing a mechanism into its various components without any sense of the biblical canon or the importance of the community's interpretive tradition of Scripture.[39] Bonhoeffer concludes,

> Regarding the form of the Bible, with this approach the concept of the canon disintegrates and becomes meaningless. Textual and literary criticism are applied to the Bible. The sources are distinguished, and the methods of the history of religions and form criticism fragment

groups into German, with philological-archeological elucidation of these results, and by means of a more or less plausible ordering of individual pieces with the help of a historical-psychological pragmatism." Contrary to their claim that they are merely establishing the text, Barth argues that historical critics are already performing the interpretive work of understanding. These critics do not proceed "scientifically" but hermeneutically in trying to *understand* Paul; they intend to show "what can not only be repeated linguistically in Greek or German but what can be *re-thought* in the *way it was meant*" ("Zweites Vorwort," in *Der Römerbrief*, Zweite Fassung, 1922, ed. Cornelis van der Kooi and Katja Tolstaja [Zürich: Theologischer Verlag Zürich, 2010], 11–12). In other words, historical critics in essence try to do the same as Luther and Calvin did, only they do it less ably, because they dismiss Calvin's teaching on inspiration. Barth recognizes that no neutral reading exists, but that all reading is interpretation based on a particular presuppositional framework.

36. Barth, "Vorwort zur fünften Auflage," in *Der Römerbrief* (Zweite Fassung, 1922), 36.

37. "Meditation über Psalm 119," in *Illegale Theologenausbildung. Sammelvikariate 1937–40, DBW* 15:524.

38. *DBW* 6:362–63.

39. "Paper on the Historical and Pneumatological Interpretation of Scripture," in *The Young Bonhoeffer: 1918–1927, DBWE* 9:286.

the larger and even the remaining short textual units into little pieces. After this total disintegration of the texts, historical criticism leaves the field of battle. Debris and fragments are left behind. Its work is apparently finished.[40]

Like Barth, Bonhoeffer champions instead a Spirit-guided (*pneumatological*) reading of Scripture that strives to hear God's word with the help of historical-critical tools. Yet, just as Barth had argued, Bonhoeffer insists that these tools are subservient to having the ancient authors and texts speak to us. Spiritual interpretation recognizes the Bible's claim to be not merely a word about God, but the word of God himself. In spiritual interpretation, "the past is made present or—better—the contemporaneity and trans-temporality of God's word are recognized."[41] Bonhoeffer follows Barth in claiming that spiritual interpretation depends on the recognition of God's presence and therefore requires divine illumination: "God can be understood only from God's Spirit," through whose work alone, "illumination can be achieved, without which *all* this is *nothing.* . . . Through this unique understanding, 'inspiration' is received by the believer. Thus the believer comes to understand the category of revelation and uses it as the foundation for all further interpretation. Here we recall Augustine: 'You would not seek me if you had not already found me.'"[42]

While Bonhoeffer articulated the principles of Spirit-guided interpretation already in 1924 as a theology student, the personal and urgent desire to hear God speak through the Bible emerged later, during what his biographer Eberhard Bethge described as Bonhoeffer's "turning point" from academic theologian to a church-oriented Christian. Bethge puts this turning point during the period 1931–32.[43] What this deepening of his faith meant for biblical interpretation is documented by a letter Bonhoeffer wrote in 1936 to his brother-in-law Rüdiger Schleicher, a prominent lawyer and liberal Protestant. Bonhoeffer tells Schleicher that "not too long ago" he came to appreciate the Bible as a book "unlike all other books" because in it "God is speaking to us."[44] The Bible, Bonhoeffer explains, is unlike other books because it is a personal address to us, to be read like a com-

---

40. *DBWE* 9:286.

41. *DBWE* 9:287.

42. *DBWE* 9:291–2.

43. Eberhard Bethge, *Dietrich Bonhoeffer: A Biography,* trans. Eric Mosbacher (Minneapolis: Fortress, 2004), 202–3.

44. *DBWE* 14:166–70.

munication from a person whom we love, whose words we simply accept and whose unfolding meaning we continue to ponder. This hermeneutical condition of relationality negates any pretensions of detached reading. "We can, after all, always seek only that which we already know. . . . Hence we must already know which God we are seeking before we can really seek that God. . . . Only if we finally dare to come to the Bible assuming that the one speaking to us here really is the God who loves us and has no intention of abandoning us with our questions will we come to rejoice in the Bible."[45] Yet the Bible is also unlike all other books because in it we encounter a God wholly transcendent of human nature, whom we cannot and should not domesticate, unless we want merely to meet our alter ego or "Doppelgänger."[46] Bonhoeffer now applies his well-known theological argument against idealism to biblical interpretation:[47] I know God either "from my own interpretation of history or nature, that is, from within myself—or I know about that God on the basis of his revelation of his own word."[48] If God himself determines how he is encountered, then we will find him in "a place that is not at all commensurate with my own nature and that does not please me at all."[49] This place is the cross of Jesus, and "the cross of Jesus fulfills Scripture, that is, the Old Testament. Hence the entire Bible claims to be this word in which God wants us to find him," but those who want to find God "must live beneath that cross just as the Sermon on the Mount demands."[50]

With these two elements in place, the trustworthy address of a God who loves us and the assurance that this God is not a mirror of our own mind, then reading the Bible becomes an interpretive quest for a concrete word rather than a preset universal message. Bonhoeffer writes, "Thus do I read the Bible. I ask every passage: what is God saying to us here? And I implore God to show us what he wants to say. Hence we are no longer even *permitted* to seek universal, eternal truths that might correspond to our own 'eternal' nature. . . . Instead we seek the will of God, who is utterly alien . . . whose thoughts are *not* our thoughts."[51] Seeking God's will

---

45. *DBWE* 14:167.

46. *DBWE* 14:169.

47. He developed this stance in his first two academic works, *Sanctorum Communio* and *Act and Being*.

48. *DBWE* 14:168.

49. *DBWE* 14:168.

50. *DBWE* 14:168.

51. *DBWE* 14:168.

in the Bible is decidedly not giving in to subjective fancy, because "God's word begins by showing us at the cross of Christ, where all our ways and thoughts—including so-called eternal ones—ultimately lead, namely, to death and judgment before God."[52] For this reason, one cannot take the Bible apart, trying to decide what may be God's word and what is merely human sentiment, because such judgments may be motivated by creating a god in our own image. For fear of self-deception, Bonhoeffer would rather allow an obscure passage to stand until perhaps "one day this passage will indeed be revealed as God's own word."[53] Bonhoeffer then describes how his new discovery of the Bible has led to a practice of regular and meditative reading: "I read it each morning and evening, often during the day as well, and every day I focus on a text I have chosen for the entire week, trying to immerse myself in it entirely that I may truly hear it. I now know that I could no longer really live properly without this. And I certainly could not believe properly. And increasingly more riddles are becoming clear to me each day; we still seem to cling wholly to the surface of things."[54]

Bonhoeffer concludes the letter to his brother-in-law with his conviction that since the Bible has answered the problems of believers for countless generations, allowing readers "to become independent and stable for a genuine life in faith," he too has made the decision "to trust the word of the Bible" to sustain him. The essential entry point into the hermeneutical circle of biblical interpretation for Bonhoeffer is "the decision whether to trust the word of the Bible, whether to allow it to sustain us as does no other word in life or death. And I believe that we will genuinely become happy and at peace only after making this decision."[55]

Bonhoeffer's often moving description of his hermeneutical practice reveals three important interpretive premises that also determine his reading of the Old Testament. First, how one approaches the Bible is based on a prior decision to take it as God's word. This decision is itself prompted by one's relation to God, a relation God himself establishes by grace.[56] Second, the same grace that allows one to enter into the relational

---

52. *DBWE* 14:168.
53. *DBWE* 14:169.
54. *DBWE* 14:169.
55. *DBWE* 14:169–70.
56. Bonhoeffer said much the same in more technical language in his earlier essay on pneumatological interpretation: "The *principle of interpretation* must derive from an already-understood scripture. Does God truly speak in scripture in such a way that only God and not humans can hear? The Spirit comes from the word and the word comes from the Spirit. Is

hermeneutical circle of the Bible as God's word predetermines God's self-revelation in Christ as the center of the Scriptures. The Bible has to be read christologically. Finally, Bonhoeffer's approach is marked by the desire for objectivity. Already Bonhoeffer's early theological work, especially *Act and Being*, is characterized by its relentless criticism of idealist philosophy as a manifestation of an egocentric epistemological stance that traps the self in subjectivism. The same theological concern with *cor curvum in se*, "the heart turned in on itself," governs Bonhoeffer's interpretive approach to the Bible. This concern becomes especially clear in the lecture "On Contemporizing New Testament Texts," which Bonhoeffer presented to fellow pastors in 1935. His main argument is that the demand for the Bible's contemporaneity springs from a proper but distorted desire to have the Bible speak to us yet to have it speak on *our* terms: "Either one understands [the Bible's relevance] to mean that the biblical message must justify itself to the present and thus demonstrate that it can be contemporized or that the present must justify itself to the biblical message and that thus the message must be made contemporary."[57] The point is, in either case, that the Bible is supposed to justify itself before our demands, to adapt to our horizon of understanding instead of shaping it. Bonhoeffer fears that when we demand the Bible's contemporaneity we really desire its correspondence to our own ideas of truth, whether these be the rationalism of the modern, autonomous individual, or the German Christians' nationalistic eisegesis.[58]

Like Barth, Bonhoeffer insists that "contemporaneity" can only mean that contemporary culture must justify itself before the Bible, not by making the message artificially relevant but by putting "the present before the forum of the Christian message; in other words, one asks the question of the content [*der Sache*], of the 'what' of the Christian message."[59] And this substance of the Christian message is essentially a "who," namely Jesus Christ. As we shall see shortly, what Bonhoeffer states here for the New Testament is also true for the Old Testament: the Bible becomes

---

there a solution, or are we, along with the concept of revelation, plummeting further and further into darkness as we search for light and enlightenment? The solution lies in the fact God opens human eyes to receive revelation in certain indescribable and undetermined moments and words. The object of understanding creates for its subject the means of recognizing in the act of knowledge. The object must become subject. God becomes the Holy Spirit" (*DBWE* 9:290).

57. *DBWE* 14:413.
58. *DBWE* 14:413.
59. *DBW* 14:403.

contemporary whenever Christ as God's word is allowed to become present. This present, says Bonhoeffer, "is not some temporal feeling, temporal interpretation, or zeitgeist; instead, the present is solely the Holy Spirit. Wherever God is present in the divine word, there one has the present [*die Gegenwart*], there God posits the present. The *subject of the present* is the Holy Spirit, not we ourselves, and that is also why the subject of *contemporization* is the Holy Spirit itself. The *concretissimum of the Christian message* and textual exposition is not a human act of contemporizing but rather always God, the Holy Spirit."[60] Thus the substance of the Bible is made present whenever "Christ speaks to us through Christ's Holy Spirit" a concrete word to his church within a particular historical context, a directive that is mediated through the words of Scripture.[61]

Bonhoeffer is adamant that this interpretive approach centered in one's reliance on the Holy Spirit is nevertheless deeply historical. The interpreter does not enter an atemporal realm of eternal ideas, but enters a transmission event in which our time horizon correlates with the historical event of God's work in history through Jesus Christ in the incarnation. Yet precisely because the God who spans present, past, and future became incarnate, the criterion for the true presence of his speaking comes from the future that Christ accomplished for us in the past. This eschatological element coming to us from the future through history requires careful exegesis to do justice to the linguistic-historical mediation of God's presence through the text: "Once we have recognized that proper contemporizing means getting to the substance and allowing that substance to come to expression, the corresponding methodology would accordingly stipulate that a contemporizing proclamation *must* essentially *be exegesis*, exegesis of the only word that has at its disposal the power of contemporizing, namely, an exegesis of Scripture."[62] Thus the proper movement of the exegete is "not from the word of Scripture to the present, but rather from the present to the word of Scripture, where it then tarries."[63]

Bonhoeffer's most directly hermeneutical reflections on christological interpretation in relation to historical criticism are his notes for a lecture on "Christ in the Psalms," given in Finkenwalde (1935). Bonhoeffer

---

60. *DBW* 14:404.

61. *DBWE* 14:417; see also *DBW* 6:362–63.

62. *DBWE* 14:418.

63. *DBWE* 14:418–19; I have modified the translation from "abides" to "tarries," to do justice to the temporary sense expressed by the German "*verharren*," connoting a provisional pausing rather than permanent dwelling.

here clearly distances himself from the position of the Lutheran theologian Ernst Wilhelm Hengstenberg (1802–69), who also tried to defend orthodox biblical teaching against the rationalism of the historical-critical school, but who did so by asserting verbal inspiration. For Bonhoeffer, this position is bibliolatry, and historical criticism rightly attacked this divinization of the Bible. For traditional Lutherans like Hengstenberg, not God but the verbally inspired Bible had become the real foundation of faith.[64] Bonhoeffer, by contrast, affirms the historicity of the Bible on theological grounds. By becoming human, God made himself vulnerable to historicity, and the true service of historical criticism is to show "the full historicity of revelation, to the point that even the existence of the son of God can be put into question."[65] The Christian, says Bonhoeffer, can accept this historicity as part of the incarnational risk and dynamic that God entered into when becoming human; yet for the Christian, this historicity, and the literary processes by which the Scriptures came into being, all stand under the sign of Christ, whose word is mediated through the historical to the contemporary reader. Both orthodox Lutherans like Hengstenberg and Bonhoeffer want to encounter God's presence in the Old Testament, but the difference is this: the orthodox want to hear Christ's verbally inspired voice at the time of David, speaking a divine word in that particular historical context and to that particular community of faith. For this approach, everything hinges on Davidic authorship and on finding New Testament faith already in the Old. No hermeneutical mediation takes place. Bonhoeffer, by contrast, seeks Christ's voice in the Psalter for the contemporary reader and for the concrete present situation.[66] Bonhoeffer makes clear that Scripture as a whole mediates God's presence, wherefore the same hermeneutic of "presencing" applies to both testaments.

Reading the Old Testament Christologically with Bonhoeffer

Bonhoeffer reads the Old Testament christologically based on his conviction that the same Trinitarian God correlates both testaments. Af-

---

64. *DBW* 14:374.

65. *DBW* 14:375.

66. *DBW* 14:375; see also Martin Kuske, *Das Alte Testament als Buch von Christus: Dietrich Bonhoeffers Wertung und Auslegung des Alten Testaments* (Göttingen: Vandenhoeck and Ruprecht, 1971), 56.

ter all, Christ is "in the Old Testament"[67] because "the God of the Old Testament is the Father of Jesus Christ. The God who appears in Jesus Christ is the God of the Old Testament. He is the triune God."[68] Reading the Old Testament christologically means "reading it through God's becoming human and his death on the cross. Otherwise we remain in a Jewish or pagan conception of the Old Testament."[69] This rigorous incarnational interpretive approach sets Bonhoeffer apart from the liberal Protestant hermeneutic. Since Jesus is no longer merely a moral exemplar but God's freely enacted affirmation, judgment, and redemption of humanity, the Old Testament is no longer merely a preliminary and expendable stepping stone to a higher morality, but an abidingly significant reflection of God's electing and redeeming work. Thus "the people and stories of the Old Testament are not moral examples but witnesses of the election and promises of God. The Old Testament testifies to God's free, merciful, and wrathful actions with his people, and not to moral examples."[70] This incarnational hermeneutic allows Bonhoeffer to read the text typologically in the patristic sense: there is deeper spiritual meaning in the historical narratives.

There are three main examples of Bonhoeffer's theological interpretation of the Old Testament: his lectures on Genesis 1–3, published as *Creation and Fall: Theological Interpretation of Genesis 1–3* (1933), his introduction to the Psalms, which appeared as his final publication under the title *The Prayerbook of the Bible* (1940), and numerous sermons, meditations on Old Testament texts, including a long fragment on Psalm 119. We will briefly sample these sources to demonstrate Bonhoeffer's theological, that is christological, hermeneutic of the Old Testament.[71]

67. Dietrich Bonhoeffer, "König David," in *Dietrich Bonhoeffer: Predigten, Auslegungen, und Meditationen*, Band 2: 1935–45, ed. Otto Dudzus (Gütersloh: Christian Kaiser Verlag, 1998), 189.

68. Bonhoffer, "König David," 215.

69. Bonhoeffer, "König David," 215.

70. Bonhoeffer, "König David," 215.

71. In his introduction to *Dietrich Bonhoeffer: Predigten, Auslegungen, und Meditationen*, Otto Dudzus (1912–2000), Bonhoeffer's student at Finkenwalde, confirms that "The most important hermeneutical principle [of the Psalms] is the christological," and this is true for all Bonhoeffer's exegesis (p. 74).

Creation and Fall

In the preface to *Creation and Fall*, Bonhoeffer provides a summary of his interpretive approach to the Old Testament. The church, as the body of Christ, exists as eschatological witness, because it cannot but view the world in light of the new creation in Christ, in whom all things were made new. Hence the church also reads the Bible, the book of the church, christologically "from the end." Bonhoeffer explains:

> Where Holy Scripture, upon which the church of Christ stands, speaks of creation, of the beginning, what else can it say other than that it is only from Christ that we can know what the beginning is? The Bible is after all nothing other than the book of the church. It *is* this in its very essence, or it is nothing. It therefore needs to be read and proclaimed wholly from the viewpoint of the end. In the church, therefore, the story of creation must be read in a way that begins with Christ and only then moves on toward him as its goal; indeed one can read it as a book that moves toward Christ only when one knows that Christ is the beginning, the new, the end of our whole world. . . . Theological exposition takes the Bible as the book of the church and interprets it as such.[72]

Reading the Old Testament christologically is thus in a sense reading it eschatologically, from the end of the new creation represented in Christ. Yet such an eschatological reading cannot step or look *behind* either the beginning or the end in an effort to rise above them, but rather the reader reads "from the middle." For example, when we contemplate the idea that "in the beginning, God created heaven and earth," Bonhoeffer insists that "only from the middle do we perceive the beginning."[73] This "middle" is not merely temporal but existential. The "middle" is our present existence either in sin or in Christ, either living in a vicious hermeneutical circle of autonomous self-understanding, which is spiritual death, or living from the "new middle," which is Christ, freed from the deadly burden of self-centered judgment.[74]

---

72. Dietrich Bonhoeffer, *Creation and Fall: A Theological Exposition of Genesis 1–3*, DBWE 3:22.

73. *DBW* 3:30.

74. *DBW* 3:87. Clearly, Bonhoeffer applies here his insights from *Act and Being* regarding the two modes of being "in Adam" or "in Christ."

Reading christologically from the "middle" of Christ's new creation also allows Bonhoeffer to read the text *allegorically* in the restricted sense of spiritual reading as defined by Henri de Lubac's account of patristic exegesis. De Lubac defines spiritual meaning as "symbolic transposition" and notes that the apostle Paul and the Latin tradition first used the word "allegory" to label this interpretive "method."[75] In this proper and good sense, allegory meant "the mysteries of Christ and of the Church as they appeared in Scripture. Hence, the allegorical meaning was the dogmatic meaning par excellence, and it was firmly rooted in history."[76] Allegory does not entail leaving history or the letter behind, but rather finds spiritual meaning in the literal, historical significance.[77] The later term "typology" was meant to express this spiritual understanding of the text more adequately, but the basic idea is the same. The letter, in short, is "the sacrament of the spirit,"[78] and this is how Bonhoeffer can also read the text. He ventures to say, for example, that "the dark abyss" over which the spirit of God hovers is "the first sounding of the power of darkness, of the passion of Jesus Christ."[79] In the subsequent section on "the Word," Bonhoeffer comments on God's creation of light through the word, that "as the former word about the dark abyss was the first pointer to the passion of Christ, so now the light that liberates the subjected, shapeless abyss into actual being points to the light that shines in darkness."[80]

Reading the creation account backward from Christ illumines the nature of God's creative power. "The world," writes Bonhoeffer, "exists from the beginning in the sign of the resurrection of Christ from the dead. Indeed it is because we know of the resurrection that we know of God's creation in the beginning, of God's creating out of nothing."[81] The deep and real break between Christ's death and his resurrection, God's free act of choosing to create life from the nothingness of death in the resur-

---

75. Henri de Lubac, *Scripture in the Tradition* (New York: Crossroad, 2000), 11–12.

76. De Lubac, *Scripture in the Tradition*, 12.

77. De Lubac, *Scripture in the Tradition*, 15, explains that the term "allegory" fell out of favor for understandable reasons in modern times. First, its etymology (that is, "speaking other") suggests that allegory is something other than the literal meaning, without any organic tie to it. Second, in modern usage, allegory is contrasted with literal or historical meaning, but this is not what the ancient use of allegory implied at all; rather, it sought spiritual meaning not behind but through the literal-historical significance of the text.

78. De Lubac, *Scripture in the Tradition*, 14.

79. *DBW* 3:35.

80. *DBW* 3:41.

81. *DBWE* 3:35.

rection, teaches us that God is indeed the utterly sovereign Creator God who has power even over nothingness. Theological, Christ-centered interpretation thus proceeds within a hermeneutical circle entered through our participation in Christ: "In the beginning—that is, out of freedom, out of nothing—God created heaven and earth. That is the comfort with which the Bible addresses us who are in the middle and who feel anxiety about the spurious nothingness. . . . It is the gospel, it is Christ, it is the resurrected one, who is being spoken of here. That God is in the beginning and will be in the end, that God exists in freedom over the world and that God makes this known to us—that is compassion, grace, forgiveness, and comfort."[82]

Bonhoeffer's theological interpretation does not abandon historical-critical tools, but makes them subservient to the consciously adopted hermeneutical framework of reading the Bible as "the book of the church." He clearly follows Barth in this assessment that "theological exposition takes the Bible as the book of the church and interprets it as such. This is its presupposition, and this presupposition constitutes its method; its method is a continual returning from the text (as determined by all the methods of philological and historical research) to this presupposition. That is the objectivity [*Sachlichkeit*] in the method of theological exposition. And on this objectivity alone does it base its claim to have the nature of a science [*Wissenschaft*]."[83] Bonhoeffer provides this example of the correlation between historical research and theological presupposition: "When Genesis says 'Yahweh,' it 'means' from a historical or psychological point of view, nothing but Yahweh; theologically, i.e., from the viewpoint of the church, however, it is speaking of God."[84]

It is also theological interpretation that leads to the *analogia relationis*, Bonhoeffer's well-known relational interpretation of the *imago dei*. He eschews any human ideal to inform our notion of what it means to be made in God's image and insists "that it is only from Christ that we can know about the original nature of humankind."[85] Such a christological and thus Trinitarian interpretation of God's image in us proceeds from God's own actions as revealed in Christ. In Christ, God has shown that he "wills not to be free for God's self but for humankind." The *pro-nobis* [for us] is

---

82. *DBWE* 3:36.
83. *DBWE* 3:22–23.
84. *DBWE* 3:23.
85. *DBWE* 3:62.

that God defines himself by using his freedom for the sake of humanity, entering into his own creation in order to free humanity for communion with the Creator: "It is the message of the gospel itself that God's freedom has bound itself to us, that God's free grace becomes real with us alone."[86] The freedom that marks our divine image is thus defined by God himself as freedom *for* others, a freedom defined as relationship. Thus, for Bonhoeffer, the divine image is not an inherent quality or substance, but essentially a relation and therefore not an analogia entis [analogy of being], but an *analogia relationis*: "The creatureliness of human beings is no more a quality or something at hand or an existing entity than human freedom is. It can be defined in simply no other way than in terms of the existence of human beings over-against-one-another, with-one-another, and in-dependence-upon-one-another. The 'image that is like God' is therefore no *analogia entis* . . . but *analogia relationis*."[87] For Bonhoeffer, in Genesis this relational image of interdependent, relational freedom is most clearly expressed in the "duality of man and woman."[88] In a later section, Bonhoeffer links the image of God in freedom and relational interdependence more closely to the body,[89] and in his subsequent book *Discipleship* yet more closely to the life, death, and resurrection of Jesus, in whom our true image is restored.[90]

The Psalms

Bonhoeffer's interpretation of the Psalms rests on many years of reading and praying the Psalms in order to immerse himself in the encounters of God and his people, as expressed in this "prayerbook of the Bible."[91] He does not hesitate to affirm the church's ancient tradition that "the Psalter is the prayer book of Jesus Christ in the truest sense. He prayed the Psalter, and now it has become his prayer for all times."[92] Bonhoeffer points out that Christ himself had claimed that the Psalms proclaimed his coming,[93]

---

86. *DBWE* 3:63.
87. *DBWE* 3:64–65.
88. *DBWE* 3:66.
89. *DBWE* 3:76–78.
90. *DBWE* 4:285–88.
91. For a fuller account of the Psalter's importance in Bonhoeffer's life, see Geffrey B. Kelly's "Editor's Introduction to the English Edition" in *DBWE* 5:143–54.
92. *Gemeinsames Leben: Das Gebetbuch der Bible*, *DBW* 5:39.
93. Luke 24:44; *DBW* 5:111.

and Christ deliberately identified his own actions with the Psalter when, for example, he expressed his anguish on the cross with words from Psalm 22.[94] Bonhoeffer concludes that the Psalter demonstrates most clearly the incarnational, christological nature of Scripture. If one wonders how a historically developed collection of prayers, not all of which may be attributed to David, can be both human prayers and also God's word, the answer is the incarnation. "How is it possible," asks Bonhoeffer, "that at the same time [David] a human being and Jesus Christ pray the psalter?" The answer is the god-man: "It is the incarnate [*menschgewordene*] son of God, who bore all human weakness in his own flesh, and who here pours out the heart of the entire humanity before God, who stands in our place and prays. For this reason it is the prayer of the human nature adopted by him that here comes before God. . . . it can become our prayer because it was his prayer."[95]

Without employing the actual term, Bonhoeffer practices in the Psalms once again the kind of spiritual (or typological) exegesis we observed in his interpretation of Genesis. As the anointed king of God's elect people, David is a "type of Christ" (*Vorbild auf Jesus Christus*). "What befalls David occurs for the sake of the one who is in him and who is to proceed from him, namely Jesus Christ. . . . David was a witness to Christ in his kingly office, in his life, and in his words." Bonhoeffer goes even further, however, claiming that Christ was *in* David: "And the New Testament says even more. In the Psalms of David it is precisely the promised Christ who already speaks (Heb. 2:12; 10:5) or, as is sometimes said, the Holy Spirit (Heb. 3:7). The same words that David spoke, therefore, the future Messiah spoke in him. Christ prayed along with the prayers of David or, more accurately, it is none other than Christ who prayed them in Christ's own forerunner, David."[96] Nowhere does Bonhoeffer come closer to the patristic sacramental way of finding Christ disclosed in the Old Testament.[97] Bonhoeffer works out the theological rationale for his typological reading in his Bible study on "King David." Drawing on the "shadow analogy" offered in the Epistle to the Hebrews, Bonhoeffer argues that *David* foreshadows Christ, but this shadow is cast retrospectively from the incarnation: "biblically, this means that the shadow exists

---

94. "More important than anything else is that Jesus died on the cross with the words of the Psalms on his lips" (*DBW* 5:116).

95. *DBW* 5:111–12.

96. *DBWE* 5:158–59.

97. Hans Boersma, *Scripture as Real Presence: Sacramental Exegesis in the Early Church* (Grand Rapids: Baker Academic, 2017), 13.

only because the incarnation exists, the becoming flesh of God's Word. David is the shadow of the Messiah having become flesh. The shadow falls on David from the incarnation. Thus the incarnation is understood as primordial. David is messianic king for the sake of and on the basis of the incarnation."[98] Bonhoeffer emphasizes that David's prayers are not merely subjective expressions of piety but are connected to and driven by the coming reality of the Messiah: "It is important for us that even David's prayer derives not from the personal excess of his heart but from the Christ who dwells in him."[99] Indeed, Bonhoeffer reads David typologically as foreshadowing the church by pointing toward the new humanity inaugurated by Christ's life, death, and resurrection. Thus the Psalter is "the vicariously representative prayer of Christ for his community. Now that Christ is with the Father, the new humanity, the body of Christ on earth, continues to pray his prayer to the end of time."[100] What makes the Scriptures both historical and timeless is our participation in the supratemporal reality of Christ and his priestly function as the head of his body, the church. In Christ, past and present, individual and community, are unified. As those who enjoy union with Christ, this participation makes possible that we pray the Psalter with David, with the church as a whole, and with Christ himself.[101]

Yet is this kind of interpretive approach really feasible? What happens, for example, with the imprecatory Psalms (Psalms of vengeance), or with Psalms that confess faults? How is one to hear the voice of a sinless Christ in verses such as these: "O God, you know my folly; the wrongs I have done are not hidden from you"?[102] Once again, the answer is God's humanity in Christ. Certainly, Bonhoeffer admits, "David spoke here of his own personal guilt. Christ, however, speaks of the guilt of all human beings, including that of David, which he took and bore upon himself, and for which he now suffers the wrath of the Father." This christological reading of the Psalms is possible "because the true human being Jesus Christ prays in this psalm and takes us up into his

---

98. Bonhoeffer, "König David," 192.

99. "Daß auch David . . . aus dem in ihm wohnenden Christus heraus betet" (*Gemeinsames Leben*, *DBW* 5:111). In *Prayerbook*, he repeats that David prayed the Psalms as one "who carried Christ in himself" (*DBW* 5:120).

100. *DBW* 5:40.

101. *DBW* 5:112.

102. Psalm 69:5 (ESV).

prayer."[103] Whatever the historical context of the Psalms may have been, their content is now taken up into the participatory prayer the church prays along with and in Christ. Just as personal guilt is taken up into Christ and resolved there, so the difficult matter of vengeance in God's name is transformed into forgiveness of one's enemy through Christ's mediation.[104] Bonhoeffer explains that "the psalm of vengeance leads to the cross of Jesus and to the love of God that forgives enemies. I cannot forgive the enemies of God by myself, only the crucified Christ can; and I can forgive through him. So the carrying out of vengeance becomes grace for all in Jesus Christ."[105] Making the Psalms Christ's prayers in this manner, Bonhoeffer moves through all the Psalms and their major thematic categories of (among others) creation, law, the Messiah, the church, life, suffering, and guilt, each time finding central relationships with the dynamics of the Christian life.

Bonhoeffer's "hermeneutic principle" for the exegesis of the Psalms is indeed "christological," but it is so in a concrete incarnational sense.[106] Christ is the center of the Psalms *as* the God-man, who assumed, redeemed, and perfected our humanity. As Otto Dudzus points out, this incarnational focus allows Bonhoeffer to claim "for the true humanity of Jesus the entire richness and polymorphy of humanity, of human self-expression as we encounter it in the Psalms. And conversely, for just this reason he [Bonhoeffer] claims Jesus Christ for all human beings in the entire breadth of their human condition."[107] Of course, as critics have pointed out, this approach cannot do full justice to the complexity and historicity of the Psalms, and the tension between historical particularity and christological exegesis is likely irresolvable.[108] Yet clearly Bonhoeffer's intelligent and textually sensitive interpretations that draw on Scripture as a whole are more adequate to the nature of the Bible as the book of a believing com-

---

103. *DBW* 5:121.

104. Bonhoeffer makes clear that the psalmist does not want to take vengeance into his or her own hands but asks God for retribution or vindication for unjust treatment.

105. *DBWE* 5:175.

106. Otto Dudzus, "Wer ist Jesus Christus für uns heute? Dietrich Bonhoeffers Versuch einer Antwort durch 20 Jahre Verkündigung," in *Dietrich Bonhoeffer: Predigten, Auslegungen, und Meditationen*, Band 1: 1925-1935, ed. Otto Dudzus (Gütersloh: Christian Kaiser Verlag, 1998), 13-93, 75.

107. Dudzus, "Wer ist Jesus Christus für uns heute?," 75.

108. Dudzus, "Wer ist Jesus Christus für uns heute?," 75.

munity that saw itself in continuity with Israel, especially when compared to a sterile and supposedly dispassionate historical approach.

Sermons and Meditations

Bonhoeffer's sermons and meditations on Old Testament texts are constructed on the basis of the same christological, Trinitarian framework that informs his whole theology. Based on his conviction that Christ constitutes the unifying center of the entire scriptures, he insisted on the correlative unity of the two testaments. He dismissed the German Christians' Marcionite rejection of the Old Testament, prepared in part by Harnack's scholarship, because of Bonhoeffer's belief that the same God reveals himself in both covenants; and he also denied the liberal Protestant notion that Hebrew morality was a preliminary stage to a higher Christian morality of which Jesus was the best exemplar. Bonhoeffer clearly believed that Christ is the fulfillment of the Old Testament promises, but this conviction did not entail supercessionism, i.e., that the Old Testament has become of merely historical importance. He avoids supercessionism by applying to intertestamental relations the same ultimate-penultimate dynamic that governs his Christ-centered view of reality in general. On this view, God's ultimate word of redeeming and renewing creation in Christ does not eliminate but affirms the penultimate, present world. As Bonhoeffer explains:

> Christian life is the dawn of the ultimate in me, the life of Jesus Christ in me. But it is also always life in the penultimate, waiting for the ultimate. The seriousness of Christian life lies only in the ultimate; but the penultimate also has its seriousness, which consists, to be sure, precisely in never confusing the penultimate with the ultimate and never making light of the penultimate over against the ultimate, so that the ultimate—and the penultimate—retain their seriousness.[109]

Neither in trying to live a Christian life nor in proclaiming the gospel may the believer skip over creational realities by, for example, preaching Christ to starving people without feeding them. For even though Christ alone creates faith, so that God's grace is not dependent on this "preparing of the way," we are called to respect and uphold for his sake the creation

---

109. *DBWE* 6:168.

affirmed in God's becoming human, reconciled in the cross, and renewed in the resurrection. In Christ, "the ultimate and the penultimate are closely bound to one another. From this perspective the task is to strengthen the penultimate through a stronger proclamation of the ultimate and to protect the ultimate by preserving the penultimate."[110] For Bonhoeffer, this interdependence of ultimate and penultimate realities means that cheapening one will also diminish the other.[111] To use more traditional theological vocabulary, we grasp the astonishing reality of God's grace only on the basis of nature; and nature is given its proper, albeit provisional, place only in light of grace.

For Bonhoeffer, this ultimate-penultimate tension also ties together the Old and New Testaments.[112] In no way has the Old Testament become superfluous in supercessionist fashion, nor is it to be read as an important but merely secondary source. To combat the theological anti-Semitism of his day, Bonhoeffer argues that the historical reality of the incarnate God in the Jewish Messiah Jesus ties Christianity and the Western world indissolubly to the Old Testament and Judaism. Reading the Old Testament within its Hebraic cultural context keeps open the question of who Christ is.[113] At the same time, if Christ is truly God's incarnate Word, the Christian reader will have to read the Old Testament story and its sources in light of this revelation.[114] In prison, Bonhoeffer restates his point that Christian theology remains forever dependent on God's history with Israel. Bonhoeffer did not deny, of course, that Jesus himself consciously takes up and transforms Israel's story by presenting himself as the fulfillment of God's messianic promises to his people. But Bonhoeffer did deny that a reader can take this transformation for granted, can accept it second-hand, as a settled truth. Rather, each reader has to work through, reexperience, and appropriate for himself this history to understand the full weight of Jesus's own affirmation that "salvation is from the Jews" (John 4:22). Only from the penultimate

---

110. *DBWE* 6:169.

111. *DBWE* 6:169.

112. Kuske, *Das Alte Testament*, 105–10.

113. I take this to mean that the Old and New Testaments are to be read in a penultimate-ultimate tension that takes seriously the possibility of not believing that Jesus is the Jewish messiah, while at the same time reading the Old Testament as fulfilled in the New Testament (see *DBW* 6:94–95).

114. Bonhoeffer thus avoids any simple successionism in his approach to the Old Testament. For a similar Catholic attempt, see Benedict XVI, *Verbum Domini* (Roma: Pontificium Institutum Biblicum, 2010), xx.

(the Old Testament) does the ultimate become comprehensible: "whoever wishes to be and perceive things too quickly and too directly in New Testament ways is to my mind no Christian. One cannot and must not speak the ultimate word before the penultimate."[115] Not by leaving the Old Testament behind but by staying within this story of which Christ is the culmination will we understand who Jesus is and who God is. "Only when one knows that the name of God may not be uttered may one sometimes speak of grace. . . . Only when one accepts the law as binding may one perhaps sometimes speak of grace."[116] For Bonhoeffer, past and present horizons are fused in a way that the whole of the past horizon constantly stands before us in its difference to elucidate our present understanding of God. According to Bonhoeffer, it is only by staying with Jesus within the Jewish narrative that we can ever grasp who Jesus really is.

German nationalist theology only served to solidify Bonhoeffer's insistence on the intrinsic role of Judaism in German culture, and the intrinsic role of the Old Testament for understanding the New Testament. Bonhoeffer openly attacks the German Christians' theological anti-Semitism when he writes, "Western history is by God's will inextricably bound up with the people of Israel, not just genetically but in an honest, unceasing encounter. The Jews keep open the question of Christ. . . . Driving out the Jew(s) from the West must result in driving out Jesus Christ with them, for Christ was a Jew."[117]

Conclusion

Bonhoeffer's Old Testament hermeneutic is christological, incarnational, and therefore historical. Bonhoeffer had a certain affinity for Rudolf Bultmann's demythologization program, because Bultmann clearly faced the hermeneutical problem of fusing the ancient biblical and cultural past with modern present horizons. Yet Bultmann's program, Bonhoeffer had complained, "did not go far enough."[118] Bonhoeffer's own biblical interpretation demonstrates that Bultmann's mistake was to bypass the historical dimension of the incarnate Christ, who is the midpoint that holds together ultimate and penultimate dimensions of both the world and the two tes-

---

115. *DBWE* 8:213.
116. *DBWE* 8:213.
117. *DBWE* 6:105.
118. *DBW* 8:414.

taments. The kind of incarnational typology Bonhoeffer employs in his readings deepens during his imprisonment and opens up a new appreciation for the Old Testament, which he read "two and a half times through" in prison.[119] He began to see how God is present in the midst of life, not when people are weak, uncertain, and looking for metaphysical crutches to lean on, but in the fullness of their abilities, in the enjoyment of life and their freedom as creatures, including their freedom to sin.

Bonhoeffer realized that the difference between the Old and New Testament is not that the resurrection removes us from our enjoyment of creation and responsibility for God's world, but rather liberates us to experience life in a new way: "This-worldliness must not be abolished ahead of its time; on this, NT and OT are united."[120] Again the penultimate-ultimate logic emerges in Bonhoeffer's insistence that "only when one loves life and the earth so much that with it everything seems to be lost and at its end may one believe in the resurrection of the dead and a new world."[121] The Old Testament now becomes for Bonhoeffer an endless source for capturing the fullness and multidimensionality of earthly life. All these stories are to be read from Christ as the midpoint.[122] Bonhoeffer essentially treats the Old Testament as wisdom literature for a truly human life in the light of Christ. Indeed, in his prison poems, we begin to see that Old Testament images help Bonhoeffer describe and confront his own situation. In his poem "Jonah," the prophet becomes an emblem of Bonhoeffer's own sense of vicarious responsibility, standing in for others and accepting the guilt for his political activities.[123] Jonah was cast into the troubled sea, which then ceased to boil. Bonhoeffer cast himself on the mercy of Christ, thus once again showing how Old Testament imagery points to the incarnate, crucified, and risen Christ. The Old Testament remained the book of the Christ and the book of the church.

---

119. *DBWE* 8:181.

120. *DBWE* 8:448.

121. *DBWE* 8:213.

122. Martin Hohmann, *Die Korrelation von Altem und Neuem Bund* (Berlin: Evangelische Verlagsanstalt, 1978), 104–6.

123. See Stephen J. Plant's interpretation of this poem in "Guilt and Promise in Bonhoeffer's Jonah," in his *Taking Stock of Bonhoeffer: Studies in Biblical Interpretation and Ethics* (Burlington, VT: Ashgate, 2015), 59–70.

Bibliography

Alexander, Denis. "How Does a BioLogos Model Need to Address the Theological Issues Associated with an Adam Who Was Not the Sole Genetic Progenitor of Humankind?" Available at http://biologos.org/uploads/projects/alexander_white_paper.pdf.

Allison, Dale C. *James: A Critical and Exegetical Commentary*. ICC. London: T. & T. Clark Bloomsbury, 2013.

Anatolios, Khaled. *Retrieving Nicaea: The Development and Meaning of Trinitarian Doctrine*. Grand Rapids: Baker Academic, 2011.

Andrews, James A. *Hermeneutics and the Church: In Dialogue with Augustine*. Notre Dame: University of Notre Dame Press, 2012.

Aquinas, Thomas. *Summa Theologica*. Christian Classics. Notre Dame: Ave Maria, 1981.

———. *Super epistolam ad Romanos lectura*. Rome: Marietti, 1953.

Asprey, Christopher. "The Universal Church and the Ecumenical Movement." Pages 3–16 in *Ecumenism Today: The Universal Church in the 21st Century*. Edited by Francesca Aran Murphy and Christopher Asprey. Burlington, VT: Ashgate, 2008.

Augustine. *Confessions*. Translated by Henry Chadwick. Oxford: Oxford University Press, 1991.

———. *On Christian Doctrine*. Translated and introduced by D. W. Robertson. New York: Macmillan, 1987.

———. *On Christian Teaching*. Translated and edited by R. P. H. Green. Oxford World's Classics. Oxford: Oxford University Press, 1997.

Aune, David E. *Revelation 6–16*. WBC 52B. Nashville: Thomas Nelson, 1998.

Ayres, Lewis. *Nicaea and Its Legacy: An Approach to Fourth-Century Trinitarian Theology*. Oxford: Oxford University Press, 2004.

———. "'There's Fire in That Rain': On Reading the Letter and Reading Allegorically." *Modern Theology* 28:4 (2012): 616–34.

Ballentine, Debra S. *The Conflict Myth and the Biblical Tradition*. Oxford: Oxford University Press, 2015.

Barbour, Jennie. *The Story of Israel in the Book of Qohelet: Ecclesiastes as Cultural Mem-*

ory. Oxford Theology and Religion Monographs. Oxford: Oxford University Press, 2012.

Barclay, John M. G., and Simon J. Gathercole, eds. *Divine and Human Agency in Paul and His Cultural Environment.* LNTS 335. London: T. & T. Clark, 2006.

Barth, Karl. *Church Dogmatics.* Edited by G. W. Bromiley and T. F. Torrance. Translated by G. W. Bromiley et al. 1st paperback edition, 4 vols. in 14. Edinburgh: T. & T. Clark, 2004.

———. "Entwürfe Zum Vorwort." Pages 581–85 in *Der Römerbrief.* Erste Fassung, 1919. Edited by Karl Schmidt. Zürich: Theologischer Verlag, 1985.

———. *The Epistle to the Romans.* Translated by Edwyn C. Hoskyns. Oxford: Oxford University Press, 1933.

———. "Vorwort zur fünften Auflage." Pages 35–39 in *Der Römerbrief.* Zweite Fassung, 1922. Edited by Cornelis van der Kooi and Katja Tolstaja. Zürich: Theologischer Verlag Zürich, 2010.

Bartholomew, Craig G. *Ecclesiastes.* BCOTWP. Grand Rapids: Baker Academic, 2009.

———. *Introducing Biblical Hermeneutics: A Comprehensive Framework for Hearing God in Scripture.* Grand Rapids: Baker Academic, 2015.

Bartholomew, Craig G., and Bruce Ashford. *The Doctrine of Creation.* Downers Grove, IL: IVP Academic, forthcoming in 2019.

Bartholomew, Craig G., and Heath A. Thomas, eds. *A Manifesto for Theological Interpretation.* Grand Rapids: Baker Academic, 2016.

Barton, John. "Historical-critical Approaches." Pages 9–20 in *The Cambridge Companion to Biblical Interpretation.* Edited by John Barton. Cambridge: Cambridge University Press, 1998.

———. *The Nature of Biblical Criticism.* Louisville: Westminster John Knox, 2007.

Batto, Bernard F. "Kampf and Chaos: The Combat Myth in Israelite Tradition Revisited." Pages 217–36 in *Creation and Chaos: A Reconsideration of Hermann Gunkel's Chaoskampf Hypothesis.* Edited by JoAnn Scurlock and Richard H. Beal. Winona Lake, IN: Eisenbrauns, 2013.

Bauckham, Richard. "James and Jesus." Pages 100–137 in *The Brother of Jesus: James the Just and His Mission.* Edited by Bruce Chilton and Jacob Neusner. Louisville: Westminster John Knox, 2001.

———, ed. *The Gospels for All Christians: Rethinking the Gospel Audiences.* Grand Rapids: Eerdmans, 1998.

Ben-Daniel, John. "Towards the Mystical Interpretation of Revelation 12." *Revue biblique* 111.4 (2007): 594–614.

Benedict XVI. *Verbum Domini.* Roma: Pontificium Institutum Biblicum, 2010.

Berger, Klaus. "Rhetorical Criticism, New Form Criticism, and New Testament Hermeneutics." Pages 390–96 in *Rhetoric and the New Testament: Essays from the 1992 Heidelberg Conference.* Edited by Stanley E. Porter and Thomas H. Ulbricht. JSNTSup 90. Sheffield: Sheffield Academic, 1993.

Bethge, Eberhard. *Dietrich Bonhoeffer: A Biography.* Translated by Eric Mosbacher. Minneapolis: Fortress, 2004.

Blount, Brian K. *Revelation: A Commentary.* Louisville: Westminster John Knox, 2009.

Bockmuehl, Markus. "Bible versus Theology: Is 'Theological Interpretation' the Answer?" *Nova et Vetera* 9.1 (2011): 27–47.

Boersma, Hans. "Joshua as Sacrament: Spiritual Interpretation in Origen." *Crux* 48.3 (2012): 23–40.

———. *Nouvelle Théologie and Sacramental Ontology: A Return to Mystery.* Oxford: Oxford University Press, 2009.

———. *Sacramental Preaching: Sermons on the Hidden Presence of Christ.* Grand Rapids: Baker Academic, 2016.

———. *Scripture as Real Presence: Sacramental Exegesis in the Early Church.* Grand Rapids: Baker Academic, 2017.

Bolman, Lee G., and Terrence E. Deal. *Reframing Organizations: Artistry, Choice, and Leadership.* 5th ed. San Francisco: Jossey-Bass, 2013.

Bonhoeffer, Dietrich. *Creation and Fall: A Theological Exposition of Genesis 1–3. DBWE 3.* Edited by John W. de Gruchy. Translated by Douglas Stephen Bax. Minneapolis: Fortress, 1997.

———. *Dietrich Bonhoeffer Werke (DBW).* 17 vols. Edited by Eberhard Bethge et al. Munich: Chr. Kaiser/Gütersloher Verlagshaus, 1986–99.

———. *Dietrich Bonhoeffer Works*, English edition *(DBWE)*. 17 vols. Edited by Victoria J. Barnett, Wayne Whitson Floyd Jr., and Barbara Wojhoski. Minneapolis: Fortress, 1996–2015.

———. "König David." Pages 189–230 in *Dietrich Bonhoeffer: Predigten, Auslegungen, und Meditationen*, Band 2: 1935–45. Edited by Otto Dudzus. Gütersloh: Christian Kaiser Verlag, 1998.

Bowald, Mark Alan. "The Character of Theological Interpretation." *International Journal of Systematic Theology* 12.2 (2010): 162–83.

———. *Rendering the Word in Theological Hermeneutics: Mapping Divine and Human Agency.* Burlington, VT: Ashgate, 2007.

Bowdler, Elizabeth Stuart. *Practical Observations on the Revelation of St. John*: Written in the Year 1775. Bath: printed by R. Cruttwell; and sold by G. G. and J. Robinson; and J. Hatchard, London, 1800.

Brown, Raymond E. *The Epistles of John.* AB 30. Garden City, NY: Doubleday, 1982.

Brueggemann, Walter. *Genesis.* IBC. Louisville: Westminster John Knox, 1982.

Burgess, Joseph A., and Jeffrey Gros, eds. *Growing Consensus: Church Dialogues in the United States, 1962–1991.* Ecumenical Documents 5. Mahwah, NJ: Paulist, 1995.

Burnett, Richard E. "Historical Criticism." Pages 290–93 in *Dictionary for Theological Interpretation of the Bible.* Edited by Kevin J. Vanhoozer, Craig G. Bartholomew, Daniel J. Treier, and N. T. Wright. Grand Rapids: Baker Academic, 2005.

Buschart, W. David. *Exploring Protestant Traditions: An Invitation to Theological Hospitality.* Downers Grove, IL: IVP Academic, 2006.

Calvin, John. *Articles by the Theological Faculty of Paris, with Antidotes.* In *Tracts Relating to the Reformation.* Translated by Henry Beveridge. Edinburgh: Calvin Translation Society, 1844.

———. *The Bondage and Liberation of the Will: A Defense of the Orthodox Doctrine of Human Choice against Pighius.* Edited by A. N. S. Lane. Translated by G. I. Davies.

Texts and Studies in Reformation and Post-Reformation Thought. Grand Rapids: Baker, 1996.

———. *Commentarius in Epistolam Pauli ad Romanos*. Edited by T. H. L. Parker. Leiden: Brill, 1981.

———. *Institutes of the Christian Religion*. LCC. Philadelphia: Westminster, 1960.

———. *Ioannis Calvini Opera quae supersunt omnia*, 59 vols. Edited by J. Baum et al. Corpus Reformatorum, vols. 29–87. Brunswick: C.A. Schwetschke & Son, 1863–1900.

———. *Opera Selecta*, vol. 4. *Institutionis Christianae religionis 1559, librum III continens*. Edited by Petrus Barth and Guilelmus Niesl. Eugene, OR: Wipf and Stock, 2010.

Carlson, Richard F., and Tremper Longman III. *Science, Creation and the Bible: Reconciling Rival Theories of Origins*. Downers Grove, IL: IVP Academic, 2010.

Carson, D. A. "Theological Interpretation of Scripture: Yes, But . . ." Pages 187–207 in *Theological Commentary: Evangelical Perspectives*. Edited by R. Michael Allen. New York: T. & T. Clark, 2011.

Castelo, Daniel, and Robert W. Wall. *The Marks of Scripture: Rethinking the Nature of the Bible*. Grand Rapids: Baker Academic, forthcoming in 2019.

———. "Scripture and the Church: A Précis for an Alternative Analogy." *Journal of Theological Interpretation* 5.2 (2011): 197–210.

Childs, Brevard S. *The Church's Guide for Reading Paul: The Canonical Shaping of the Pauline Corpus*. Grand Rapids: Eerdmans, 2008.

———. *Myth and Reality in the Old Testament*. SBT, First Series, No. 27. Eugene, OR: Wipf and Stock, 2009. Orig., London: SCM, 1962.

Clifford, Richard J. *Creation Accounts in the Ancient Near East and in the Bible*. CBQMS 26. Washington, DC: The Catholic Biblical Association of America, 1994.

Collins, Adela Yarbro. *The Combat Myth in the Book of Revelation*. Missoula, MT: Scholars Press, 1976.

———, ed. *Early Christian Apocalypticism: Genre and Social Setting*. Semeia 36. Atlanta: Scholars Press, 1986.

Collins, Francis S. *The Language of God: A Scientist Presents Evidence for Belief*. New York: Free Press, 2006.

Collins, John J. *The Bible after Babel: Historical Criticism in a Postmodern Age*. Grand Rapids: Eerdmans, 2005.

———, ed. *Apocalypse: The Morphology of a Genre*. Semeia 14. Missoula, MT: Scholars Press, 1979.

Couenhoven, Jesse. "St. Augustine's Doctrine of Original Sin." *Augustinian Studies* 36.2 (2005): 359–96.

Crenshaw, James L. *Ecclesiastes: A Commentary*. OTL. London: SCM, 1988.

———. *Qoheleth: The Ironic Wink*. Columbia, SC: University of South Carolina Press, 2013.

Dahood, Mitchell. *Psalms II: 51–100*. AB 17. New York: Doubleday, 1968.

Daly, Robert J. "Introduction." Pages 1–26 in *Origen, Treatise on the Passover* and *Dialogue of Origen with Heraclides and His Fellow Bishops on the Father, the Son, and the Soul*. Translated and edited by Robert J. Daly. ACW 54. New York: Paulist, 1992.

Daniélou, Jean. *From Shadows to Reality: Studies in the Biblical Typology of the Fathers.* Translated by Wulstan Hibberd. London: Burns & Oates, 1960.

Davids, Peter H. "Catholic Epistles." Online at *Oxford Bibliographies.* Oxford University Press, 2015. Available at http://www.oxfordbibliographies.com/view/document/obo-9780195393361/obo-9780195393361–0018.xml.

Dawkins, Richard. *The God Delusion.* New York: Bantam, 2006; Boston: Mariner, 2008.

———. *The Greatest Show on Earth: The Evidence for Evolution.* New York: Free Press, 2009.

Dawson, John David. *Christian Figural Reading and the Fashioning of Identity.* Berkeley: University of California Press, 2002.

De Lubac, Henri. *Medieval Exegesis: The Four Senses of Scripture.* Vol. 2. Translated by E. M. Macierowski. Grand Rapids: Eerdmans, 2000.

———. *Scripture in the Tradition.* New York: Crossroad, 2000.

———. "Typology and Allegorization." Pages 129–64 in *Theological Fragments.* Translated by Rebecca Howell Balinski. San Francisco: Ignatius, 1989.

deSilva, David A. *Seeing Things John's Way: The Rhetoric of the Book of Revelation.* Louisville: Westminster John Knox, 2009.

DiMattei, Steven. *Genesis 1 and the Creationism Debate: Being Honest to the Text, Its Author, and His Beliefs.* Eugene, OR: Wipf and Stock, 2016.

Dudzus, Otto. "Wer ist Jesus Christus für uns heute? Dietrich Bonhoeffers Versuch einer Antwort durch 20 Jahre Verkündigung." Pages 13–93 in *Dietrich Bonhoeffer: Predigten, Auslegungen, und Meditationen,* Band 1: 1925–1935. Edited by Otto Dudzus. Gütersloh: Christian Kaiser Verlag, 1998.

Dunn, James D. G. *Romans.* 2 vols. WBC 38A–B. Dallas: Word, 1988.

East, Brad. "The Hermeneutics of Theological Interpretation: Holy Scripture, Biblical Scholarship, and Historical Criticism." *International Journal of Systematic Theology* 19.1 (2017): 30–52.

Enns, Peter. *The Evolution of Adam: What the Bible Does and Doesn't Say about Human Origins.* Grand Rapids: Brazos, 2012.

———. *Inspiration and Incarnation: Evangelicals and the Problem of the Old Testament.* 2nd ed. Grand Rapids: Brazos, 2015.

———. *The Sin of Certainty: Why God Desires Our Trust More Than Our "Correct" Beliefs.* San Francisco: HarperOne, 2016.

———. "Spinning Our Wheels: A Response to a Review of 'The Evolution of Adam' (with apologies to those with a 500 word, 1.6 minute internet attention span)." Available at http://www.peteenns.com/spinning-our-wheels-a-response-to-a-review-of-the-evolution-of-adam-with-apologies-to-those-with-a-500-word-1-6-minute-internet-attention-span/.

Evans, G. R. *The Reception of the Faith: Reinterpreting the Gospel for Today.* London: SPCK, 1997.

Evans, Vyvyan, and Melanie Green. *Cognitive Linguistics: An Introduction.* Edinburgh: Edinburgh University Press, 2006.

Falk, Darrell R. *Coming to Peace with Science: Bridging the Worlds Between Faith and Biology.* Downers Grove, IL: IVP Academic, 2004.

Farthing, John L. *Thomas Aquinas and Gabriel Biel: Interpretations of St. Thomas Aquinas in German Nominalism on the Eve of the Reformation.* Durham, NC: Duke University Press, 1988.

Fishbane, Michael. *Biblical Interpretation in Ancient Israel.* Oxford: Clarendon, 1985.

———. "Jeremiah iv 23–26 and Job iii 3–13: A Recovered Use of the Creation Pattern." *Vetus Testamentum* 21.2 (1971): 151–67.

Flint, Thomas P. "Two Accounts of Providence." Pages 147–81 in *Divine and Human Action: Essays in the Metaphysics of Theism.* Edited by Thomas V. Morris. Ithaca, NY: Cornell University Press, 1988.

Ford, J. Massyngberde. *Revelation.* AB 38. Garden City, NY: Doubleday, 1975.

Fowl, Stephen E. *Engaging Scripture: A Model for Theological Interpretation.* Oxford: Blackwell, 1998.

———. "Historical Criticism, Theological Interpretation, and the Ends of the Christian Life." Pages 173–86 in *Conception, Reception, and the Spirit: Essays in Honor of Andrew T. Lincoln.* Edited by J. Gordon McConville and Lloyd K. Pietersen. Eugene, OR: Cascade, 2015.

———. "Scripture." Pages 345–61 in *The Oxford Handbook of Systematic Theology.* Edited by John Webster, Kathryn Tanner, and Iain Torrance. Oxford: Oxford University Press, 2007.

———. "Theological Interpretation and Its Future." *Anglican Theological Review* 99.4 (2017): 671–90.

———. *Theological Interpretation of Scripture.* Eugene, OR: Cascade, 2009.

Fox, Michael V. *Ecclesiastes.* JPS Bible Commentary. Philadelphia: Jewish Publication Society, 2004.

———. "Frame-Narrative and Composition in the Book of Qohelet." *Hebrew Union College Annual* 48 (1977): 83–106.

———. *A Time to Tear Down and a Time to Build Up: A Rereading of Ecclesiastes.* Grand Rapids: Eerdmans, 1999.

Frazer, James G. *Adonis, Attis, Osiris: Studies in the History of Oriental Religion.* London: Macmillan, 1906.

Frye, Northrop. "Historical Criticism: Theory of Modes." Pages 33–67 in *Anatomy of Criticism: Four Essays.* Princeton: Princeton University Press, 1969.

Ganoczy, Alexander. *The Young Calvin.* Translated by David Foxgrover and Wade Provo. Philadelphia: Westminster, 1987.

Giberson, Karl W., and Francis S. Collins. *The Language of Science and Faith: Straight Answers to Genuine Questions.* Downers Grove, IL: InterVarsity, 2011.

Goodacre, Mark. *The Case Against Q: Studies in Markan Priority and the Synoptic Problem.* Harrisburg, PA: Trinity Press International, 2002.

Gorman, Michael J. *Elements of Biblical Exegesis: A Basic Guide for Students and Ministers.* Rev. and exp. ed. Grand Rapids: Baker Academic, 2009.

Green, Joel B. "Embodying the Gospel: Two Exemplary Practices." *Journal of Spiritual Formation and Soul Care* 7.1 (2014): 11–21.

———. *Practicing Theological Interpretation: Engaging Biblical Texts for Faith and Formation.* Grand Rapids: Baker Academic, 2011.

———. "Re-thinking 'History' for Theological Interpretation." *Journal of Theological Interpretation* 5.2 (2011): 159–73.

———. *Seized by Truth: Reading the Bible as Scripture.* Nashville: Abingdon, 2007.

Gregory, Andrew. *Ancient Greek Cosmogony.* London: Bristol Classical, 2011.

Gregory, Andrew F., and C. Kavin Rowe, eds. *Rethinking the Unity and Reception of Luke and Acts.* Columbia, SC: University of South Carolina Press, 2010.

Gregory of Nyssa. *Gregory of Nyssa: Commentary on Ecclesiastes, An English Version with Supporting Studies.* Edited by Stuart George Hall. New York: Walter de Gruyter, 1993.

Gros, Jeffrey, Harding Meyer, and William G. Rusch. *Growth in Agreement II: Reports and Agreed Statements of Ecumenical Conversations on a World Level, 1982–1998.* Grand Rapids: Eerdmans, 2000.

Gros, Jeffrey, Thomas F. Best, and Lorelei F. Fuchs. *Growth in Agreement III: International Dialogue Texts and Agreed Statements, 1998–2005.* Geneva: WCC; Grand Rapids: Eerdmans, 2007.

Gunkel, Hermann. *Creation and Chaos in the Primeval Era and the Eschaton: A Religio-Historical Study of Genesis 1 and Revelation 12.* Translated by K. William Whitney Jr. The Biblical Resource Series. Grand Rapids: Eerdmans, 2006.

———. *The Legends of Genesis: The Biblical Saga and History.* Translated by W. H. Carruth. Chicago: Open Court, 1901.

Güttgemanns, Erhardt. *Offene Fragen zur Formgeschichte des Evangeliums: eine methodologische Skizze der Grundlagenproblematik der Form- und Redaktionsgeschichte.* München: C. Kaiser Verlag, 1970; ET *Candid Questions Concerning Gospel Form Criticism: A Methodological Sketch of the Fundamental Problematics of Form and Redaction Criticism.* Translated by William G. Doty. PTMS 26. Pittsburgh: Pickwick, 1979.

Hainsworth, John. "The Force of the Mystery: Anamnesis and Exegesis in Melito's *Peri Pascha.*" *St. Vladimir's Theological Quarterly* 46.2–3 (2002): 107–46.

Hall, Christopher A. "Creedal Hermeneutics: How the Creeds Can Help Us Read the Bible." Pages 109–26 in *Serving God's Community: Studies in Honor of W. Ward Gasque.* Edited by Susan S. Phillips and Soo-Inn Tann. Vancouver: Regent College Publishing; Singapore: Graceworks, 2014.

Halverson, James L. *Peter Aureol on Predestination: A Challenge to Late Medieval Thought.* Studies in the History of Christian Thought 83. Leiden: Brill, 1988.

Hamilton, Victor P. *The Book of Genesis: Chapters 1–17.* NICOT. Grand Rapids: Eerdmans, 1990.

Harlow, Daniel C. "After Adam: Reading Genesis in an Age of Evolutionary Science." *Perspectives on Science and Christian Faith* 62.3 (2010): 179–95.

———. "Creation According to Genesis: Literary Genre, Cultural Context, Theological Truth." *Christian Scholars Review* 37.2 (2008): 163–98.

Harrington, Wilfrid J., O.P. *Revelation.* SP 16. Collegeville, MN: Liturgical Press, 1993.

Harrisville, Roy A., and Walter Sundberg. *The Bible in Modern Culture: Theology and Historical-Critical Method from Spinoza to Käsemann.* 2nd ed. Grand Rapids: Eerdmans, 2002.

Hauser, Alan J., and Duane F. Watson, eds. *A History of Biblical Interpretation*, vol. 3: *The Enlightenment through the Nineteenth Century*. Grand Rapids: Eerdmans, 2017.

Hays, Richard B. "Reading the Bible with the Eyes of Faith: The Practice of Theological Exegesis." *Journal of Theological Interpretation* 1.1 (2007): 5–21.

Hendel, Ron S. "Farewell to SBL: Faith and Reason in Biblical Studies." *Biblical Archaeology Review* 36.4 (2010): 70–74.

Hohmann, Martin. *Die Korrelation von Altem und Neuem Bund*. Berlin: Evangelische Verlagsanstalt, 1978.

Humphrey, Edith M. *The Ladies and the Cities: Transformation and Apocalyptic Identity in Joseph and Aseneth, 4 Ezra, the Apocalypse and The Shepherd of Hermas*. JSPSup 17. Sheffield Academic, 1995.

———. *Scripture and Tradition: What the Bible Really Says*. Grand Rapids: Baker Academic, 2013.

———. "Which Way Is Up? Revival, Resurrection, Assumption, and Ascension in the Rhetoric of Paul and John the Seer." Pages 328–39 in *Essays in Honour of Frederik Wisse: Scholar, Churchman, Mentor*. Edited by Warren Kappeler. ARC: *The Journal of the Faculty of Religious Studies*, McGill University, Volume 33, 2005.

Irons, Lee, and Meredith G. Kline. "The Framework View." Pages 217–56 in *The Genesis Debate: Three Views on the Days of Creation*. Edited by David G. Hagopian. Mission Viejo, CA: Crux, 2001.

Janz, Denis R. *Luther and Late Medieval Thomism: A Study in Theological Anthropology*. Waterloo, ON: Wilfrid Laurier University Press, 1983.

Jenkins, Allan K., and Patrick Preston. *Biblical Scholarship and the Church: A Sixteenth-Century Crisis of Authority*. Aldershot: Ashgate, 2007.

Jerome. *St. Jerome: Commentary on Ecclesiastes*. Translated by Richard J. Goodrich and David Miller. ACW 66. New York: Newman, 2012.

Josephus. *Antiquities. The Works of Flavius Josephus*. Translated by William Whiston. 1737. Available at http://www.sacred-texts.com/jud/josephus/.

Juel, Donald. *Messianic Exegesis: Christological Interpretation of the Old Testament in Early Christianity*. Philadelphia: Fortress, 1987.

Kaufmann, Yehezkel. *The Religion of Israel*. New York: Schocken, 1972.

Kiddle, Martin. *The Revelation of St. John*. London: Hodder & Stoughton, 1940.

Kirk, J. R. Daniel. *Unlocking Romans: Resurrection and the Justification of God*. Grand Rapids: Eerdmans, 2008.

Klink, Edward, III, ed. *The Audience of the Gospels: The Origin and Function of the Gospels in Early Christianity*. LNTS 353. Edinburgh: T. & T. Clark, 2010.

Kloppenborg, John S. *The Formation of Q: Trajectories in Ancient Wisdom Collections*. Philadelphia: Fortress, 1987.

Knapp, Henry M. "Melito's Use of Scripture in *Peri Pascha*: Second-Century Typology." *Vigiliae Christianae* 54.4 (2000): 343–74.

Knobel, Peter S. *The Targum of Qohelet: Translated, with a Critical Introduction, Apparatus, and Notes*. In *The Aramaic Bible*, vol. 15: *The Targums*. Collegeville, MN: Liturgical Press, 1991.

Koch, Klaus. *The Rediscovery of Apocalyptic: A Polemical Work on a Neglected Area of*

Biblical Studies and Its Damaging Effect on Theology and Philosophy. Translated by Margaret Kohl. SBT 2.22. London: SCM, 1972.

Krodel, Gerhard A. *Revelation.* ACNT. Minneapolis: Augsburg Fortress, 1989.

Kugel, James L. *Traditions of the Bible: A Guide to the Bible as It Was at the Start of the Common Era.* Cambridge: Harvard University Press, 1998.

Kugel, James L., and Rowan A. Greer. *Early Biblical Interpretation.* Philadelphia: Westminster, 1986.

Kuske, Martin. *Das Alte Testament als Buch von Christus: Dietrich Bonhoeffers Wertung und Auslegung des Alten Testaments.* Göttingen: Vandenhoeck and Ruprecht, 1971.

Lamoureux, Denis O. *Evolutionary Creation: A Christian Approach to Evolution.* Eugene, OR: Wipf and Stock, 2008.

———. *I Love Jesus & I Accept Evolution.* Eugene, OR: Wipf and Stock, 2009.

Lane, A. N. S. "Calvin and the Fathers in *Bondage and Liberation of the Will.*" Pages 67–96 in *Calvinus Sincerioris Religionis Vindex*: *Calvin as Protector of the Purer Religion.* Edited by Wilhelm H. Neuser and Brian G. Armstrong. Kirksville, MO: Sixteenth-Century Journal Publishers, 1997.

———. *Justification by Faith in Catholic-Evangelical Dialogue: An Evangelical Assessment.* London: T. & T. Clark, 2002.

Lauha, A. "Omnia Vanitas: Die Bedeutung von hbl bei Kohelet." Pages 19–25 in *Glaube und Gerechtigkeit: In Memoriam Rafael Gyllenberg.* Edited by Jarmo Kiilunen et al. SFEG 38. Helsinki: Vammalan Kijapaino Oy, 1983.

LaVallee, Armand Aime. "Calvin's Criticism of Scholastic Theology." PhD diss., Harvard University, 1967.

Legaspi, Michael C. *The Death of Scripture and the Rise of Biblical Studies.* Oxford Studies in Historical Theology. New York: Oxford University Press, 2010.

Leithart, Peter J. *Deep Exegesis: The Mystery of Reading Scripture.* Waco, TX: Baylor University Press, 2009.

Levenson, Jon. *Creation and the Persistence of Evil: The Jewish Drama of Divine Omnipotence.* 2nd ed. Princeton: Princeton University Press, 1994.

Levering, Matthew. *Engaging the Doctrine of Revelation: The Mediation of the Gospel through Church and Scripture.* Grand Rapids: Baker Academic, 2014.

———. "Linear and Participatory History: Augustine's City of God." *Journal of Theological Interpretation* 5.2 (2011): 175–96.

———. *Participatory Biblical Exegesis: A Theology of Biblical Interpretation.* Notre Dame: University of Notre Dame Press, 2008.

———. "Readings on the Rock: Typological Exegesis in Contemporary Scholarship." *Modern Theology* 28.4 (2012): 707–31.

Lewis, C. S. "Introduction." Pages vii–viii in *Letters to Young Churches: A Translation of the New Testament Epistles.* Translated by J. B. Phillips. New York: Macmillan, 1953.

———. *Till We Have Faces: A Myth Retold.* New York: Harcourt, Brace & Company, 1984.

Lockett, Darian R. *An Introduction to the Catholic Epistles.* London: T. & T. Clark Bloomsbury, 2012.

———. *Letters from the Pillar Apostles: The Formation of the Catholic Epistles as a Canonical Collection.* Eugene, OR: Pickwick, 2016.

Lohfink, Norbert. *Qoheleth*. Translated by Sean McEvenue. CC. Minneapolis: Fortress, 2003.

Long, Steve A. *Natura Pura: On the Recovery of Nature in the Doctrine of Grace*. Minneapolis: Fortress, 2010.

Longenecker, Richard N. *Biblical Exegesis in the Apostolic Period*. 2nd ed. Grand Rapids: Eerdmans, 1999.

Longman, Tremper, III. *The Book of Ecclesiastes*. NICOT. Grand Rapids: Eerdmans, 1998.

Lord, Albert B. *The Singer of Tales*. Cambridge: Harvard University Press, 1964.

Luther, Martin. "Prefaces to the Old Testament." Pages 263–64 in *Luther's Works*, vol. 35. American ed. Edited by E. Theodore Bachman. Philadelphia: Fortress, 1960.

Madueme, Hans. "Some Reflections on Enns and *The Evolution of Adam*: A Review Essay." *Themelios* 35.2 (2012): 275–86. Also available at http://themelios.thegospel coalition.org/article/some-reflections-on-enns-and-the-evolution-of-adam-a -review-essay.

Madueme, Hans, and Michael Reeves, eds. *Adam, the Fall, and Original Sin: Theological, Biblical, and Scientific Perspectives*. Grand Rapids: Baker Academic, 2014.

Maier, Harry O. *Apocalypse Recalled: The Book of Revelation after Christendom*. Minneapolis: Fortress, 2002.

Mangina, Joseph L. *Revelation*. Brazos Theological Commentary on the Bible. Grand Rapids: Brazos, 2010.

Martens, Peter W. "Revisiting the Allegory/Typology Distinction: The Case of Origen." *Journal of Early Christian Studies* 16.3 (2008): 283–317.

Melito of Sardis. *On Pascha and Fragments*. Translated and edited by Stuart George Hall. Oxford: Clarendon, 1979.

———. *On Pascha: With the Fragments of Melito and Other Material Related to the Quartodecimans*. Translated and edited by Alistair Stewart-Sykes. Popular Patristic Series 20. Crestwood, NY: St. Vladimir's Seminary Press, 2001.

Merrick, J., and Stephen M. Garrett, eds. *Five Views on Biblical Inerrancy*. Grand Rapids: Zondervan, 2013.

Mettepenningen, Jürgen. *Nouvelle Théologie—New Theology: Inheritor of Modernism, Precursor of Vatican II*. London: T. & T. Clark, 2010.

Miller, Keith B., ed. *Perspectives on an Evolving Creation*. Grand Rapids: Eerdmans, 2003.

Mitchell, Margaret M. "Patristic Counter-Evidence to the Claim that 'the Gospels Were Written for All Christians.'" *New Testament Studies* 51.1 (2005): 36–79.

Moberly, R. W. L. "Biblical Criticism and Religious Belief." *Journal of Theological Interpretation* 2.1 (2008): 71–100.

———. "'Interpret the Bible Like Any Other Book'? Requiem for an Axiom." *Journal of Theological Interpretation* 4.1 (2010): 91–110.

———. "What Is Theological Interpretation of Scripture?" *Journal of Theological Interpretation* 3.2 (2009): 161–78.

Moessner, David P. "Luke's 'Witness of Witnesses': Paul as Definer and Defender of the Tradition of the Apostles—'from the beginning.'" Pages 117–47 in *Paul and the Heritage of Israel: Paul's Claim upon Israel's Legacy in Luke and Acts in the Light of the Pauline Letters*. Edited by David P. Moessner et al. LNTS 452. London: T. & T. Clark Bloomsbury, 2012.

Mounce, Robert H. *The Book of Revelation*. Rev. ed. NICNT. Grand Rapids: Eerdmans, 1998.

Moyise, Steve. *Paul and Scripture*. London: SPCK, 2010.

Muller, Richard A. "Demoting Calvin: The Issue of Calvin and the Reformed Tradition." Pages 3–17 in *John Calvin, Myth and Reality: Images and Impact of Geneva's Reformer*. Papers of the 2009 Calvin Studies Society Colloquium. Edited by Amy Nelson Burnett. Eugene, OR: Cascade, 2011.

———. "Scholasticism in Calvin: Relation and Disjunction." Pages 247–66 in *Calvinus Sincerioris Religionis Vindex*: *Calvin as Protector of the Purer Religion*. Edited by Wilhelm H. Neuser and Brian G. Armstrong. Kirksville, MO: Sixteenth-Century Journal Publishers, 1997.

———. *The Unaccommodated Calvin*: *Studies in the Foundation of a Theological Tradition*. Oxford: Oxford University Press, 2000.

Murphy, Roland E. *Ecclesiastes*. WBC 23A. Dallas: Word, 1992.

Mussner, Franz. *Der Jakobusbrief*. Freiburg: Verlag Herder, 1964.

Nelson, R. David, and Charles Raith II. *Ecumenism: A Guide for the Perplexed*. London: Continuum, 2017.

Newman, John Henry. *An Essay on the Development of Doctrine*. Notre Dame: University of Notre Dame Press, 1989.

Niebuhr, H. Richard. *Christ and Culture.* San Francisco: Harper & Row, 1951.

Nienhuis, David R. *A Concise Guide to Reading the New Testament: A Canonical Introduction*. Grand Rapids: Baker Academic, 2017.

Nienhuis, David R., and Robert W. Wall. *Reading the Epistles of James, Peter, John, and Jude as Scripture: The Shaping and Shape of a Canonical Collection*. Grand Rapids: Eerdmans, 2013.

Noonan, John T., Jr. *A Church That Can and Cannot Change: The Development of Catholic Moral Teaching*. Notre Dame: University of Notre Dame Press, 2005.

Oberman, Heiko A. *Forerunners of the Reformation: The Shape of Late Medieval Thought*. Cambridge: James Clarke & Co., 1967.

O'Keefe, John J., and R. R. Reno. *Sanctified Vision: An Introduction to Early Christian Interpretation of the Bible*. Baltimore: Johns Hopkins University Press, 2005.

Ong, Walter J. *Orality and Literacy: The Technologizing of the Word*. New Accents. New York: Routledge, 2002.

Origen. "Letter to Gregory." Columns 88–89 in Patrologia graeca. Vol. 11. Edited by Jacques-Paul Migne. Paris, 1857–86.

———. *The Song of Songs Commentary and Homilies*. Translated by R. P. Lawson. ACW 26. New York: Newman, 1957.

———. "Treatise on the Passover (*Peri Pascha*)." Pages 27–56 in *Treatise on the Passover* and *Dialogue of Origen with Heraclides and His Fellow Bishops on the Father, the Son, and the Soul*. Translated and edited by Robert J. Daly. ACW 54. New York: Paulist, 1992.

Orr, James. *The Christian View of God and the World as Centring in the Incarnation: Being the Kerr Lectures for 1890–1891*. 2nd ed. Edinburgh: Elliot, 1893.

Osborne, Grant R. *Revelation*. BECNT. Grand Rapids: Baker, 2002.

Overbeck, Franz. "Über die Anfänge der patristischen Literatur." *Historische Zeitschrift* 48.3 (1882): 417–72.

Paddison, Angus. "The History and Reemergence of Theological Interpretation." Pages 1–25 in *A Manifesto for Theological Interpretation*. Edited by Craig G. Bartholomew and Heath A. Thomas. Grand Rapids: Baker Academic, 2016.

—. "Theological Interpretation and the Bible as Public Text." *Journal of Theological Interpretation* 8.2 (2014): 175–92.

Padilla, C. René. "The Interpreted Word: Reflections on Contextual Hermeneutics." *Themelios* 7.1 (1981): 18–23.

Pelikan, Jaroslav. *The Vindication of Tradition*. New Haven: Yale University Press, 1983.

Perhai, Richard J. *Antiochene Theōria in the Writings of Theodore of Mopsuestia and Theodoret of Cyrus*. Minneapolis: Fortress, 2015.

Perry, Peter S. *The Rhetoric of Digressions: Revelation 7:1–17 and 10:1–11:13 and Ancient Communication*. WUNT 2.268. Tübingen: Mohr Siebeck, 2009.

Plant, Stephen J. *Taking Stock of Bonhoeffer: Studies in Biblical Interpretation and Ethics*. Burlington, VT: Ashgate, 2015.

Poirier, John C. "Jewish and Christian Tradition in the Transfiguration." *Revue biblique* 111.4 (2004): 516–30.

—. "'Theological Interpretation' and Its Contradistinctions." *Tyndale Bulletin* 60 (2009): 105–18.

Porter, Stanley E. "What Exactly Is Theological Interpretation of Scripture and Is It Hermeneutically Robust Enough for the Task to Which It Has Been Appointed?" Pages 234–67 in *Horizons in Hermeneutics: A Festschrift in Honor of Anthony C. Thiselton*. Edited by Stanley E. Porter and Matthew R. Malcolm. Grand Rapids: Eerdmans, 2013.

Powell, Mark Allan. *What Do They Hear? Bridging the Gap between Pulpit and Pew*. Nashville: Abingdon, 2007.

Provan, Iain W. *Ecclesiastes, Song of Songs*. NIV Application Commentary. Grand Rapids: Zondervan, 2001.

Rad, Gerhard von. *Genesis*. Rev. ed. Philadelphia: Westminster, 1972.

Rae, Murray. "Reading as Formation." Pages 258–62 in *Ears That Hear: Explorations in Theological Interpretation of the Bible*. Edited by Joel B. Green and Tim Meadowcroft. Sheffield: Sheffield Phoenix, 2013.

—. "Theological Interpretation and Historical Criticism." Pages 94–109 in *A Manifesto for Theological Interpretation*. Edited by Craig G. Bartholomew and Heath A. Thomas. Grand Rapids: Baker Academic, 2016.

Raith, Charles, II. *After Merit: John Calvin's Theology of Works and Rewards*. Refo500 Academic Studies, vol. 34. Göttingen: Vandenhoeck & Ruprecht, 2016.

———. *Aquinas and Calvin on Romans: God's Justification and Our Participation.* Oxford: Oxford University Press, 2014.

———. "Calvin's Critique of Merit, and Why Aquinas (Mostly) Agrees." *Pro Ecclesia* 20.2 (2011): 135–66.

Reno, R. R. "Using the Fathers." *Journal of Theological Interpretation* 7.2 (2013): 163–70.

———. "What Makes Exegesis Theological?" *Nova et Vetera* 9.1 (2011): 75–90.

Resseguie, James L. *The Revelation of John: A Narrative Commentary.* Grand Rapids: Baker Academic, 2009.

Rhee, Helen. *Early Christian Literature: Christ and Culture in the Second and Third Centuries.* London: Routledge, 2005.

Robinson, B. P. "The Two Persecuted Prophet-Witnesses of Rev 11." *Scripture Bulletin* 19.1 (1988): 14–19.

Root, Michael, and James J. Buckley, eds. *The Morally Divided Body: Ethical Disagreement and the Disunity of the Church.* Eugene, OR: Cascade, 2012.

Rowland, Christopher C. "The Book of Revelation: Introduction, Commentary, and Reflections." Pages 501–736 of *The New Interpreter's Bible*, vol. 12. Edited by Leander E. Keck. Nashville: Abingdon, 1998.

Rummel, Erika. *The Humanist-Scholastic Debate in the Renaissance & Reformation.* Harvard Historical Studies 120. Cambridge: Harvard University Press, 1995.

Sanders, E. P. *Paul and Palestinian Judaism: A Comparison of Patterns of Religion.* Minneapolis: Fortress, 1977.

Sarisky, Darren. "What Is Theological Interpretation? The Example of Robert W. Jenson." *International Journal of Systematic Theology* 12.2 (2010): 201–16.

Schroeder, Joy A. "Female Figures and Figures of Evil." *Word and World* 15.2 (1995): 175–81.

Schüssler Fiorenza, Elisabeth. *The Book of Revelation: Justice and Judgment.* 2nd ed. Minneapolis: Fortress, 1998.

Scurlock, JoAnn. "*Chaoskampf* Lost—*Chaoskampf* Regained: The Gunkel Hypothesis Revisited." Pages 257–68 in *Creation and Chaos: A Reconsideration of Hermann Gunkel's Chaoskampf Hypothesis.* Edited by JoAnn Scurlock and Richard H. Beal. Winona Lake, IN: Eisenbrauns, 2013.

———. "Searching for Meaning in Genesis 1:2: Purposeful Creation out of *Chaos* without *Kampf*." Pages 48–61 in *Creation and Chaos: A Reconsideration of Hermann Gunkel's Chaoskampf Hypothesis.* Edited by JoAnn Scurlock and Richard H. Beal. Winona Lake, IN: Eisenbrauns, 2013.

Scurlock, JoAnn, and Richard H. Beal, eds. *Creation and Chaos: A Reconsideration of Hermann Gunkel's Chaoskampf Hypothesis.* Winona Lake, IN: Eisenbrauns, 2013.

Seitz, Christopher R. "Canonical Approach." Pages 100–102 in *Dictionary for Theological Interpretation of the Bible.* Edited by Kevin J. Vanhoozer, Craig G. Bartholomew, Daniel J. Treier, and N. T. Wright. Grand Rapids: Baker Academic, 2005.

———. *The Character of Christian Scripture: The Significance of a Two-Testament Bible.* Grand Rapids: Baker Academic, 2011.

———. *Colossians.* Brazos Theological Commentary on the Bible. Grand Rapids: Brazos, 2014.

———. "Scripture Becomes Religion(s): The Theological Crisis of Serious Biblical Interpretation in the Twentieth Century." Pages 40–65 in *Renewing Biblical Interpretation*. Edited by Craig C. Bartholomew, Colin J. D. Greene, and Karl Möller. Grand Rapids: Zondervan, 2000.

Seow, Choon-Leong. *Ecclesiastes: A New Translation with Introduction and Commentary*. AB 18C. New York: Doubleday, 1997.

Sheehan, Jonathan. *The Enlightenment Bible: Translation, Scholarship, Culture*. Princeton: Princeton University Press, 2007.

Sider, J. Alexander. *To See History Doxologically: History and Holiness in John Howard Yoder's Ecclesiology*. Radical Traditions. Grand Rapids: Eerdmans, 2011.

Simonetti, Manlio. *Biblical Interpretation in the Early Church: An Historical Introduction to Patristic Exegesis*. Edited by Anders Bergquist and Markus Bockmuehl. Translated by John A. Hughes. Edinburgh: T. & T. Clark, 1994.

Sommer, Benjamin D. *A Prophet Reads Scripture: Allusion in Isaiah 40–66*. Stanford, CA: Stanford University Press, 1998.

Speiser, E. A. *Genesis*. AB 1. New Haven: Yale University Press, 1964.

Steinberg, Julius, and Timothy Stone, eds. *The Shape of the Writings*. Siphrut 16. Winona Lake, IN: Eisenbrauns, 2015.

Steinmetz, David C. "The Superiority of Pre-Critical Exegesis." *Theology Today* 37.1 (1980): 27–38. Reprinted in *Theological Interpretation of Scripture: Classic and Contemporary Readings*. Edited by Stephen E. Fowl, pp. 26–38. Oxford: Blackwell, 1997.

Stewart-Sykes, Alistair. "Introduction." Pages 1–35 in Melito of Sardis, *On Pascha: With the Fragments of Melito and Other Material Related to the Quartodecimans*. Translated and edited by Alistair Stewart-Sykes. Popular Patristic Series 20. Crestwood, NY: St. Vladimir's Seminary Press, 2001.

———. *The Lamb's High Feast: Melito, "Peri Pascha," and the Quartodeciman Paschal Liturgy at Sardis*. Leiden: Brill, 1998.

Svigel, Michael J. "The Apocalypse of John and the Rapture of the Church: A Reevaluation." *Trinity Journal* 22.1 (2001): 23–74.

Tabor, James D. "'Returning to the Divinity': Josephus's Portrayal of the Disappearances of Enoch, Elijah, and Moses." *Journal of Biblical Literature* 108.2 (1989): 225–38.

Tanner, Kathryn. "Cultural Theory." Pages 527–42 in *The Oxford Handbook of Systematic Theology*. Edited by John Webster, Kathryn Tanner, and Iain Torrance. Oxford: Oxford University Press, 2007.

Tavo, Felise. *Woman, Mother and Bride: An Exegetical Investigation into the "Ecclesial" Notions of the Apocalypse*. Leuven: Peeters, 2007.

Thiselton, Anthony C. "Communicative Action and Promise in Interdisciplinary, Biblical, and Theological Hermeneutics." Pages 133–239 in *The Promise of Hermeneutics* by Roger Lundin, Clarence Walhout, and Anthony C. Thiselton. Grand Rapids: Eerdmans, 1999.

———. *New Horizons in Hermeneutics: New Testament Hermeneutics and Philosophical Description*. Grand Rapids: Zondervan, 1992.

———. *The Two Horizons: New Testament Hermeneutics and Philosophical Description with Special Reference to Heidegger, Bultmann, Gadamer, and Wittgenstein*. Grand Rapids: Eerdmans, 1980.

Tjørhom, Ola. "An 'Ecumenical Winter'? Challenges in Contemporary Catholic Ecumenism." *Heythrop Journal* 49.5 (2008): 841–59.

———. *Embodied Faith: Reflections on a Materialist Spirituality*. Grand Rapids: Eerdmans, 2009.

Treier, Daniel J. *Introducing Theological Interpretation of Scripture: Recovering a Christian Practice*. Grand Rapids: Baker Academic, 2008.

Tromp, Johannes. *The Assumption of Moses: A Critical Edition with Commentary*. SVTP 10. Leiden: Brill, 1993.

Tugendhaft, Aaron. "Bible-Babel-Baal." Pages 190–98 in *Creation and Chaos: A Reconsideration of Hermann Gunkel's Chaoskampf Hypothesis*. Edited by JoAnn Scurlock and Richard H. Beal. Winona Lake, IN: Eisenbrauns, 2013.

Van den Hoek, Annewies. "Etymologizing in a Christian Context: The Techniques of Clement of Alexandria and Origen." *Studia Philonica Annual* 16 (2004): 122–68.

Vanhoozer, Kevin J. "What Is Theological Interpretation of the Bible?" Pages 19–25 in *Dictionary for Theological Interpretation of the Bible*. Edited by Kevin J. Vanhoozer, Craig G. Bartholomew, Daniel J. Treier, and N. T. Wright. Grand Rapids: Baker Academic, 2005.

Wall, Robert W. "Acts of the Apostles: Introduction, Commentary, and Reflections." Pages 1–368 in *The New Interpreter's Bible*, vol. 10. Edited by Leander E. Keck. Nashville: Abingdon, 2002.

———. "A Canonical Approach to the Unity of Acts and Luke's Gospel." Pages 172–91 in *Rethinking the Reception and Unity of Luke-Acts*. Edited by Andrew F. Gregory and C. Kavin Rowe. Columbia, SC: University of South Carolina Press, 2010.

———. "The Canonical View" and "The Canonical Response." Pages 111–30 and 188–200 in *Biblical Hermeneutics: Five Views*. Edited by Stanley E. Porter and Beth M. Stovell. Downers Grove, IL: IVP Academic, 2012.

———. "Epilogue: A Reflection." Pages 199–211 in *Muted Voices: Readings in the Catholic Epistles and Hebrews*. Edited by Katherine M. Hockey, Madison N. Pierce, and Francis Watson. LNTS 565. London: T. & T. Clark Bloomsbury, 2017.

———. "The Function of the Pastoral Letters within the Pauline Canon of the New Testament: A Canonical Approach." Pages 27–44 in *The Pauline Canon*. Edited by Stanley E. Porter. Pauline Studies 1. Leiden: Brill, 2004.

Wall, Robert W., and Eugene E. Lemcio. *The New Testament as Canon: A Reader in Canonical Criticism*. JSNTSup 76. Sheffield: JSOT Press, 1992.

Walton, John H. *The Lost World of Adam and Eve: Genesis 2–3 and the Human Origins Debate*. Downers Grove, IL: InterVarsity, 2015.

Watson, Francis. "Does Historical Criticism Exist? A Contribution to Debate on the Theological Interpretation of Scripture." Pages 307–18 in *Theological Theology: Essays in Honour of John Webster*. Edited by R. David Nelson, Darren Sarisky, and Justin Stratis. London: T. & T. Clark Bloomsbury, 2015.

Wawrykow, Joseph P. *God's Grace & Human Action: Merit in the Theology of Thomas Aquinas*. Notre Dame: University of Notre Dame Press, 2016.

Weaver, Rebecca Harden. "Introduction." Pages xi–xxvi in *Grace for Grace: The Debates after Augustine & Pelagius*. Edited by Alexander Y. Hwang, Brian J. Matz, and Augustine Casiday. Washington, DC: The Catholic University of America Press, 2014.

Webster, John. "Canon." Pages 97–100 in *Dictionary for Theological Interpretation of the Bible*. Edited by Kevin J. Vanhoozer, Craig G. Bartholomew, Daniel J. Treier, and N. T. Wright. Grand Rapids: Baker Academic, 2005.

———. *Holy Scripture: A Dogmatic Sketch*. Cambridge: Cambridge University Press, 2003.

Weinfeld, Moshe. "God the Creator in Genesis 1 and in the Prophecy of Second Isaiah." *Tarbiz* 37 (1968): 105–32 [Hebrew].

Weinrich, William C., ed. *Revelation*. ACCS 12. Downers Grove, IL: InterVarsity, 2005.

Wendel, François. *Calvin: The Origins and Development of His Religious Thought*. Translated by Philip Mairet. New York: Harper & Row, 1963.

Wenham, Gordon J. *Genesis 1–15*. WBC 1. Waco, TX: Word, 1987.

Westermann, Claus. *Genesis 1–11: A Commentary*. Translated by John J. Scullion. Minneapolis: Augsburg, 1984.

Whybray, R. N. *Ecclesiastes: Based on the Revised Standard Version*. NCB. Grand Rapids: Eerdmans, 1989.

Wilhite, David E. *The Gospel According to the Heretics: Discovering Orthodoxy through Early Christological Conflicts*. Grand Rapids: Baker Academic, 2015.

Wilken, Robert L. "Historical Theology." Pages 225–30 in *A New Handbook of Christian Theology*. Edited by Donald W. Musser and Joseph L. Price. Nashville: Abingdon, 1992.

———. "Melito, the Jewish Community at Sardis, and the Sacrifice of Isaac." *Theological Studies* 37.1 (1976): 53–69.

Williams, A. N. *The Ground of Union: Deification in Aquinas and Palamas*. Oxford: Oxford University Press, 1999.

Williams, Rowan. "Historical Criticism and Sacred Text." Pages 217–28 in *Reading Texts, Seeking Wisdom: Scripture and Theology*. Edited by David F. Ford and Graham Stanton. Grand Rapids: Eerdmans, 2003.

Wingren, Gustaf. *Creation and Gospel: The New Situation in European Theology*. Toronto: Edwin Mellen, 1979.

Witherington, Ben, III. *Revelation*. Cambridge: Cambridge University Press, 2003.

Wolterstorff, Nicholas. *Reason within the Bounds of Religion*. 2nd ed. Grand Rapids: Eerdmans, 1984. Repr., 1999.

Wrede, William. "The Tasks and Methods of 'New Testament Theology.'" Pages 68–116 in *The Nature of New Testament Theology: The Contribution of William Wrede and Adolf Schlatter*. Edited by Robert Morgan. SBT 2.25. London: SCM, 1973.

Wright, Addison G. "The Riddle of the Sphinx: The Structure of the Book of Qoheleth." *Catholic Biblical Quarterly* 30.3 (1968): 313–34.

Wright, N. T. *What Saint Paul Really Said: Was Paul of Tarsus the Real Founder of Christianity?* Grand Rapids: Eerdmans, 1997.

Author Index

Subject Index

Adapa, Babylonian myth of, 72

"aesthetic excellence" and the Catholic Epistles collection, 20–22, 116n, 123

allegorical interpretation: Bonhoeffer's reading of Genesis 1–3, 210; Daniélou's distinction between allegory and typology, 164–65; patristic interpretations of Exodus 12 and Passover narrative, 151–52, 157–61, 163–65, 170, 173–74. *See also* Exodus/Passover narrative, allegorical/typological readings of; spiritual interpretation of the Bible; typological interpretation of the Bible

Apocalypse of John. *See* Revelation (Apocalypse of John)

Apollo-Python-Leto myth, 142–44

Aquinas, Thomas: on Augustine's reading of Genesis 1:2 and doctrine of creation, 92; and Calvin, 180–92; and Calvin's reading of Romans, 182–92; on justification, 22, 183–84, 189–91; nonparticipatory and participatory elements in theology of salvation and justification, 189–91; reflections on interpretive methods, 34; understanding of merit/grace and relationship between divine and human causality, 186–88

Atrahasis, epic of, 72

Augustine: on Bible as the "writing of the mysteries," 163–64; and Catholic Epistles collection in New Testament

canon, 121n; interpretation of Genesis 1:2 and God's action of creation, 89, 92; on Romans 5:12, 74, 75; theological interpretive methods, 34–35

Babylonian creation myths, 72, 88, 91–92, 98

Barth, Karl: and Bonhoeffer, 85–86, 197, 201–2; *Church Dogmatics*, 85, 90; *Epistle to the Romans*, 85; on Genesis 1:2 and Gunkel's *Chaoskampf* motif, 87–89; on Genesis 1:2 and Isaiah, 89–90, 95–96; on Genesis 1:2 and the doctrine of creation, 85–86, 87–90, 92–97; and historical criticism, 199–202; theological interpretation of the Bible, 85–86, 87–90, 92–97, 199

Bonhoeffer, Dietrich, 23, 85–86, 90–97, 193–219; allegorical/typological readings of Old Testament, 210, 213–14; and Barth, 85–86, 197, 201–2; "Christ in the Psalms," 206–7; christological biblical hermeneutic, 193–98, 204–6; christological interpretation of the Psalms, 212–16; christological reading of the Old Testament, 85–86, 194–96, 207–18; on contemporizing biblical texts, 205–6; *Creation and Fall: A Theological Exposition of Genesis 1–3*, 85–86, 90–92, 209; eschatological reading of Old Testament, 209; *Ethics*, 194, 195–97; on Genesis 1:2 and the doctrine of creation,

241

Scripture and Other Ancient Literature Index